I KISSED THE BOSS

LINDSEY HART

COPYRIGHT

～

Cover by Oliviaprodesign.
You can contact the author, Lindsey Hart at:
team@lindseyhartromance.com

CLAIMED BY THE BOSS

BOOK 1

BOOK DESCRIPTION

My hot sexy EX is back and wants me to work for him.
The nerve he has to even show me his gorgeously annoying face all these years later.
He wants me to organize the most luxurious Christmas party for him.
And I just want to toss a big bag of poop at him.

If he thinks his big fat check is going to make me agree to stay in his close proximity for longer than needed to throw that sack of poop, he can dream again.
And that smoldering gaze of his as it roams over my body tells me he definitely has other plans on his agenda.
It probably includes melting me back into his arms and bed.
Which is totally absolutely never ever going to happen again.
The only problem, he keeps kissing me "by mistake" at every turn.

AMBERINA

*N*o matter which way she looked at it, Trey Hartford would always have been her downfall.

Ambi's hands shook as she held the black phone receiver away from her face. She closed her eyes and took a breath. One. Another. Two. A shaky third. Three. She kept going, all the way to ten. When she hit the magical marker that was supposed to calm everything down and make the world brand spanking new and sparkly, all her problems still remained. She knew she couldn't put off the call any longer. It only takes so long to check if a date is open.

As much as she would like to say that November twenty-seventh was taken, it unfortunately, wasn't. While she was busy with other parties leading up to it, it wasn't wedding or grad season and while a few people hired an event planner to help with Christmas functions, it wasn't exactly a hot time of year.

Not only was she free, she knew that no matter what, no matter how much she hated Hartford & Heatherford Assured Investment Group- their stupid name was reason enough to hate them- she knew she'd take the job. A high-profile client like that could really help her business and she'd work hard to get a good reference.

Ambi punched the red hold button and mustered up her sweetest, *I don't give a shit* tone.

"Sorry for the hold. We'd be delighted to help you plan your event." *I'd rather die a slow, agonizing death choking on a party popper.* "If you want to set up a time to meet, we can go over the details. I have an office, or I can come to you." *I'd rather munch on broken glass and rusty nails than ever go to H&H.*

She was pretty sure their name shouldn't have been Hartford and Heatherford. Those two H's should have been dumbed down to Hell and Heller. Or double hell. Not that their name wasn't shitty enough on its own. Dale Hartford had probably been searching for just the right business partner for years, one with a name so close to his that it would look resoundingly ridiculous on a sign or card and sound even worse, not to mention the *assured* part of the name, which was misleading, since investment was never a sure thing.

"Oh, well, I can give you some of the details now, as my schedule is quite full over the next little bit. That way we can just get started if that's alright?"

Ambi closed her eyes. Normally, she loved keeners. People who had their shit together enough to avoid making her life a living hell. This girl though, Sarah, was grating on her already shredded nerves. Which wasn't her fault. Sarah couldn't help that she was probably blonde, beautiful and bubbly, the three B trifecta. It was that she worked at H&H that was the annoying part.

"Yeah. Sure." She reached for her notepad, the one with

llamas dancing at the top in various frilly outfits and polka dot dresses. "Shoot." *As in please shoot me now before I can ruin myself taking this job.*

"Well, we wanted something that could include anyone, so please no references to ethnicity or religion. We want this to be as neutral as possible, so we would prefer no reference at all to Christmas. If it has to say something, happy holidays would be preferred."

"Great. Not a problem." *You do realize you started this conversation telling me you wanted me to plan a Christmas party?*

"The budget is pretty wide open. This is the first real office party we've had in ages and we want it to become an annual thing. Mr. Hartford Sr. has eighty thousand set aside for decorations, food, games, entertainment. You know. Basically, think of an upscale wedding. All the good stuff. What do you normally charge for your services of something of this magnitude?"

"How many people again?" Ambi choked out. She scrawled eighty thousand across the top of her notepad in huge, blocky numbers. Who the fuck spent eighty K on an office Christmas party? Oh, right. A happy holiday party. And double right. Dale Hartford, douchebag of the century.

"There are eighty in the office."

How perfect. A grand for each of you. I'm sure no one could use that extra thousand on things that actually matter like food or paying down credit card debt. All employees want a freaking party they're forced to go to instead of a well-deserved bonus.

Maybe they were getting that too. Ambi shook her head, trying not to be uncharitable. Maybe Dale Hartford didn't run his business like he ran his life. And his son. Maybe he wasn't such a dick when it came to his company and he actually treated his employees quite a bit better than he treated his son's (at the time) girlfriend.

"Eighty. Right." Ambi realized she had to say something. Awkward pauses on the phone didn't make anyone comfortable.

"We were thinking of renting out a nice hall type place. Having a dinner, hopefully catered, some live entertainment during that, maybe a magic show or someone who plays piano, then having dessert and a live band. Drink tickets would be up to the hall pricing, as we don't want people to get completely wasted on the company's dollar if you know what I mean."

"Of course. Yes. That all sounds very doable for your budget. I'd require a deposit of ten percent to get started, non-refundable. My services for something of this size, given that it's only a month away and that's kind of last-minute in the event world, would be around six thousand. Is that alright?" She winced after, wishing she would have quoted double the price, just to stick it to H&H. She was too honest.

"Yes. Perfect." Sarah didn't even miss a beat.

"Great. I'll come down to your office for a cheque and I'll have a couple of packages put together for you by then. Does tomorrow afternoon work?"

"That would be perfect. Thanks so much."

"Thank you for calling. Can I ask how you heard about me?"

"Oh." Sarah giggled into the phone. She was probably twirling a strand of her hair around her index finger at the moment, leaning back in her desk chair, her pink sky-high heels perched on her appointment book. "I don't know. Someone in the head office just gave me your name and asked me to call about planning this. I guess word of mouth? Or maybe they looked you up online?"

Right. Because her company was at the top of every search result in Minneapolis. Not. Ambi wasn't starting out or anything, but it took years to build a successful business. She'd only been doing event planning for a few years. Not long enough that she'd be someone's choice in a cold search. Maybe it was word of mouth. Maybe someone worked at H&H and she'd helped plan their wedding or their daughter's or son's wedding or grad or something. It sure as hell wasn't Dale Hartford or his son. One hated her and the other she hated- okay, maybe hate was a strong word and maybe she disliked them both- so that was a big nope on their part.

"Yeah. Sounds good. Thank you. I'll be in touch tomorrow."

"Super." Sarah drew out the s, making it sound really snake-like. "Do you know where we're located?"

Unfortunately, yes. "I do. Thank you. I'll be by tomorrow afternoon, likely around three, if that's alright?"

"That's perfect. Thanks a bunch. Have a super day." There was that snakey s again.

"You too."

Ambi put the phone back down in the cradle on her desk and leaned back in her chair so far the thing nearly snapped. Yes, she was still one of those people who had an office phone. She wasn't about to give her freaking cell number out to potential bridezillas and the like. She was perfectly capable of ducking into her office at all hours of the day and night to check her messages, seeing as she lived in a small apartment right above the even smaller retail space.

The shittier, evil, horrible parts of herself wanted to plan the worst, most bland, horrible office Christmas party in history, just to stick it to the Hartfords. For being such dicks. For treating her like she was garbage just because she didn't come from a line of blue-blooded assholes. Pedigree. That was the problem. The whole reason Dale Hartford told his son that if he didn't end things with her, it would be the end of him and his inheritance. Like she was a dog or something, which in Dale's eyes, she likely was.

She was some poor college kid with student loans, working her way through a Business Degree, hoping to graduate and go into event planning, a humiliating career in which she worked for and served others menially for fairly low pay. It didn't matter that she was good at it or that she loved it and always had. That she'd planned most of her high school fundraisers and was involved in a ton of different activities and groups in college.

No. To someone like Dale Hartford, she was trouble. Or troubled. Not that it mattered. She was beautiful enough to ensnare his son. Trey had to be pried from her claws before she brought them all to ruin. Imagine. Trey Hartford married to someone who was raised by a single mother after her alcoholic father ran out on them. She'd probably lift a finger to plan their wedding, which would be absolutely shameful. And she wasn't a size zero, so while she was pretty enough, the whole trophy wife thing was off the table. She could do nothing to advance H&H. She wasn't suitable. If she was a dog, she wasn't the right breed.

So, Trey gave her the boot. He chose his family, his inheritance, and H&H over her.

Ambi slammed her open palm on top of her notepad so hard that tears welled up in her eyes. She was definitely producing that moisture because of the desk slap she'd just handed out and not because it hurt to think about Trey, even five years after the fact.

She'd stick it to H&H by doing an amazing job. By being the best event planner they ever freaking had. By doing her job so well that she'd prove them both wrong. She was a success in her own right. She might have worked for three years after college to save up and pay off her student loans before she could open her business, but she was rolling now. Plus, she'd be taking six grand of their money for doing pretty minimal work.

A huge bonus.

Another huge bonus was that people like Dale and Trey didn't get their hands dirty. They sat up in their glass tower and watched while the rest of their menial little ants ran around all day, doing their bidding. She knew for a fact she wouldn't see either of them. She'd just make sure that they knew that it was her who had planned the party everyone was raving about after. *After*. She'd send a thank you card with her signature on it and they'd know that not only had they given her company business, they'd also hired and paid her, the woman that Dale Hartford looked at as scum.

She'd make sure that everyone fell in love with her. That there was no chance she wouldn't get a good reference or repeat business. She'd work her butt off for it and then, she'd have her revenge in the only way she could get it short of sending a steaming bag of shit to Trey's doorstep. She hadn't exactly ruled that one out, even half a decade later.

She just needed to find an anonymous pooper and an anonymous delivery guy willing to drop off a sketchy package. Maybe she'd use the six grand from planning the happy holiday party to do just that.

Ambi grinned as she picked up her pen and scrawled

the happiest thought she'd had in a long time along the bottom of the notepad's page.

Steaming hot pile of dung. Dubious package. Clueless delivery guy.

She underlined it after. Twice.

Revenge was a dish served piping hot. Piping hot and smelly.

2

TREY

There were a few things in life that he regretted. Amberina Danby was one of them. His father threw down an ultimatum. He'd taken the bait. He had money now. He was VP right under his father, who was President, of a very wealthy, healthy, thriving company. He had a sprawling house in one of the nicest neighborhoods in Minneapolis. He had a collection of antique cars that would make most museums salivate. Sometimes, he even drove them.

In short, life was good. Life was really, really good, and Trey enjoyed the hell out of it. He believed in living.

He also had a shithead side that believed in sticking it to his father.

Daddy dearest told him to get rid of Amberina or lose his inheritance and spend his days penniless. Not that it would have happened. He was smart and he could have made his own money. Because he was stupid and young and a little afraid of a man who'd always been more like a dictator than a father, and because Dale had always played the mother card, invoking how disappointed Violet would be if he walked away from his duties and his family over a pretty face. Trey had loved his mother just about more than anything in the world, so he finally caved.

He'd also made just about every eligible bachelor list, magazines, and even a few billboards in the past five years. It was a big flip off to his father when that shit came out.

Dale Hartford had made stipulations about Ambi. But he hadn't made stipulations about marriage, and sadly enough for him, that's where he'd gone wrong.

To add fuel to the fire, when his father announced his intentions to throw a big office Christmas party to show just how well H&H treated their employees, he'd gone right along with it, knowing full well exactly who he'd get to plan that party.

He may have also done a little creeping- er- digging, in which he paid some very unsavory character to find out the finer details of Amberina's life. She was still single. She owned her own business, Ingenuity & Imagination Event Planning. She was the sole employee as far as he knew.

Trey told himself this was just a nice way to make his father pay. He also wanted to see Ambi and apologize. He'd never been able to properly tell her how sorry he was. For everything.

He knew she wouldn't listen. Ambi was Ambi. She was gorgeous, compassionate, kind, and also, tough as nails. He figured she'd rather kick him in the balls by way of an apology than listen to anything he had to say. Hell, he might just let her try.

Trey adjusted his tie for the millionth time. He had a cheque in his hand, compliments of Sandy in accounting. Ten percent and the six grand Ambi demanded for her services. Sarah was more than a little shocked when he'd breezed by her desk that morning and told her he'd be handling the event planning from here on out. She'd gladly passed over a yellow lined page with the few details she scrawled down and told him the event planner, someone named Annie, was going to be dropping by at three for the deposit.

He'd told her to show *Ambi* to their board room, stressing that her name wasn't Annie, even if it was a dick move.

It was ten after three and Sarah had just called his office to inform him that his appointment, *Ambi*, was there. At least she'd got her name right. He'd thanked her and hung up while she was still talking. He then proceeded to pace the hallway outside the board room for a good five minutes, the check growing sweaty and clammy in his palm.

He could practically smell Ambi's scent lingering in the hall. She hated perfume and only wore natural products. She disliked deodorant and chose instead to use lemons-yes, real lemons. It was crazy, but it worked for her and she always smelled delicious. Clean and fresh with the under-lying scent of lemon and the floral tang of her natural sham-poo. Mixed with her own special blend of pheromones and whatever else she was putting out there, she was always this heady, intoxicating mix of perfection.

Finally, he took a deep breath, one he swore was lemon tinged, squared his shoulders, and pushed open the solid door to one of their larger meeting rooms.

The thing was fully stocked with its own coffee bar, large screen TV mounted on the wall, projector, a massive table surrounded by at least twenty expensive leather office chairs, and a myriad of abstract art purchased straight from some gallery in New York that neither he nor his father gave a shit about.

His house was pretty much the same story. Entirely soulless. Put together by a designer more interested in a commission than in what he truly wanted.

Trey had just a second between the time his hand left the door handle and Ambi's head jerked up from the notepad in front of her to observe her.

She'd always had this incredible head of raven black hair. She hated haircuts and it was pretty obvious that she still had that strange opinion that hairdressers were akin to the devil. A river of sleek silky hair flowed down her back, spilling over the table and chair in long blue-black currents. She was dressed professionally, at least from what he could see of her above the table. A black dress that was tight enough to show off the fact that she had nice breasts, but not tight enough to be in bad taste for a business meeting. It nipped in at her narrow waist. She'd always looked good in dark and bright colors and she'd paired the dress with a fire engine red cardigan and a vintage gold necklace with a bold pendant that boasted a cluster of jade stones.

"Miss Danby," Trey said, letting the words roll off his tongue, smooth and delicious like burnt sugar.

Her head snapped up at the sound of his voice. It only took about three seconds for her beautiful features- and god, she was beautiful- to contort in horror. Her huge blue eyes nearly popped out of the sockets. Her dark brows shot straight up her forehead. A bright flush of pink appeared on her delicate skin right above the high slashes of her cheekbones. Her nostrils flared and her perfect bow lips, done in a shade of bright red to match her sweater, parted in shock.

"You!" She exclaimed, half accusation and half slur before she scrambled to push her chair back.

The thing was huge and Ambi flailed as her feet kicked, which was a mistake, given that the chairs were ergonomic, obscenely expensive and all that bullshit. They were quite springy at the back and instead of holding up Ambi's weight and stalling her momentum, the chair kicked back, sending her tumbling head over heels straight to the floor.

"Holy shit!" Trey cursed under his breath.

Ambi let out a scream of surprise as he rounded the table. It only took him a second to reach her and she was indeed wearing a dress. And it was not tight enough to hide the fact that she had bright red lace panties on beneath.

Who the hell wore bright red lace panties to a business meeting? *Fuck*. Now he wasn't just nervous as hell, he was also hard as hell. He bent, taking care to hide the fact that there was a fucking camping party going on in his pants, tents pitched all over the place and stared at Ambi.

He offered his hand, the one not still clutching the cheque, but she looked at him like she'd rather eat a shit sandwich than accept his help.

She pushed herself to her feet, pulled down her dress, adjusted her sweater, and brushed the clinging strands of her hair from her face. God, her hair. It trailed well past her waist.

Trey straightened, threw the cheque down on the table, and slammed his hands into his pockets to hide the fact that his dick really appreciated her being there. It was like the bastard wanted to greet her after five long years. Shake her hand, maybe. Her mouth...

Fuck again. Trey did his best to block out the mental images that came to mind the second he saw Ambi. It wasn't his fault. They had a history. There was enough material there for him to draw on for years to come. Even if they didn't, she was gorgeous. Five nine, but curvy in every place that mattered. Annnnnnd apparently wearing red lace panties. Maybe she'd known all along he was going to crash her meeting and she'd come dressed to slay.

"What the hell are you doing here?" she hissed, and there went that assumption. She bared her teeth, genuinely pissed.

"It's good to see you too, Ambi."

"Don't Ambi me," she shot back, her face suffused with rage. "It's Amberina for you. Better yet, don't address me at all. You have no right to use my name in any capacity. What are you doing here? I'm not meeting with you."

"Well, I work here," Trey started, being purposely obnoxious. Neither of them moved to take a seat.

God. Seeing Ambi was like a punch right to the throat. It stole all his breath and made even the most basic functions, like swallowing impossible. He was pretty sure he might actually have a river of saliva trailing out of the corner of his mouth, but he didn't want to take his hands out of his pants pockets to check seeing as that would give away just how *much* he enjoyed seeing her.

"And secondly, you *are* meeting with me. I've decided to be your contact for this. Sarah is busy with other things and I thought I'd help her out where I could."

Ambi blinked. "Help out your admin assistant? Or whoever's assistant she is? Doubtful. People like you don't get your hands dirty and you don't stoop to mingle with the common folk." The words were venomous and before he could react, Ambi grabbed up her black tote from the floor. She swept her flowing hair over her shoulder. "See you. Enjoy finding someone else to plan your party."

"What? No!" Ambi might be fast, but he was faster. Trey pretty much ran to block the door and he stood there, an obnoxious as hell tree that he knew Ambi couldn't budge even if she tried. Judging by the way she looked at him like she wouldn't touch him with a hundred-foot pole, she wasn't going to try.

Her brows knitted together, and her lips pursed. "I am not under any obligation to take this contract. Nothing was signed or agreed on. No money was exchanged. I would never, ever work for you. Ever. So, dream fucking on, Trey. Nice try."

He slowly crossed his arms, praying that Ambi wouldn't look down, because he was pretty sure that he was still indecent south of the border. Thankfully, Ambi always had been one for maintaining eye contact, even when she was pissed.

She was even prettier when she was in a rage like someone opened her up and filled her full of fire, sunshine, and life. She'd always lived in a way that most people didn't. Like she floated instead of walked, sparkled and dazzled in bright color when everyone else was shades of foggy grey.

He had to admit that he felt a little drunk, like his head was going to lift right off his shoulders, and no, it wasn't because Ambi was looking at him like she'd rather see his head on a pike.

"I'll double your asking price. And I'll make sure that every contact we have in this city and beyond knows who planned our very successful event. I'll make sure your business increases tenfold this year. You'll have to hire some real employees."

Ambi's eyes sparked. "How do you know I don't have any employees?"

He shrugged as casually as he could while he cursed himself inwardly for being massively stupid. Then again, he'd always been pretty stupid when it came to Ambi. At least in the tongue-tied, fall over your feet, hopeless kind of way. She'd owned him, every bit of him, from the first time he set eyes on her crossing the college campus with a butt load of books in her arms, her black hair trailing behind her like a gothic cloak.

"I don't. I was just saying. You'll have to hire more, you'll have so much business coming in. I imagine that since you're here in person, you do most of the work yourself."

Ambi cocked her head to the side. She gave him two seconds in which she pretended to consider his offer before she lifted her right hand and flipped him off. Right there in his own conference room after she'd just tumbled so ungracefully to the floor. In a freaking dress. She had the nerve to flip him off and laugh in his face. Except she wasn't laughing. She was dead serious. She'd rather spit on him than accept his money or his offer to help her.

"Please. Let me make it up to you in any way I can. Ambi I-"

"Stop." Her bird changed to a flat open palm that she held up like a stop sign. "Nope. Not taking your money. Not taking anything from you. I tried that once. It didn't work out so well. Really, that was your loss and not mine." She swept up to him, so close that the intoxicating scent of lemons reached him when he breathed in. He pressed a little harder into the door. "Oh, and Trey," Ambi murmured. "It really is your loss. Now. Get out of the way before you embarrass yourself." Her eyes flicked down, down to his slacks where his cock was trying to high five her for taking a stand.

Fuck, fuck, fuck. None of this whole meeting had gone down how he thought it was going to go. The cheque still sat, the amount unfilled, on the board room table. Worse, he was pretty sure that his normal bronzed complexion was ten shades of scarlet.

"Fine." He stepped to the left, leaving the door open. "But you *will* plan this party. We're not done here."

"Maybe you aren't, but I am." With another pointed glance at his groin, and a loud scoff, like what was there

didn't impress her at all, Ambi flipped her hair, set her t
on her shoulder, and stalked out of the room.

Trey wanted to go after her, but he'd had about as much
humiliation as he could handle for the hour. Cursing under
his breath, he slapped the cheque off the table and slammed
it into his pocket. Ambi's sea glass eyes still haunted him as
he stomped his way back to his office.

3

AMBERINA

*G*ross. Just- just gross. *Fucking Trey Hartman.*

No, just Trey Hartman. The f-bomb and Trey's name didn't belong in the same sentence. It was bad enough the creep tried to trap her into some stupid contract, planning a wretched party. It was bad enough that he'd obviously looked into her. That was creepy in itself, but then he had to come into that board room looking like a gorgeous stalker and she had to react all wrong and get so flustered that she literally flipped right off her chair, and then he had to go and make it obvious that for the past five years, he'd probably used her as spank bank material by popping a very obvious hard-on right in front of her.

Ambi smacked her steering wheel with an open palm. She relished the sting and focused on the pain. Anything was better than thinking about Trey and his slacks. Or about anything they'd done in the past. She would have liked to say he had a small dick and she'd faked it every single time. She could lie to herself about a lot of things, but that wasn't one of them.

"Why?" She smacked her steering wheel again. Then again. A third time. A fourth. "Why, why, whyyyyyy?"

Overnight she'd made some plans for that money that was supposed to be coming her way. She actually did plan on hiring someone. Worse, she was going to bonus herself and treat her mom to a week in Mexico right after Christmas as a surprise. She'd even found a perfect resort for a budget price.

A rap at her window scared her out of her skin. She realized she probably looked wild-eyed and crazed as she rolled down her window to find a middle-aged man with a big paunch and a complexion that was a tad too red along the cheeks and nose, bending at her window.

"Scuse me, ma'am, I noticed your meter's run out. I figured you were moving, so I wouldn't have to write you a ticket."

The guy's breath was rancid. It smelled like onions and stale coffee and Ambi's stomach lurched. The meter dude, a middle-aged guy with beady, sharp eyes and oily hair protruding from beneath his ball cap, ran his tongue along his bottom lip like he'd relish writing her a ticket for the least infraction. She resisted the urge to snap all over the guy's ass. You win more flies with honey than with vinegar, but at the moment she just wanted to get the hell out of there.

"I'm sorry. Yes. I'm moving. Right now." She moved her hand to the keys dangling from the ignition and was ready to turn it when a deeper, smoother voice, overrode any good sense she had left. Her hand fell away.

"She's actually staying parked there for a few more minutes. Here. This should cover it."

Trey. Effing Trey Hartman. Her worst nightmare. God. He deserved a *double* steaming poo pile for this.

Ambi turned her head just enough that it looked like she was still looking forward, but she could see Trey peel off a bill with a large number in the corner and hand it over to the parking creep. She could have sworn her meter wasn't out of time at all. She'd planned for a much longer meeting in H&H.

The guy, creep number two of the day after Trey himself, pocketed what was probably a hundred-dollar bill, flashed a crooked smile at Trey and sauntered off whistling. Ambi's stomach lurched again.

Trey leaned into her open window and she wasn't fast enough to crank it back up. "Your meter still has half an hour left on it." He purred in his liquid velvet voice. "Looks like I just saved you from- well- who knows."

"What the fuck?" Ambi shoved her door open so hard that it bumped against Trey's shins. He didn't back up on time and winced, shifting from foot to foot. She stayed seated in the car, clutching the door. "That guy was just doing a bit of disgusting flirting or something. He was likely just checking to see if I was alright, seeing as I was going a little apeshit on my steering wheel." She swallowed hard. She shouldn't have admitted that. "He was not going to molest me. The door was locked anyway, shithead. You, on the other hand, stalked me, creeped me, and then made it pretty obvious you had some molesting of your own in mind."

Trey sighed so hard it sounded like it hurt. "Look, Ambi..." he raked a hand through his gorgeous mahogany hair. It was always just a tad past needing a haircut. Not shaggy. No, it was sexy. The kind of hair every woman dreams of running her fingers through.

The rest of him was insanely gorgeous too. Unfortunately, Trey didn't just inherit a ton of money from his parents. He'd got the best of their DNA too. It was beyond her how two mortals could make someone who looked like a god.

He knew it though, so it kind of spoiled his bronzed skin, sharp cheekbones, angled jaw, perfect nose, and lips. He was well over six feet and jacked, naturally athletic and rich enough to make up for anything he lacked with personal trainers and someone to cook all his meals for him. He made that two-thousand-dollar suit look good. It looked *really* good. Again, all that deliciousness was basically like the package she wanted to send him. Shit wrapped in a pretty box with a shiny bow. Gorgeous and flawless on the outside. Stinking and nasty on the inside.

"Don't use my name," she barked. "We are not on a first name or even a last name basis and we never will be again. As far as I'm concerned, we have no history. The only thing you taught me was not to trust assholes, and I learned my lesson well, so yeah. We're done here."

Unfortunately, Trey parked one of his massive legs in front of her car door so that when she tried to shut it, she couldn't budge it. He was too close, and she had to let her hand fall away or she'd risk grazing his leg and that was *not* going to happen.

"I was serious when I said I'd double the price. I know you have something you could do with that money. I'll even throw in a trip somewhere nice as a bonus."

"You can't buy me! You had me once, Trey. You had me. Body, heart, soul, everything else. Everything I was and would be. You traded me away for your bank account, a nice house and some cars, so no. You won't buy me with that money."

Trey didn't budge. Worse, he leaned down so that they were level. She had to meet his gaze or risk admitting defeat by letting him know what his proximity was doing to her. It was throwing her into the worse internal disarray. Her insides cramped into a jumbled mess. Her hands were so clammy she was amazed they didn't slip off the wheel. Her heart pounded into a mess all over the place.

"Don't be too proud. You need this. You always wanted to own your own business. This is your chance to really succeed."

"I'd rather go under than take any help from you."

Trey shook his head and made a tsking sound. "Always so proud. If I truly don't mean anything to you and you're over what we were, then you wouldn't mind taking this job. The old Ambi would do it just to stick it to me. To prove that she could. To prove that I was the idiot and I was wrong and she'd take my money just so I had less of it, she'd go on that vacation, enjoy the hell out of it, and send me a photo of her flipping me off while drinking twelve dollar beers by the pool."

"You'd probably like that, wouldn't you? Me in a bikini next to the pool."

"I wasn't imagining you in a bikini, but if that's the photo you wanted to send, I wouldn't object."

Trey had the best eyes. He'd always had the best eyes. Dark green. Sharp and pretty, deep and serene, like a cross between emeralds, cut grass, and a tropical pool.

Her hands tightened on the wheel. He was right. He was freaking right, and he knew it. Trey was the enemy and it was a dangerous enemy who knew every single one of her weaknesses. She had to figure out a way to beat him at his own game. Maybe he was right. The old Ambi wouldn't let someone walk all over her. She wouldn't let her pride get in the way of her dreams. She would have taken that money and laughed about how it grew her business. How Trey was the loser at the end of it. And she'd take that damn trip, on his dollar. He had her and he knew it. She couldn't say no, because that would now mean admitting defeat. It wasn't a matter of pride or taking the moral high ground at all.

"Fine," she huffed. "I want twelve grand to plan your dumb office party. I'll make sure everyone even gets little fartsy favors. The live band will be the best in Minneapolis, and I'll hire a fucking magician. The hall will be spectacular, and people will talk about the food and the amazing desserts for the rest of the year. You'll look like a genius and everyone will sing your praises instead of realizing what cold-hearted, depraved bastards you and your father really are."

Trey winked one of those gorgeous eyes at her. His eyelashes were sinful. Too thick and long to belong on a man at all. "Sounds like a plan, Stan."

Fuck you and Stan too. Or no. No, rather, just fuck off. "I want two tickets to the nicest resort in Mexico for a week. All inclusive. Everything paid for. In January, when it's too cold here to even live."

Trey's dark brows drew together and for a split second, there was a shimmer of hope that made that aching pinch in her belly so much worse. Her hands nearly strangled the wheel. She was so disgusted with herself she wanted to send her own self a bag of shit.

"I've wanted to take my mom on a holiday since forever."

Instead of looking disappointed, Trey's gorgeous face broke into a huge grin. He had a resting non-bitch face. He was so handsome it was painful. When he smiled. *God.* It was like someone switched on a generator inside and fired up the lights. It was potent, that grin, and he knew it. He used it as a weapon, and it worked. Ambi felt cut to shreds just seeing it.

Trey produced the cheque that he'd thrown on the table earlier from his pocket. He pulled out a pen and filled in the amount on the top line. When he handed it over to her, she took it without her hands shaking- the world's biggest accomplishment. She nearly gasped when she noticed he'd made it out for seventeen thousand.

"That should cover the Mexico thing. Or take her anywhere. Wherever you decide." He stuck out his hand. "It's going to be a pleasure working with you, Miss Danby."

Ambi threw the cheque carelessly onto her passenger seat. She brought her palm up and spat on it before she slapped it to Trey's. He never broke eye contact with her, even when his fingers closed around hers and lingered for a second too long. Payback for the spit trick.

"A real pleasure," he repeated as he let her hand go.

He stepped back and she slammed her car door. "I'd have more pleasure eating turds," she hissed and then she peeled out of her parking spot and down the street before Trey could see right through her and realize that it wasn't true at all.

4

TREY

*T*rey almost couldn't believe Ambi agreed to meet with him. Then again, she'd cashed the cheque a day ago, and when he'd called what he assumed was her office phone to ask about cake testing, something so stupid even he couldn't keep a straight face when he called, she'd reluctantly agreed. She was a true professional and she'd made it clear, by rattling off a place and time in a curt voice and hanging up on him, that she wanted as little to do with him as humanly possible.

He planned to stretch that little out as far as he could. He'd get as much mileage out of that cheque as anyone else, and then some. He still couldn't believe that once she found out she was going to be dealing with him, she'd actually taken the money. Ok, so maybe he played her a little bit but he seriously never expected it to work. Which meant she was either desperate for the business, really wanted a vacation for her mum, or he meant that little to her that she figured the extra money was well worth having to put up with him. If he had to bet on it, Trey would put his money on the latter. College was years ago. They were a couple for like, two seconds. Okay, it was almost a year, but still. Ambi had obviously moved on.

So why couldn't he?

When he arrived at the giant freaking bakery, he felt like a pathetic puppy waiting. She was not there yet.

The bakery had that industrial feel, a small counter at the front with baked goods and a menu stating prices, but most of the activity was taking place behind the scenes. The building was large, a brick construction that extended far past the small frontage.

The hum of conversation, the clang of baking sheets and pans, and the delicious smells of freshly baked breads, pastries, and cakes reached Trey as he stood by the window, arms crossed over his thick black wool pea coat. He tapped one square-toed leather shoe in slight annoyance.

He hated lateness and Ambi knew it. It was always the one thing he couldn't stand, even when they were together. Nothing picked his ass faster than someone not respecting his time. So of course, she showed up twenty minutes late.

Trey watched her nondescript black sedan edge into a parking spot that was huge, but she made it look too small. She'd always hated parallel parking. She got out, dropped some money in the meter, pulled out her phone with one gloved hand, and checked it.

He didn't miss the secret smile that blossomed over her coral-pink lips or the puff of satisfied breath that wafted above her head after.

Ambi swept into the bakery like a queen. Her head held high, her glorious raven black hair cascading down her houndstooth coat in the front and the back. The coat was cute, so *Ambi* style that Trey almost choked on his own spit. It nipped in at the waist and flared out. She had a set of tight black skinny jeans on that were tucked into sensible winter dress boots with no heel.

"Trey." She said his name in a neutral tone as soon as she spotted him, which was right away, but somehow the word hung in the air like it left a bad taste in her mouth and she was glad it was out.

Ambi's eyes roamed over his figure boldly, and when she turned her nose up like he was nothing special and this was just another meeting, his chest compressed. *Yeah.* He knew her better than that. Her indifference was worth a thousand fucking words. She liked what she saw, that's why she didn't want to look at him. He jammed his hands in his pockets even though his coat hid any kind of repeat action of the embarrassing office incident from a few days ago.

"Well? Are we going to taste cakes or are you going to stand there all morning pretending that you hate me?"

Ambi didn't look back at him. She kept her eyes trained on the bakery counter. "First of all, your arrogance knows no boundaries. Second, I'm here because this is a business meeting. Third, I figured you couldn't be civil so I'm just going to leave instructions for several cakes to be set out. You can taste them and tell me what your final decision is."

Fuck that. If Ambi thought she was walking out that door within the next hour, she was sadly mistaken.

"Actually, that's not how this is going to work. I have this cold. Been fighting it for a few weeks now. I can't taste anything at the moment. Can't smell anything either. You'll have to do the honors and tell me which one you prefer."

Ambi scrunched her nose at him. Her eyes swept over his face frankly, which made him want to press her up against the counter and let her get real up close and personal. He wanted to plunder her lips, to kiss off that coral lipstick until it was her much lighter, prettier lips below.

They were already plump and full, but they'd be much more beautiful ravaged and swollen from his kiss.

"You look fine to me. Sounds fine too."

He shrugged. "Looks can be deceiving."

"Right. They can be." Ambi clutched her tote a little tighter, her knuckles whitening with the effort. She wasn't as calm and composed as she was letting on. "For example, I know that you're nothing better than a steaming pile of turds candy-coated with a pretty shell and expensive clothing."

"Most people go for a wolf in sheep's clothing."

Ambi blinked at him and answered in her most sugary tone. "That would be to imply that you're the type of animal that is strong, powerful, independent, *alpha* when we both know you're just a little boy who does his daddy's bidding. So, no. Turds is a much better analogy."

"I think it's a metaphor actually."

Ambi blinked again. "Whatever, Turds. A shit in sheep's clothing has a nice ring, actually. Do you want to play at this? Fine. We can do that. At the end of the day, I'll be seventeen grand richer and you'll still be working at a company you despise, letting your daddy run your life."

Her barb dug deep. The Ambi he knew never would have stooped so low. The Ambi he knew also loved him. Now? He was public enemy number one in her books. He didn't blame her and her fire only made her that much more attractive. He hadn't broken her spirit. She was still alive and kicking and ready to stick it to him. Fuck, if she knew how sexy that was, she'd paste on a happy smile and do his orders willingly. Her easy compliance and capitulation would be so much less thrilling and dangerous than the wildcat in front of him.

"Amberina!"

Ambi spun at the sound of her name and his attention was dragged up to the counter where an ancient woman stood. She was so short that only her grandmotherly wrinkled face with her shining eyes and flushed wrinkled cheeks topped by an enormous white chef's hat, were visible behind the counter.

"Marcella. Good morning." Ambi's face broke into a radiant smile that wasn't at all forced.

For a split second, Trey was actually jealous of a granny with flour smeared all over her wrinkled cheeks. There was a time when Ambi reserved those smiles just for him. Or at least, he was included on the list of sunny radiance she gifted the world. Now? Now he was just a turd on her shitlist. He deserved to be there, but it didn't stop him from wishing.

"You're here for the cake tasting. I have three set aside for you. The usual and two new ones we've been experimenting with. You'll be the first to try them."

"So, we're your guinea pigs?"

Ambi shot him a dirty look while Marcella blinked. Obviously, his attempt at humor fell flat.

"No, sir, we've been working on these cakes for months. We wouldn't feed them to anyone if they weren't ready," Marcella corrected like he was too dense to understand. To make it worse, she had one of those sweet granny voices that said that it wasn't her first rodeo when it came to dealing with idiotic individuals.

"Turd," Ambi muttered under her breath as she swept past him. The sweet fragrance of *her* trailed in her wake, lemons, and flowers, intoxicating him, turning his knees to something close to goo.

Trey shook his head. Right. He'd asked for this. He could damn well play along. Ambi was a formidable foe, but she had her weaknesses. He used to know just about all of them. He didn't plan on keeping her as a foe for long.

Marcella showed them to the back, a small room that looked very officey, with tiled floors and generic white walls. There were three collapsible tables set up and each one contained a huge, four-tier cake fully done up.

"These are just models," Marcella explained. She was dressed all in white, white chef's coat, white pants, and a huge hat. She kind of looked like an adorable granny-style snowman.

Trey had never had a grandma. Both his sets of grandparents died either before he was born or right after. He thought that if he'd had a grandma, he would have wanted her to look like Marcella. Sugary, sweet, and soft looking, a little round with the softest loving arms, but with an acerbic wit of steel.

"Models?" Okay, this was new to him.

"They don't set out freshly baked cakes to sit and spoil for months," Ambi hissed. She rolled her eyes. "This is what they'll look like. They're just cardboard. But if you want to taste one of those, go ahead."

"You're the one doing the tasting," Trey grumbled.

Ambi turned to Marcella and her smile was back. It was like it was on auto-pilot. As soon as she wasn't looking in his direction, it was safe to use it.

"What are the new flavors?"

"Well, we have a dark chocolate with buttercream frosting, a red velvet with cream cheese, but it's not your regular red velvet and a gingerbread egg nog latte for Christmas."

"The cake is gingerbread eggnog latte?" Trey stared at Marcella in disbelief.

She broke into a smile that gave her wrinkles wrinkles. In short, she was entirely adorable. She was entirely too charming, the perfect warm kind of granny and he could see why Ambi chose this bakery instead of some big corporate machine.

"Yes, that's right."

"I'll have a taste of that then," Ambi said.

Marcella nodded. "I'll go get you a plate. One minute."

Ambi dug the toe of her boot into the tile while Marcella was gone. She turned and showed him her back, which was still the sexiest back on the planet. She refused to talk to him and for once, he didn't know what to say. He was still trying to come up with something when Marcella swept back into the room.

"Here you are, sweetheart." She handed Ambi the plate. "How's business going? And your family? Everyone's well?"

Ambi's back was to him, but he could hear the joy in her voice. It hurt. It shouldn't, because he'd done it to himself, but it did.

She received the plate from Marcella, with a single slice of cake on it. It came with a metal fork. Trey's entire world narrowed to the point of watching her scrape that fork across the glass, gather up a small piece of cake. That fork. The cake. Her hand never wavered as she brought the fork to her mouth. To those full, lush, coral-hued bow lips. Her mouth parted and the fork slipped inside. Her lips caressed the tines and her eyes closed in pleasure.

When the fork popped out again, it was licked clean. He nearly died on the spot.

"This is amazing, Marcella. Not that anything I've ever tried wasn't, but I think you've really outdone yourself this time."

It caught Trey off guard. Something so simple, so mundane as tasting something, shouldn't be so- so... sexual. He felt lightheaded, the rest of his body just as light, like he'd float off to the ceiling and dissipate there, amongst the fluorescent lights and white speckled rectangular tiles. Something warm and ridiculous blossomed in his chest. It leaked into other parts right after, his stomach, his limbs, his heart. He was suffused with it, flooded, and it erased all the common sense he should have had. The barriers between him and Ambi crumbled, at least in his mind.

He was moving, stepping towards her. She stood there, too shocked to move as he drew near. He had no business being there, in her physical space. It felt too private. Too real. Yet there he was.

"I changed my mind," he said huskily. Darkly. "I do want a taste."

Ambi's eyes fluttered shut, just for a second. He should have stopped. He should have, but he didn't. He gripped Ambi's jaw, so warm and delicate and alive, between his thumb and index finger, tilted her face up and slammed his lips over hers.

5

AMBERINA

*H*e's kissing me. Oh my god, he's actually freaking kissing me right now.

Ambi's brain seriously checked out, because that was her first thought. Not anything along the lines of that he was her mortal enemy, that he tasted like a shit sandwich, that he was foul and gross and evil, and she needed to shove him away.

In fact, her brain was so messed up that her default reaction was to shut off all common sense, let down her guard to a pathetic new low, and lean into him like she was freezing to death and he was some lifesaving kind of fire. Her instincts should have kicked up and kicked into flight mode, but they chose a different mode entirely. Instead of running, she was taking in the body heat seeping through his jacket. She was shutting her eyes and drowning in the sensations. Firm lips, demanding and unyielding, going to war with hers. Fingers that were just as unyielding yet gentle on her jaw. His fingers were scalding. His lips were even hotter.

When Trey's tongue butted up against her lips, she crashed back to reality. Trey was horrible. She'd loved him and he'd shattered her heart so he could get rich instead. He'd never tried to stand up for her. For them. He'd left her crushed and broken-hearted without so much as a backward glance.

As the facts crashed in and crushed her all over again, she got her scrambled wits together enough to pull back, since both her hands were full. Trey's lips detached from hers. His body heat left her, but he'd planted his insidious warmth inside of her like a virus. Her lips burned. Her entire body burned. Her brain felt like it was boiling inside her skull.

"You asshole!" Ambi stabbed out with the fork in her right hand, barely missing Trey's chest. "Get away from me!"

He stepped back but shot her a shit-eating grin that made her stomach churn and set fires in all the wrong places and a volley of cold tingles to other, worse spots. Namely the one throbbing between her thighs. Trey had strings anchored in her belly, in her thighs and legs, in her lips and the traitorous parts of her heart that couldn't get over him and the stupid mush of her brain that couldn't forget him. He was pulling those strings, yanking on them.

It couldn't happen. She could never let that happen. This was a job. That was it. Trey was an asshole. He had been and always would be.

"Ambi, come on, I was just-"

"You were just nothing!" She was aware that Marcella was watching the whole heated exchange, probably with no small amount of interest, but she couldn't get away with letting Trey freaking kiss her. She took a menacing step forward. "I told you not to use my name," she hissed as she drew back her other hand.

It was a shitty use of cake, but fuck it, she'd already tasted it. She was going to order it no matter what Trey thought about it. What she didn't eat would just go in the garbage anyway and she'd been taught never to waste food.

Trey might be a good six inches taller than her, but she had the power of rage behind her arm. She launched the big piece of delicious, frosted, amazing, gourmet cake right into the center of his face. And smooshed. She rubbed and twisted until she could feel his nose and lips grinding against the plate. When she pulled back, plate in hand, the cake didn't come with it. It remained mashed all over his smug, asshole face.

"Well, that's a vast improvement, I must say." She grinned as Trey blubbered and scrubbed at his face with one big, strong hand, trying to clear his eyes. "I thought I'd give you that taste. Marcella doesn't have a public bathroom, so you can do double duty and lick it off yourself."

Marcella tsked and cooed behind her. She swept in and brushed Ambi aside, taking Trey's arm. It looked hilarious, little old Marcella, who was probably all of five feet tall, leading Trey, who looked like a giant next to her, out of the room.

"You can use our staff bathroom in this case," she cooed, all worried, loving grandmother.

Ambi rolled her eyes. She would rather have rubbed dog poo in Trey's face. The thrill of getting back at him was already wearing off and she was left with the tingling in some really unwanted parts. Okay, her parts weren't unwanted. The tingling, however, was.

"We'll take that one, Marcella," she called out of the room, down the hall. "Thanks, I'll stop by later on to pay for it and give you all the details."

"Okay, dear, take care," Marcella called back and Ambi had to smile.

She slipped out while Trey was occupied. There was no

way she was giving him the satisfaction of seeing how flus-tered she was. Her face was probably red. He knew her well enough that even if it wasn't, he'd see right past the mask to the desire that kiss awoke. Okay, truthfully, the desire was always there. It was hard not to see Trey and want him. He was beautiful, but it was the kind of beauty that was wrecked by getting to know him. By the festering horrible-ness of who he really was that lay beneath that gorgeous exterior.

Ambi let herself out, the bells above the door jingling merrily.

She pretty much ran back to her car, even though the sidewalk was icy, and she nearly landed on her head. When she shut herself inside, it was a full minute before she could stop her rapid-fire breaths from steaming up the windshield and another before she could actually find her keys and get them in the ignition. This time Trey didn't pop out to stop her.

She made her escape. It might be a brief reprieve, but it was an escape all the same. She knew she'd have to give Marcella an explanation. That the old woman would prob-ably hoot and holler and laugh her butt off about the whole thing. Worse, she knew she had to face Trey again, and soon. She wanted to pick out the venue, but he'd insisted on seeing it first. She had an appointment set up for Wednesday morning, less than two days away.

Which gave her about forty-six hours to arm herself, put her walls back together, and bring it.

If Trey wanted war, she'd give him war.

There really wasn't any other option.

6

AMBERINA

*O*f course, when Ambi dropped the cheque off for Marcella, the older woman was there at the counter waiting. She actually leaned in when Ambi set the cheque down as if she just couldn't wait for the juicy details.

"I didn't know you had a boyfriend," Marcella winked. "You should tell this old woman all your juicy secrets. All I have left in my life is this bakery and gossip. Only one of them keeps me young and it sure isn't running my butt off baking cakes for a bunch of ungrateful brides, picky eaters, and toddlers having meltdowns when they should be having birthdays."

"He's not my boyfriend." Ambi pressed her lips together. "Yeah. No. He's not."

"For shame! You shouldn't let men you aren't dating kiss you. You know what they say about milking the cow and all that."

Ambi stifled a groan. "I don't know if you noticed, but he ended up wearing your cake for that little stunt he pulled. I didn't let him do anything."

"It sure looked like you did. You let him for a good

minute before you pulled away. He must be a really good kisser. Did he taste like mint? I thought I could smell mint on him when I took him to show him where the bathroom was."

"No- argh. Marcella! He didn't taste like mint. He tasted like disappointment and entitlement. We dated once, for like, five minutes five years ago. It wasn't anything. I moved on. Apparently, Trey is still a troll. He trapped me into planning this work Christmas office party thing. I didn't want to do it, but he made me an offer I couldn't refuse. He's paying me good money-"

"So, you let him take liberties?"

"No. No liberties! That kiss was a mistake. I was too shocked to react at first, that's all it was. It was nothing and I made him pay for it. I'm pretty sure he got the memo."

Marcella laughed like that was the funniest joke she'd heard in her entire life. "Oh, good lord, child, he didn't get any such thing. He was practically glowing when he came out with all that cake wiped off. If you want to get a man to want you, just play hard to get."

"That's not what's happening here."

"I don't think he knows that. He seems like a determined young man. A handsome one too!" Marcella tittered and her cheeks, incredibly enough, actually flushed pink.

"You don't like him, do you?" Ambi asked, disbelief coloring her words.

"Oh, of course not. He seems like a scoundrel."

"He is. And much worse."

Marcella laughed so hard that tears formed in the corners of her eyes. Something funny formed in Ambi's stomach too. A hot wave followed by an intense cramp. God, she must have eaten too much bread that morning or something. Maybe it was the banana she'd eaten too quickly on her way over to the bakery.

"He might be a scoundrel, but he's in love with you. I can tell."

"Marcella!" Ambi had to turn her face away to hide the redness she was pretty sure was creeping its way up her neck. "Don't say that! The only thing Trey is in love with is money. Well, his big house and his fancy cars and money. That's it. That's all."

"Sweetheart, whatever happened in the past, things can always be fixed. I wouldn't put it out of the question. I saw the way he looked at you like you hung the moon. Like you were the moon in his universe. Brighter than the sun, lighting the way in his darkness."

"Yeah right," Ambi snorted, so flustered that she could barely see straight. "That's very poetic of you, but that's not me and Trey." She winked at Marcella. "Save that for your starstruck brides and grooms who come in here." Her hands had started to shake so she jammed them into the pockets of her coat. She'd picked the bright red three-quarter-length coat. It was wool, vintage, and super warm. The weather was just crap. So cold it hurt to breathe.

"I know what I saw," Marcella insisted. She picked up the cheque and glanced at it for a moment before she shuffled over to the ancient antique register she used even though the thing was so old it never functioned properly. It was ornate and gold and did look really cool though.

"Well, I don't know what you think you saw, but I know it wasn't love. Trey could have had me five years ago. He chose to dump me and go work for his dad after he threatened to disinherit him. I think the choice was pretty clear. So was the message he sent. He's just playing around now. I don't honestly know why. Maybe because he's a jerk. Maybe because he's a man and he's obsessed with his dick, like all men are. I- I don't know. Maybe he's just doing it because he feels guilty about what happened. Who knows. I don't. I don't want to. I just want to get his job done and over with and move on to the next. That's all this is about for me. My business."

Marcella tittered to herself. "This bakery is a passion of mine. There were two things I loved in life. Making cakes and my Frank. He loved my cakes. Always encouraged me. After he passed, I needed something to do. A way to pay the bills, but also a way to fill up all the long hours. I loved him. All forty-six years we had together. The moral of the story is that when you find a good one, don't let him go, no matter how stupid he was in the past. People make mistakes. Maybe he's trying to tell you he's sorry. I know what I saw, and that boy is head over heels in love with you."

Ambi knew she wasn't going anywhere by arguing. Okay, she'd probably argue herself straight into a migraine and that part of the day was still coming. She had to go meet with Trey at the hall she wanted to use as the venue for the party in less than an hour. She couldn't afford to explode what remained of her brain cells.

Or to go soft. No, she definitely couldn't afford that. Thoughts about Trey in any capacity other than him being a massive jerk who wasn't good enough to lick the bottoms of her boots were strictly off-limits.

"Thanks for making the best cakes, Marcella. I'll see you in a couple of weeks to pick it up."

Marcella nodded and smiled knowingly like she and Trey were in on some big secret that Ambi didn't want to be a part of. Fricking Trey. He even got Marcella to like him. Not that it was hard. Marcella was an extremely nice lady. She was as grandmotherly as she looked. Ambi wished that she would have been one of those mean grannies when it came to Trey. The kind who lured a person in with pastries then shoved them in the oven or baked them into a pie.

Trey pie.

It would probably be delicious.

Just like the rest of him.

Shit. Shit on a freaking stick. Her brain was already betraying her. Her body was doing that stupid buzzing thing like she'd just stuck a knife in a toaster and jumped in the tub with it.

Ambi shook her head and waved to Marcella as she turned and started for the door.

"Wish your mother Merry Christmas from me," Marcella called.

Ambi turned and waved again. "I will. See you in a few weeks, Marcella. Thanks again for everything."

She made a hasty exit before Marcella could sing any more of Trey's praises. As she slipped into her car, she had to grip the wheel to keep her hands from shaking and the frigid cold had nothing to do with it. Ambi sank her teeth into her bottom lip and worked it until she could taste blood. She had to be composed. On her game. She still had to meet with Trey at the stupid hall and she wasn't going to walk in there with anything less than the toughest poker face in place.

She was filled with resolution when she started driving, but by the time she reached the first red light, something more than dread was churning in the pit of her stomach.

Marcella's words were like seeds from the most insidious weeds. They planted themselves in the barren garden of her heart and refused to give up, sprouting and growing without sunlight or water or even warmth.

7

TREY

The hall. Yet another convenient excuse to meet with Ambi.

Trey knew he could be a first-rate asshole. Usually, he tried to keep that shit to a minimum. He made a point of not treating people the way his father did, like he owned them just because he paid their salaries. He didn't want to treat Ambi that way. He didn't want to be a jerk. He didn't want her to think he was trying to assert ownership over her just because he was paying for some stupid party.

He just wanted to spend time with her. A few minutes here and there was so much more than he'd had in the past five years. Those few minutes were everything. She'd always been what he thought about at the end of the day, his last thought, and his first thought in the morning.

That kiss- that kiss at the bakery- it had been two days and he still couldn't stop thinking about it. He felt it with every fiber of his being. Every shred of who he was wanted a repeat, even if it was glaringly obvious that Ambi hated him.

She acted like she did. She said she did. Then there was the hesitancy in her kiss. She hadn't pulled away. Slapped him. Kneed him in the balls. All of the things he deserved. No. She'd let him kiss her until her better judgment kicked in and she remembered that she was *supposed* to hate him.

Waiting for Ambi to show in the hall's entrance made Trey feel like he was going to explode, at least on the inside. He'd pretty much been a wreck for the past two days. He tossed and turned all night, trying to come up with a game plan, but there was nothing. He was still winging it and with Ambi, that was far from good enough.

He almost thought she was going to stand him up just to teach him a lesson, but then she breezed through the door, twenty-five minutes late. He was more annoyed at this pathetic puppy dog reaction to her than he was about her being purposely late. He wanted to wag his tail, jump all over her legs barking wildly, and pee all over the floor in his excitement.

Yup. He'd reached new lows alright.

Ambi was gorgeous, as always. She had a red vintage coat on that had a set of gold buttons at the breast, nipped in at the waist, and ended in pleats. Her hair was done in some fancy braid that trailed well down her back. She'd left a few wisps down at the front to frame her beautiful face. Her cheeks were flushed pink from the cold and she clapped her gloved hands, totally oblivious to the inner turmoil that was turning him inside out.

God, did she have to be so blindingly beautiful? Did she have to smell so damn good? Did she have to be so indifferent to him?

"Good to see you made it," Ambi said politely as she glanced around the hall.

The building was huge, a modern square thing that was black and white on the outside with red accents. The yard was probably manicured in the summer, but the snow blanketed any appeal that might have had. Trees were planted here and there, almost as an afterthought. The inside, from what he could see, was designed to be as white and cold as possible. Glass railings, white tile, and white walls made the place so sterile that it could have been a hospital.

His father would find the place appealing. Maybe that's why Trey hated it.

"Of course I made it. Why would I not make it? I was the one who said that I wanted to see the hall before I committed to it."

Ambi brushed at her hair before she remembered that it was braided and dropped her hand away. She tugged at her black leather gloves instead, ripping them from her hands and tucking them into the pocket of her coat.

"Really? I find it hard to believe that you'd be willing to commit to anything."

Something wild and irrational built up in his chest. Ambi wasn't looking at him. She'd hurled the insult so casually, almost like someone drawing back a bow and firing an arrow straight into the sky. Somehow it fell and hit the intended target right in the bullseye.

Trey studied his shoes while his chest compressed his lungs into the point of total incapacity. Breathing was apparently going to be a no-go.

"Anyway, I have a few backups if you don't like this one," Ambi went on, oblivious or uncaring.

No, she wasn't either of those things. She wasn't oblivious to what she was doing. She was doing it intentionally and he deserved the beat down. He'd left her five years ago. It wasn't exactly what she thought, but it was enough of what she thought that she was justified in her rage. He'd pretty much forced her into this when she'd made it more than obvious she wanted nothing to do with him. He'd kissed her when he had no right to her body or her personal space. He'd stolen something that wasn't his. No matter how much he wished he could undo all the shit from the past, it was already done.

"Right. Well, lead the way," Trey choked out. His voice sounded almost normal, a little harsh, but Ambi just nodded.

She walked off in the sea of white, her flat-soled boots scraping across the white tile. His heart thundered in his chest as he followed her. Ambi led the way up a set of stairs and down two narrow hallways before she finally came to something marked Ballroom A.

Trey guessed she planned a lot of events at the Centre, seeing as she was showing him around herself and there was no manager or staff in sight.

The room was done in neutrals. More white tile. White walls. A huge bank of floor to ceiling windows made up the far wall, letting in sunlight. It was magnified on the white. At least it was bright and airy. There was even a small second level, overlooking everything.

God, his father would love this place. Everyone would. They'd all be impressed by how pretty and new and future forward it was.

Did it make him a huge fucking asshole that he wanted to request a hole in the wall dive instead?

"Well?" Ambi turned, eyes glistening naturally, the sunlight from the windows playing over her features, high-lighting the delicate curl of her cheekbones, the fullness of her lips, and the slope of her jawline.

He cleared his throat when his heart stuttered painfully, but he didn't say anything. Ambi swallowed hard, obviously unnerved by his silence. She took a step back, then another, putting distance between them. It didn't matter. He still felt like she was inside of him, flowing through his veins. His throat closed up.

"Okay, well, the place has excellent food. The catering is actually affordable, even though it's pretty high end. There are some great menu choices and they do all the options like vegan, vegetarian, gluten free- anything people need. They have a great bar system. Drinks are generally six dollars a piece so people won't likely be getting smashed. It's very professional and the place is classy, so you don't even need to bother with spending money on decorations. It's well within the budget."

Ambi trailed off. She stood there, a few feet from the entrance to the mostly empty room. She looked nervous suddenly.

"Uh- they do all the setup and takedown. Their tables and chairs are nice. Everything is new. It's all very modern, to match the building itself. Like I said. Classy. I think it's a good fit."

Trey wanted to argue with her. He wanted to tell her to pick something shittier, something that people would complain about, something that required tacky decorations. He'd rather honestly host the whole thing in an old gym somewhere with a space for a dance floor and potluck style tables set up at the back. At least people would have fun then.

"There's more than enough room for a band and other entertainment. I brought a list of contacts with me that I thought were suitable. I'd have to book soon, as most people are already busy this time of year. I'm going to have to call in a favor as it is."

Trey flexed his hands. He opened and closed his fists, his palms disgustingly damp. His heart did something wild in his chest. God. Ambi had no idea how fucking hot it was that she was doing this. What she'd always wanted to do. That she was so... put together. So in charge. So good at this.

When he still didn't answer, her liquid eyes traveled slowly to his face. Something in the air shifted between them. The room became awkwardly charged again, like the floor was filled up with live wires, sparking and dangerous around their ankles like a viper waiting to strike.

When she blinked it was like it happened in slow motion, one dark sweep of even darker lashes. Finally, she sighed.

"Well, if you don't like it, I have two other places that aren't booked up. They're not as nice as this one though, and they won't give me as good of a price. This really is the best option."

Trey blinked back. Ambi was too much of a professional to let him in. She had a good mask in place. The kind of mask that gave nothing away. She looked at him like she was seeing through him, like he was anyone else. Like they'd never shared anything. Not a life, not an apartment, not hopes and dreams. Not even a moment.

It absolutely gutted him. Was there really nothing there? Did he imagine the whole hesitant couple of seconds on her part when he'd kissed her? The instant he swore she'd been about to kiss him back? Had she moved on? Just because she didn't have someone didn't mean that she wasn't happy. She'd obviously carved out a life for herself. Started a business from scratch. She was well on her way to becoming a success.

He wanted to kiss her again, to try to convince her that there was something. Something unfinished. Something, anything. A shred of what they were. That it wasn't just alive for him. He needed to convince himself that he wasn't the only one that had battled five long years to put out the fire and lost. That she felt just a little of that inferno, somewhere in her being. That there wasn't enough water on earth to put it out for either of them.

"Hello? Trey? Anyone home in there?" Ambi snapped her fingers right in front of his face. "If you're not going to answer me, I'm going to take your silence as a yes and just book the place." She rolled her eyes. "God, I don't even know why you insisted on coming down here. You hired me to do this all for you and yet you're here. Making my life difficult. As per usual."

"So, you do still feel something." As soon as he put it out there, he knew it was the wrong thing to say.

Ambi's eyes widened, and not in a good way. In the kind of telltale way that said she knew exactly what he was doing and that it was a pathetic stab in the dark on his part. She looked at him like he was the fly who had been pissing her off for the past two days. The one she'd finally lined up in the crosshairs of her fly swatter and would be only too happy to smush.

Ambi inhaled sharply, but when she spoke her voice was strong and even. "We're talking about the hall. I'm doing a job. The job I was paid to do. There is nothing else. There will never be anything else. I'm a professional, which is why I'm here. Because I care about my business. Because this is a huge opportunity to me, and honestly, because you made it impossible for me to say no. I'm not a bad person, Trey, so just tell me. Is this place okay or not?"

Fuck. How had he managed to screw everything up in a matter of minutes? Oh right. He'd done that five years ago when he'd dumped Ambi for a multi-billion dollar company that was set to be his empire as soon as his father passed away, and a six-figure bank account in the interim.

"Yeah." His voice was foreign to his own ears. "The hall is fine. I guess."

Ambi breathed a sigh of relief. He literally watched the shiver roll through her, watched her shoulders sag and her body curl into itself. Was she that glad that she didn't have to deal with him? Was it really just business for her or was she really good at pretending?

"Right. I'll book it then. I'll have the menus emailed to you for tomorrow morning so you can pick what you want. Let me know if there are alternative options you need, as I mentioned. I'll also have a list of potential entertainment and links to samples of their work to you by noon tomorrow. I'll need a decision soon, since the party isn't far away, and this is a busy time for everyone."

Trey nodded woodenly. The way Ambi rattled off facts like that really was impersonal. It was all business. There wasn't a scrap of feeling behind it. Not even anger. It was all *indifference*. He hated indifference. That lack of feeling anything at all.

Ambi nodded at him, tucked her hands back into her pockets, and whirled. She stalked confidently out the door, banking hard to head down the hall.

Hell no. He wasn't going to let her go like that. There was something in him, something raw and broken, like salt in already shredded wounds, stinging and chaffing and burning. He couldn't let her leave like that. Like any other person in the world would have. He couldn't let her, because he wasn't any other person in her world, and she wasn't in his.

He caught up to her right at the front entrance. There were only two big sliding doors, one for entry and one for exit, and a bank of windows surrounding it all. He ran after Ambi, his shoes slapping against the tiles so hard that she whirled right by the door.

"Trey- what-"

He couldn't stop himself. He gripped her arm with one hand, curling her into him. He caught her off balance and her hands slapped against the black wool of his coat as her body melded against his. She capitulated from the shock and his other arm encircled her back. He dipped his head at the same time her lips parted.

The instant their lips met, fire erupted between them. She was the gasoline and he was already roaring. The burn ate at them, the intensity wild and alarming and disarming. He plundered her mouth, licking at her lips with burning passes of his tongue until they parted for him on an exhale, granting him entrance.

It was wrong. It was totally wrong, but nothing had ever felt so fucking right.

Trey swept his tongue in and stroked Ambi's. His whole body reacted, hardening, melting into hers, as he devoured and claimed. He wanted to back her up against a wall, kiss her until she couldn't breathe. He wanted her in his arms. Always. He wanted her surrender. He wanted to give her back everything she'd taken and ask for all the parts of himself that she still held locked up within all the parts of her. All the parts that had once been *them*.

While he was still kissing her, Ambi's hands balled into fists against his chest. She beat at him before she even pulled away. He nipped her as she pulled back, by accident, but he couldn't stop the groan that vibrated through his chest when copper blossomed and exploded on his lips.

He let her fall away when she pushed. He let her step back, let her break the magic. It didn't feel like being saved from drowning. It felt like the exact opposite. Like her absence was the lead weight that dragged him down back into darkness.

"What are you doing!" She held a shaking hand up to her lips. She pressed her fingers there and pulled them away after, to check for blood. There was no evidence of the copper he'd tasted and he breathed a small sigh of relief. It was short-lived since her eyes flashed and crackled with rage. "What do you think you're doing?" she spat out again.

Trey pointed up at the door, where a bough of something as modern as the rest of the place was strung up. "There's mistletoe above the door. I was just doing my duty and all."

Ambi's eyes flicked upwards then her nostrils flared, and her lips thinned out. "That's not a mistletoe! You wouldn't know a mistletoe if it bit you in the fucking dick!"

They were still standing close, even with the step back she took. Trey felt drunk on her, drunk on the sensation of kissing her, of the sweet vanilla taste of her still in his mouth, of the lingering warmth of her body that had just been pressed against his. He wanted to keep drinking. To keep drinking her in until he blacked out from her beauty.

She could lie to him. She could lie to him with her words, but her body gave her away. Her lips were swollen, her hands were shaking at her sides. Her entire body was vibrating, and her pupils were blown so wide there were almost no iris left.

Ambi's shoulders heaved. He thought for a second that she was going to say something. To tell him off. That she'd do something. Anything. Instead, she whirled and ran out the door. Ran. She wasn't someone who fled from her problems. She wasn't someone who ran away from anything. She stood and faced it. Not without fear, but with bravery. She didn't *run*.

Yet there she was, racing through the parking lot, her braid streaming out behind her. Trey stood rooted next to the window by the door, breathing so hard and sharp that it felt like glass going in and out of his lungs. He watched Ambi get in her car and peel away. He kept watching, long after she was gone. He stood in the same spot for so long that it felt like he wasn't human any longer, like he'd been turned into some version of a statue, as ultra-modern as the rest of the building.

When he finally forced himself to walk out to his own car, his heart was still racing. Everything felt wild and wrong and torn up inside. He was bleeding out. Not slowly, but violently. He waited another half hour, sitting in the cold of his car without it running. He waited until it started to pour. Raining. Freezing raining. It barely even registered with him.

He waited until he was sure Ambi was back at the office, or at least safely pulled over somewhere else, then he texted her private number. The one she hadn't ever given out. The one the PI he'd hired to look into her handed him as a little extra gift.

Ambi was Ambi and she wasn't going to give in without a fight.

Which was why he'd take her off guard with a truce.

8

AMBERINA

Somehow a storm snuck up on Ambi and took her by surprise. A vile storm. A genuine storm. A storm raged, brutal and as ugly as the one going on in her heart.

First, the city was blanketed with freezing rain that fell for hours, turning the streets and sidewalks alike into skating rinks. For the grand finale, the wind kicked up and the temperature dropped, and the rain turned to snow. The wind furiously swirled and tossed the fat flakes about until it was nothing more than a good old-fashioned blizzard with whiteout conditions.

Travel wasn't advised. People were being warned to stay off the streets when and if at all possible. The whole thing had come up in a few hours and by the time evening rolled around, the snow was so mounded up that most people probably couldn't get around anyway.

The storm wasn't forecasted, but right after her meeting with Trey at the hall, the weather warnings started dinging away on the weather app. Ambi canceled her plans for the afternoon, which included grocery shopping and a few other personal errands and went straight back to the office. Sometimes it was lucky that she lived where she worked. She parked her car in her spot in the back and hunkered down to work on some unplanned accounting for the afternoon.

She tried not to think about the text Trey sent her earlier.

He was sorry. Bullshit he was sorry. He wasn't freaking sorry. Sorry that she'd run out on him, maybe. Sorry that she had more than a couple thousand dollars of his money in her pocket and she could choose to just call the whole thing off and slap him with a sexual assault charge. Yeah. He was freaking sorry all right.

He'd texted her personal number, which meant that somehow, he had it. He said he wanted to apologize in person and that he'd come by her office after work. Around six.

Trey was never late. It was six-thirty and when he still hadn't showed up, Ambi leaned back in her office chair, propped her feet up on the desk and stared at her pink socks with the flamingos. She'd locked the door at four when she normally closed. No one could get around the city in the terrible weather anyway. She'd still sat down at her office, forcing herself to do catch up work and paperwork that she hated.

She stared past her socks, out into the darkness. The window was getting foggy and frosted and there really wasn't much to see except a blanket of white anyway. The rain had frozen to the glass earlier, smudging and smearing and blocking out most of the world anyway.

Trey was never late. That was his thing. She knew it.

She'd purposely shown up late for their past two meetings just to pick his ass.

Ambi picked her phone off the desk, toyed with it in her hand for a bit, turning it over and over, and finally dialed the number Trey texted her from. The call went straight to voice mail, which usually meant that someone's phone was off or dead. She tried texting anyway, even though she felt ridiculous doing it.

Are you still coming?

The message stayed marked unread, so five minutes later, she sent another.

As fun as it would be to watch you eat crow and humble pie for half an hour, I'm done. It's late. You're late. Don't bother coming. You probably won't get here anyway.

She waited ten minutes, even though she wanted to slip up the back stairs to her apartment, slip into some really fuzzy pajamas, make herself a cup of tea and camp out in front of the TV to binge watch something totally uninteresting while she purposely didn't think any thoughts involving Trey.

Ambi picked up her phone again, just to check to see if the blizzard had been downgraded, which wasn't likely given that the wind was still screaming out there. She just happened to check and see if her texts had been marked as read. They hadn't, but maybe Trey turned that feature off.

Why was she even still down there waiting, three hours past her closing time? She didn't want to think about Trey, yet that's all she was doing. When she realized how pathetic that was, that even though she'd finished her accounting and the extra hours had been about work, they'd also been about something they should never have been, she bit down hard on her bottom lip. She chewed it until it hurt. It was better to concentrate on the bite of pain than to think about Trey's lips on hers.

Had she been hoping for an apology or something else?

Before she could begin an inner monologue with herself, which was sure to be filled with conflict and a heck of a lot of berating herself for just about everything that had happened in the past week, something hard banged against the front window.

Ambi let out a gasp and shot to her feet. The banging came again, sharper, more brutal, this time from the front door. She didn't have a doorbell and the pounding continued long past what was normal. The hair on the backs of her arms stood on end. Thank god she'd locked the door. Who the heck was out there?

She debated about charging up the stairs to her apartment, since it separated her and whoever was out there by two doors with locks, one of them thick, industrial, and steel, but then she shook her head.

Trey wouldn't have been dumb enough to try and get there in the crazy weather, would he?

"Ambi?" As if in answer, her name floated through the door. It was muffled and garbled, but it was definitely Trey's voice.

"You asshat! What the hell?" She figured it would serve Trey right to stand out there and freeze. On second thought, she didn't want to be responsible for him really freezing. Trey was so unpredictable that if he knew she was there, which obviously he did given that the lights were on and he could probably make out her shadowy shape inside, he'd likely be too stubborn to leave.

Ambi stalked to the door, flipped the lock and pushed it open. It took all her strength given that mother nature seemed to be pushing with equal force from the other side.

Trey was there. He practically fell through the open door. He looked like some version of a winter monster, caked in snow, breathing hard, his breath frosted and frozen all over his face, his coat cloaked in ice and snow. His eyebrows and eyelashes were frosted over and beaded up with ice. Even his hair was coated and stiff with white.

"What the hell?" Ambi stumbled back. "Why were you stupid enough to try and make it in this? Don't you know that they're not advising travel?"

"Y-yeah," Trey gasped. A violent shiver wracked him so hard that particles of ice and snow actually fell off his coat and dropped onto the floor to melt in little round puddles like he was a shaggy dog shaking himself.

Ambi rolled her eyes to hide the fact that she was more than a little concerned. She stepped past Trey and locked the door. A drift of snow had blown in and was melting on her tiled floor. She whirled and took in Trey. He stared back, his massive shoulders heaving with every breath. His wool coat was sodden, and his black slacks looked soaked through. His square-toed dress shoes were terribly inadequate for the drifts out there and snow still clung up to his knees. His face was cherry red, right along with his ears and when he rubbed his hands together, his fingers were the same angry hue.

"Jesus. What happened?"

"In- in short," Trey panted. He stopped and gulped in a breath. "In short I ignored the weather warnings and went out anyway. My car got stuck a couple of miles from here. I called for a tow, but apparently, half the city is under snow and they said it would be hours if they could even get to me before morning. I stayed in the car, idling it for as long as I could, but I only had less than a quarter of a tank and it ran out in an hour. I gave up on the tow and decided to walk. It was only a few miles which wouldn't have been bad, but I didn't have boots and I got soaked through right away, there were so much snow and wind. I tried to call you after I tried calling a tow, but my phone died, and I didn't have a charger in the car."

Ambi stared at the pathetic sight that was Trey. She should be happy to see him washed in looking like a miserable, drowned rat. She wished she could say that she hoped that he'd contracted pneumonia and died prematurely, but she didn't wish that at all. Trey's hands looked painful. His feet might have frostbite. She wouldn't laugh if he lost a couple of toes at her expense. She wouldn't laugh at all. Despite everything, she didn't want Trey to be miserable.

She just wanted him to leave her alone.

Except honestly, she wasn't even sure she wanted that either. She had been, but now... after two days and two kisses, she had no idea where she stood. She wasn't as resolute as she should have been. She wasn't resolute at all.

"You're an idiot," she mumbled. "A complete dumb ass. Who drives around in winter with less than a quarter tank and without a survival kit with a candle and a set of warm clothes?"

Trey blinked. Water clung to his eyelashes, starring them above his ridiculously gorgeous jade eyes. He looked pathetic, but still unfortunately gorgeous.

"You're right." He shrugged. "It was stupid. All of it. I shouldn't have come."

"No. You shouldn't have." It occurred to her that now that he was there, Trey was likely there for the night. She wasn't going to send him back out into the cold. Getting a cab would likely be impossible until the streets were plowed, and she wouldn't fare any better in her car than he had in his. "You shouldn't have."

She debated about making him sleep in the office overnight. The floor would be good enough for him. It was better than being out in the blizzard. Really, that's all he should hope for. He could get his rich daddy to send a freaking driver to come pick his ass up sometime between now and morning, plowed be damned. Maybe they could land a helicopter or their private jet on the top of the building.

Ambi winced internally at herself. She was being petty. She knew it, but she just couldn't help it. She was ten seconds away from telling Trey to make himself at home before she bolted up the stairs to her own comfy apartment, but then a big glop of snow melted off his hair and ran down his face like a really unfortunate bird shit or a raw egg.

She was horrified to find a smile playing over her lips. God, she'd pay money to see Trey get shit on by a bird. She wondered if she could find one for hire.

"You better come up." She pointed to the ceiling. "I live up there, but then again, you probably know that given that you stalked me. You must have. You have my private cell number."

Trey tried to muster up his signature smirk, but instead, his lips wobbled, and his teeth knocked together loudly as a violent shiver swept through him.

"Anyway. I don't want to be the one responsible for you getting pneumonia or something. Two wrongs don't make a right and two turds don't make anything good. We've already decided that you're a turd. I don't want to be a turd. I want to be the better person. So- if you- can- uh- promise me a truce, I'll make you a cup of mint tea and you can get out of those wet clothes."

Trey groaned. "You k-know I h-h-hate mint tea." He had

trouble with the words, given that he was shivering so hard that his whole body was shaking.

Ambi grinned wickedly. "I know no such thing. You know, I don't remember much of anything at all from when we went out. It was such a long time ago and it wasn't very long or meaningful. When you ended things, I just kind of forgot about all of it. What I did remember, I viewed as kind of a really low point in my life, so I tried to block out as much as I possibly could."

Trey practically growled at her, but the effect was spoiled by the fact that he still looked like a wet mop and was shivering so violently his teeth were on the verge of shattering each other.

Ambi smiled back innocently. She imagined it was innocent, at least. In reality, she probably looked like the guilty cat who had just swallowed its owner's favorite canary whole and wasn't sorry at all.

"Anyway, you can have a bath while I dry out your wet clothes."

"Those clothes are d-dry c-c-clean o-only," Trey shivered.

"Good." Her smile grew wider. "I'll throw them in the dryer."

Trey's eyes widened in horror. *Please.* Surely there were worse things than a two-thousand-dollar suit and an expensive wool coat hitting the dryer. Just because things said they were dry clean only, didn't mean that they actually *were*.

She followed up with the best part of all. The part she had no doubt that Trey would be absolutely thrilled about. The icing on the cake, the item that would seal the deal.

"While they're drying, I just so happen to have a nice, fluffy, pink quilt for you."

She turned and left Trey dripping all over the tiled floor

of her office, shivering and breathing heavy. She went straight to the stairs to her apartment. It only took Trey a few seconds to do the whole suck it up, buttercup routine and follow.

Ah, humble pie had never been so freshly baked or smelled so delicious.

9

TREY

*I*t turned out that there were few things better in life than a warm shower. He stripped out of his sopping wet clothes, left them outside the bathroom door as instructed, and cranked the shower on to something somewhere between scalding and fucking unbearable. The water was hot enough to melt him and hurt like hell on his frozen feet, hands, and face, but it also felt pretty damn near heaven.

He was so enraptured by getting warm again when he felt cold straight to his bones, the kind of cold that can't actually be properly eradicated without being so hot that sweat beaded his brow even under the pounding water, that he didn't actually stop to take in any details of the bathroom until after he'd shut the water off.

Black spots danced in front of his eyes from the brutal temperature change, then the boiling alive. His blood was probably sizzling, and he figured passing out on top of everything else wouldn't be smart or conducive to anything. He kind of wanted to keep his skull in one piece.

He stepped out of the tub and grabbed for the towel on

the rack. Of course, it was pink. Pink and fluffy. Ambi always did like pink. She liked her towels big enough to wrap around her three times since she was always cold.

Thinking about the towel now wrapped around his hips on Ambi's body worked miracles for his dick. It was good to see that the bastard hadn't frozen off in the whole frigid trek from hell he'd forced himself to undergo. Then again, desperation made people do really stupid shit. He'd let Ambi go once. He wasn't going to make the same mistake again.

Trey glanced slowly around the bathroom, breathing in the colder air. The mirror was fogged up, even with the fan clanking away overhead. The office was one of those old brick buildings that must have had a few thousand previous lives. The apartment on top was large, but it was old and unique with tons of character. Brick walls, exposed ceiling beams, beat up hardwood floor. Exactly what Ambi liked.

The bathtub was a claw foot, number one on her bathtub wish list, and an old cast iron one at that, none of the fake plastic shit. The sink was a simple pedestal and the toilet was nothing special, but the exposed gold radiator at the end of the bathroom was pretty cool. The whole thing screamed Ambi.

Footsteps sounded in the hall outside the bathroom. Trey could practically hear Ambi breathing through the old wood door- also the real deal with the five panels and the antique knob that looked like it might fall off at any given minute.

"Yo, Ambi? My clothes are done in the dryer yet?"

She snorted through the door. It was muffled, but he could imagine her face, half pissed off, half annoyed. No, wrong. A third pissed off, a third annoyed, a third trying to hide that she actually didn't find his company that repulsive.

That might be wishful thinking, but he knew for a fact that if she did, she would have told him to go fuck himself and left him downstairs to thaw out in her office and figure out his own way home.

Fuck. He couldn't think about the term fuck himself at the moment. Not with Ambi so close and nothing more than her towel wrapped around his hips. His dick throbbed at the idea of any kind of action.

Trey gripped the towel tighter, trying to figure out how to tuck his cock up or block it so that it wasn't obvious that he had a damn two by four going on under there. Ambi would probably burn that towel if she found out.

"The dryer?" Ambi snorted again. "They aren't even done in the wash yet."

"You're washing my suit?" Trey slammed his eyes shut. That was probably the end of his hopes of wearing clothes out of there. Everything would likely be shrunk eight sizes too small when Ambi was done with it. Maybe that was her end game. Revenge. Humiliation. Not that he could fault her.

"Yeah. Everything. Your coat too."

Trey groaned. Wool and washers and dryers didn't mix. That coat cost him over a thousand dollars and Ambi likely knew it.

"Do you have anything I could put on in the meantime?" He was glad his eyes were closed so he didn't have to watch his balls wither up.

"I have a robe. A pink one. I think it would be way too small on you though."

Ambi's. Pink. Robe. The fact that the idea wasn't as hideous as it should have been said a lot for his testosterone level. He imagined slipping that warm fuzzy pink object against his skin and bringing it to his face, smelling Ambi's fresh scent all over it. On the other hand, his dick was trying to reach up and give him a high five over the idea, so maybe he was still a dude after all, bathrobe fantasies included.

"Or I have a quilt. Take your pick."

"I'll take the quilt. I don't want to ruin your robe."

Ambi let out a laugh that was too harsh to be a real laugh at all. "Oh really? You don't want to ruin my robe, but you have no qualms about ruining my life? Not that I remember anything about that. I've blocked that right out of my mind. I just think that's really fucking rich."

Trey winced. Right. He deserved that. He deserved so much worse.

He didn't have a good comeback for any of it, so he stood there stupidly, staring at the pink towel wrapped around his waist. A minute later the door cracked open and something multicolored was shoved inside before the door slammed shut again.

He stared at the heap of fabric. It wasn't hand sewn. It was one of those cheap puffy looking things from the department store that ruined on the first wash. It was ten different shades of pink and purple. Apparently, his humiliation for the night wasn't complete yet.

He cringed as he slipped off the towel, hung it back on the rack since he knew Ambi hated towels left on the floor or flung over the shower bar or tub side, and pulled on the quilt. He wrapped it around himself the best he could before he opened the bathroom door and stepped out.

He was greeted with another laugh, this time a real one. It started out small and turned into a full-on cackle. It was such a beautiful sound, Ambi full-on doing that crazy belly laugh of hers that sounded totally like an evil witch cackling about a spell, that he was instantly warmed all over again.

"You look like a freaking burrito," she giggled. He finally

turned his head, just to watch her brush tears from the corners of her eyes. "Just wait. Let me get my phone. I have to get a picture."

"Hell no. No pictures," Trey grumbled. "I won't be black-mailed over this. I came here to apologize for what happened. I nearly froze to death out there. I'm lucky I didn't lose my toes or my fingers or something worse."

Her eyes immediately tracked to his waist. Thankfully, his dick wasn't choosing that moment to make a tent out of the middle of the quilt. Small mercies did indeed still exist. His eyes flicked to her face right after and she was blushing a deep shade of scarlet. She ripped her eyes away immediately and stalked down the narrow hall, muttering something about it being a service to all mankind if it had happened.

Trey followed Ambi, struggling to keep the quilt in place. He was very aware that he had absolutely nothing on underneath and that she picked the kitchen to have their conversation. Of course. The kitchen. A room filled up with all sorts of sharp and dangerous objects like knives and frying pans if he should choose to get out of line again.

Like the bathroom and the hallway, which was lined with colorful artwork, the kitchen and living room combo, which opened up into each other, was pretty much exactly what she'd always wanted. Not just the architecture of the place, but the furnishings. She'd picked mostly antique stuff and carried the eclectic artwork into the living room and even the kitchen. The living room had a big red woven rug and a curved vintage green sectional that screamed sixties. The kitchen was complete with a farmhouse table, big planks on the top and chipped yellow paint on the thick legs. The appliances were some kind of retro deal. They were a strange seafoam color and didn't look safe to use at all.

Of course, Ambi was right in her element. She threw a kettle on the stove and indicated the table. There were four different chairs surrounding it, all upholstered beasts that he had a fuck ton of trouble pulling out without the quilt dropping off. When he plunked down in a black brocade chair which was extremely uncomfortable and thrust a spring right into his left ass cheek, she set a steaming mug of mint tea in front of him.

So, she'd made good on her word.

God, he hated tea. He hated all tea, but he knew Ambi loved it. She didn't drink coffee. Never did. She was a true tea granny through and through.

"I like the place," Trey said awkwardly, while he tried not to inhale the minty vapors coming from the mug in front of him.

"Thanks." She pulled out a chair and sat down across from him. She thumped a water bottle on the table and added a good portion to her half-full mug. It was something she always did. Added cold water so she could drink her tea right away without waiting for it to cool.

It was amazing how five years hadn't changed her at all. She'd accomplished and found everything she wanted. All without him.

If that wasn't humbling, he didn't know what was.

"It's nice. Your style. The brick. The wood beams. The décor. The tub. It's everything you ever described."

"Yeah." She took a big gulp of tea. "And my office is right below so it's really convenient. Thanks for making it possible, you know, with your twenty grand and the amazing reference you're going to give me to ensure I can keep affording the rent on the place. I haven't told Mom about Mexico yet, but when I do, I know she's going to be thrilled."

Underneath her acerbic words, spoken with way too much sweetness for him to mistake her intent, was a big fucking guilt trip. She was basically flipping the bird right in his face without raising a hand at all.

"Look... I'm here to make peace. I wanted to say that I'm sorry. For everything. God..." Trey reached up and ran a hand through his wet hair. He removed it, but not before spraying water droplets all over the place. "You have no idea how many times I wanted to call and tell you that. Text. Email. Send a fucking letter. Do something. Anything."

Ambi's one eyebrow curled a little at that. "Yeah?" Her hand paused on the handle of her mug. She didn't pick it off the table. Instead, she nailed him with a direct gaze that was so full of emotion he couldn't begin to get his head on straight enough to unravel the mystery of it. "Then why didn't you?"

10

AMBERINA

*T*rey in her apartment wasn't a good idea. Trey soaking wet, sitting three feet away, very naked under a quilt that was trying its best to fall off, was a terrible, terrible idea. As in, the Worst.

The problem was, no matter how hard she tried, she couldn't erase the memories of their time together. She'd lied about that. About not remembering. About forcing herself to forget. She remembered it all. Every single detail. She wanted to peel back that quilt and find the scar on Trey's left pec, compliments of when he fell out of a tree when he was six. A branch caught him and cut him, leaving him with a two-inch scar that hadn't faded as he grew up.

She wanted to see how five years had changed him, if at all. She didn't care if he was still cut or as broad or ridiculously chiseled, veiny, and delicious. She could pretty much see that he was all of those things, even with the quilt covering everything but his arms. His arms. God, his arms.

Those arms, with their sinful golden skin, their bulging muscles at the top and the striated longer ones at the forearms, the corded ropes of veins that traversed it all and the crisp dark hairs... they were good enough to rip off and eat. They'd probably be an extremely delicious accompaniment to mint tea.

That was the problem.

Trey was the problem.

She hadn't forgotten. Any of it. It hadn't died with time. She couldn't will it away no matter how hard she tried, and damn it, she'd really, really tried. The thing about hatred and rage was that it was too potent and powerful and close to other really extreme feelings and emotions. Like lust. Like desire. Like- well- like *like*. She couldn't even think of any other L words.

Trey cleared his throat and she remembered that she'd asked him a question.

"Well," he said gruffly. "I- I guess I thought that- that- you'd wait."

"Wait?" Ambi snorted. "Wait?" God. It was a good thing that Trey was so good at killing her feelings for him. She didn't even have to do it on her own anymore. "You just thought that I'd wait for you? For *five years*?"

"I didn't mean it like that-"

"Oh, no, you definitely meant it like that. You thought that I was pathetic. That I didn't have a life? That I didn't have any meaning other than you? That you- you- that just because you were rich, I'd gladly take you back? Jesus, Trey, how conceited can you be?"

Trey thumped his hand down on the tabletop. Not hard enough to be violent or scary, but hard enough to make the tea in her mug jump a little. Hard enough that she might have jumped a little too.

"I. Didn't. Mean. It. Like. That." Trey ground every word

out, enunciating each one. "I came here to talk. You might want to try listening."

Ambi slammed her arms over her chest. "Why the hell would I want to listen to anything you have to say?"

"Great. Well. This isn't going to go anywhere if you refuse to have an open mind."

"That would make two of us."

Trey's nostrils flared. His jade greens turned to that darker shade, something closer to emeralds. "Here. I'll prove that I have an open mind." He picked up his mug and even though his tea was still steaming, he chugged back the whole thing. He kept the quilt tucked under his armpits and wiped at his mouth with the back of his hand. "There. I drank your foul tea. I tried it again, even though I knew I'd hate it. It wasn't half bad. I drank the whole thing. Yeah. It actually wasn't that bad at all. Can I have another? Is that proof enough for you? How many mugs of this do I have to drink to get you to hear me out? Because I'll do what it takes, even if I have to down a hundred of those."

"You'd puke before then."

"It would be my pleasure if you'd hear me out."

She didn't want to just capitulate, so she shoved back her chair and put the kettle on. She kept her back to Trey until she put a second mug in front of him. It was even worse than mint. He hated chai tea with a passion. She had milk and sugar to make it more palatable, but she kept it out of it.

"Here's the deal," she said roughly, not letting him in on the fact that she might have been softening just a little. "You drink that, and I'll hear you out."

"It's scalding," Trey protested.

Ambi wasn't letting him off the hook that easily. She got up, walked to the fridge, popped a few ice cubes out of the tray, and let them fall into Trey's cup back at the table. She waited a minute until they dissolved.

"There. Problem solved."

Trey looked like he really was going to be sick just looking at the tea. He picked up the mug though and downed it like he'd down the mint tea. It really wasn't fair. He was too good at just opening his throat and pouring it down. He could shotgun a beer like that too, in under a minute.

He thunked the mug down on the table when he was done and wiped his mouth with the back of his hand again. A mouth she tried really hard not to look at because it reminded her of kissing him and thinking about kissing him made her uncomfortably warm and that made her want to do something crazy, like leap across the table and maybe try it again. It didn't help that he drew the tip of his pink tongue over his bottom lip. His mouth was outright *sexual*. He stared at her with an *if it's war you want, it's war you'll get* expression.

"You have to hear me out now," he said, his voice uncharacteristically soft, not demanding at all. IT was almost more like a question.

She sighed like she was bored. She sipped at her tea like it was the last thing she wanted to do when really, she did want to hear what Trey had to say. She did and she hated that she did, so she kept her careful mask in place.

"I thought you'd wait," he started, but it didn't come out as terrible as before. "I thought that you wouldn't move on with someone else. I knew how focused you were on starting your own business. When you want something, you throw your whole self into it. I didn't think there'd be room for you for distractions."

"Glad you clarified." Unfortunately, even though her words dripped sarcasm, they'd lost most of their heat.

Trey continued on like she hadn't said anything at all. "I didn't choose money over you. I know that's what you think, but you don't know the half of it."

"It is what I think because it's true. You're now rich. Your dad asked you to break up with me. He gave you an ultimatum. Pick me and kiss your inheritance goodbye or pick the company and him and a really good, cushy, padded life over me. It's pretty obvious what choice you made. Explaining it five years after the fact is a little late." Ambi's foot started vibrating and she pressed down on her thigh to keep her leg from jumping nervously all over the place.

"It wasn't just about the money." Trey set his hands on the tabletop. Strong hands. Beautiful hands. With lean, strong fingers.

Ambi couldn't look at his hands so she looked at hers, pressing down on her thighs, instead. She couldn't think about what his hands had done to her. How at first, they'd twined through hers and she'd felt a flurry of butterflies just from that brief contact. How they'd rested on the small of her back, brushed her tears away, massaged her temples and her shoulders when she was stressed. How they'd brought her pleasure. So. Much. Pleasure.

"My dad- he..." Trey swiped at his wet hair again. He brushed the back of his hand over his forehead like he was sweating, even though when Ambi looked up, he wasn't shiny and there wasn't sweat beaded there. "He used my mom against me. Said she'd always wanted me to take over the family business. Focus on it. Grow it. Advance everything we have now. He said she would have wanted me to focus on that and keep my options open, not tie myself down young and regret it for the rest of my life."

"Oh really? Tie yourself down and regret it? Give me a break. If your mom really thought that, then it was only because she married an asshole and she regretted the hell out of it."

"My dad might be an asshole sometimes, but my parents had a happy marriage."

"Right." Ambi dropped her eyes at about the same time the bottom of her stomach dropped out. "I'm sorry. That was uncalled for."

Trey sighed. Hard. "Look, Ambi. I'm sorry too. I loved my mom. You know that. You know that her death when I was sixteen fucked me up. She didn't get to see me graduate high school. She didn't get to see me go to college. I knew the company was her and my dad's life. They built it from scratch. They were happily married. No one expected her to have a fucking brain aneurysm and die. My dad is an asshole partly because he still doesn't know how to deal with that, even though it's been a really long fucking time."

"What did he have against me?" Ambi folded her arms over her chest again. She felt safer that way. "Why did he tell you that you had to pick?"

"He wanted me to be focused. He wanted me to work hard, to earn everything. He wanted me to be hungry and want it. It's why he paid for me to go into business and nothing else. I could have gone to school for something of my choice, but he wouldn't have footed the bill. I- he- the company really is his life. It's all he has left of my mom other than me. In a way, and it might be a fucked-up way, I think he needs to control both because he's grasping at straws. He didn't want to lose me. He wanted to see the company go to me and the only way to ensure that was to threaten to disinherit me if I didn't choose that path."

"That's a really shitty way. Almost a sure way to make you hate all of it."

"Yeah," Trey agreed readily. "It really was. Is. I hate working there. It took me a few years to finally admit that to myself. If it was up to me, I'd see it go in a different direction completely. This Christmas party was my idea. We've never had one. I wanted it to be good as a thank you to everyone who puts in long hours for us. I had to fight my dad tooth and nail to get it to happen."

"And of course, you chose me. As a big fuck you to him."

"Actually, I chose you because I thought you'd do a good job and I figured that if I was going to give the money to anyone, it should be you. My dad doesn't know anything about it. I said I'd take it on. He doesn't care. He doesn't want to know."

"Yes, well, here we are." Ambi couldn't keep the bitterness from leaching into her voice. "No matter what reason you did it, you still didn't stand up to him. You could have proven to him that you could do both. Be with me and be a part of the company."

Trey laughed, but it wasn't happy sounding. It was sad and lost and pathetic, and it made her want to look up at him, but she refused. She couldn't. It would be dangerous. She might crumple under the weight of the pain swimming in his jade eyes.

"That's the thing. My dad was perfectly right. If I'd have been with you, I wouldn't have worked for the company. I would not have spent years doing things that made me unhappy. I wouldn't live in a soulless shell of a house that doesn't feel like home at all. I wouldn't go on the road half a year to business meetings I don't believe in. I wouldn't have thrown away the last five years of my life. I wouldn't have a big house or the fancy cars or any of it, because I wouldn't have tried to make myself feel whole."

"Please-"

Trey wouldn't let her interrupt him though. "He saw you as a threat and he was right because you never would have let me do something that made me so unhappy. You would have got me to see reason and then we would have been poor, living together, but we would have been happy. You would have built up your business and I would have done everything I could to support you. We'd be regular people working at regular jobs. The only thing that stayed the same about me was that I never moved on. It was always you, Ambi. Always. That's why there are all those magazines, billboards and fucking eligible bachelor lists. My father thinks I do it to rub it in his face because he never made marriage a stipulation of my inheritance and now, I'm so invested in the company and I have my own money and my own life. I'm powerful enough now that he can't threaten me again."

"So, you took a chance. You found out I was still single. You're single. You thought that if we reconnected, that there'd still be this fire. That you'd tell me you were sorry and that you made a mistake and we could just pick up where we left off?"

Trey cleared his throat loudly. "Yeah," he admitted.

Her head cranked up so hard that her neck actually cracked audibly when he didn't say anything else. "Yeah?" Her mouth dropped. "Yeah? Just like that?"

Trey's jade green gaze held hers. She couldn't tear her eyes away if she tried. Not that she wanted to. There he was, the Trey she used to know and love, on display in all his beautiful, broken, battle-scarred glory. It hurt. It hurt her in every single place a person could hurt, but still, she couldn't stop looking at him. He was letting down his guard, letting her peek inside, letting her see how absolutely genuine he was.

"If there's one thing I learned, it's that you can't keep living in the past." Trey's voice was hoarse. The shadows shifted in his gaze like clouds peeling away from the sun.

"That's very inspirational of you." Ambi laid the sarcasm on thick. "Put that on a billboard." She stamped her foot since it was vibrating again. She hated nervous ticks. She didn't want to be nervous. She wanted to be sure of herself. "You're very full of yourself. None of what you said matters. I don't need you to apologize. I'm not living in the past. I've moved on. I didn't need someone else to do that with. I did it by myself and I'm happy being single. I like my life. I have my business, my friends, my family. It's not complicated, and I like it that way. I don't have any feelings for you, Trey. Not like that. I'm happy with my life how it is and that's not going to change no matter what you say or how you try and tempt me."

If there was one thing she should have remembered about Trey, it was that he loved a challenge. He lived for the thrill of it. Which meant that maybe he'd had a game plan all along. Or maybe, people really did fuck up and make shitty mistakes and spend years trying to fix it. Maybe dumping her was his lowest point and he'd spent years building up after that, waiting for the time he could make things right because he knew her. He freaking *knew* her.

He knew.

Trey shoved his chair back in one fluid motion and stood slowly. His eyes never broke from hers. "Tempt you? I haven't done anything to tempt you. If you're so sure, though... I'll just get my clothes on and leave."

She was about to mutter something about them not

being dry yet, but then Trey lifted his arms and the edges of the quilt that were safely tucked up under them fell away. Right along with the rest of it.

Suddenly Trey didn't look like the world's sexiest burrito. Nope. Suddenly he was absolutely. Freaking. *Nude*.

11

TREY

*P*ulling the whole naked thing probably wasn't fair. Okay, it wasn't fair, and he knew it, but he was desperate. He could tell that Ambi was sitting there lying through her teeth about that last bit. About not having feelings. About being happy by herself. He could see it in her eyes. The truth. She still wanted him. She still had some kind of feelings for him, even if they weren't exactly love. The spark of desire was still there.

He had to take the chance. Either he was going to get the cops phoned on his ass or something else would happen. Either way, Ambi would be forced to tip her hand. Either way, she'd be forced to stop lying to herself.

"Argh!" She screamed and slapped her hands over her eyes. "You asshole! Put that quilt back on right now! I'll get your clothes. They're not dry, but you can go out and catch your death. Freeze your dick off. I don't care. It would serve you right."

Ambi shoved back her chair and took off down the hall. Trey knew he might have made the biggest mistake of his life, pushing her like that, like the worst kind of perverted douchebag. Dropping that quilt was a real dick move, no pun intended. What was he thinking? He might have been desperate but stunning her wasn't appropriate. Not that her eyes went there. She'd kept them trained, like a true professional, above his waist.

"Ambi wait!" Trey turned, ready to grab up the quilt and chase after her. He was going to apologize to her, get his clothes on, and leave. He'd keep it strictly professional from here on out. He'd even let his secretary, Sarah, deal with Ambi from now on just to assure her that the truce he was going to put out there was real.

He had good intentions. Honestly, he did. And then his foot caught in the puddle of the quilt on the floor and instead of some glorious chance at redemption and a white flag between them, he ended up flat on his face. Literally. His cheek hit the hardwood floor and his teeth cracked together so hard that if his tongue had been between them, he might have bitten it right off.

"Trey? Oh my god, are you okay?"

Ambi was back. God, she was back, and her hand was on his shoulder. Her touch was delicate, light, burning into him.

He groaned, but the groan turned into a chuckle and that turned into a full belly laugh. He knew what he looked like. How absolutely ridiculous he was. To his surprise, Ambi laughed too. She laughed a real laugh, that gorgeous, light, summery, sunny sound that he loved so much. He'd forgotten just how beautiful it was because memory wasn't adequate to contain something that amazing.

He planted his palms on the floor and shoved himself into a sitting position. Ambi's hand never left his shoulder. Not until he curled into her. He shouldn't have done it, but he swiveled and pulled her into him. He gave her a chance to get away. To punch him in the dick or the jaw or the nose. To call him an asshole and hurl other insults that were generally true.

Instead, she set her warm palms on either side of his jaw and melted against him. This time, when their lips met, she was the one who kissed him. It wasn't just kissing. They were drowning in each other. Trey had a hell of a lot of lost time to make up for. He might be a Turdmaster, but he didn't kiss like one.

He swept his tongue along Ambi's lower lip, sucking it into his mouth before he bit down gently. She moaned and writhed against him. Her lips parted and he swept his tongue inside, finding hers and warring with it. He'd never kissed her like that when they were dating. He'd never kissed her with enough determination and desperation to slay an entire army and win the battle. That's what he was doing. He was fighting for her. Fighting for her silently, since his words had failed. Fighting with all that he had left. Eating her whimpers, stealing her breath, breathing for her, stroking her tongue, nibbling and sucking her lips.

Ambi's still clothed hips rocked into him and he knew it wasn't enough. She needed more. They both needed more. Trey thrust his knee between her legs, parting them easily. Ambi mewled and ground down against him. God. He was naked and she was fully clothed and somehow this was just about the hottest thing they'd done. Ever.

While he plundered her mouth, Trey's hands flew to Ambi's jeans. He undid the button with ease and slid the zipper down. She didn't stop him. She didn't tear her lips from his and tell him that he was the last person on earth she'd do this with, even if they were the last people on earth. She didn't tell him that he looked like turds, smelled like turds, and tasted like turds.

She kept kissing him, desperately, her hands clawing at his naked shoulders until her nails sunk into the skin and muscle. She bit his lip right after and swiped her tongue over the wound, flooding both their mouths with hot copper. It was like someone had replaced all the blood in his veins with violent lightning.

Trey couldn't stop. He shifted, lowering Ambi to the floor where he stripped away her jeans and her socks. He left her panties on since he didn't just want to assume that she was up for this. For all of it. He was, though. Obviously. His cock kicked straight up and throbbed.

Ambi was breathing heavy, her shoulders heaving. She stared at him with wonderment in her eyes. It was a heady feeling, watching her lids lower and seeing her pupils blown with desire. Those passion drenched eyes raked over his body in frank appreciation, which made every single second he'd ever set foot in a gym worth it. They dipped below his waist, and the tempo of her breathing increased before they flew back to his face.

Trey's hand slid up Ambi's creamy white thigh, so smooth, like silk, that his fingertips felt rough against her skin. He'd touched her like this before. Years ago. Why did it seem like it was the first time? His cock ached and throbbed. He wanted to take himself in his hand and stroke himself at the same time, but when Ambi's head lolled back against the floor and her eyes slammed shut, he was done.

She was giving him permission. Silent permission to keep going.

Trey knelt between her gorgeous legs, staring at her yellow cotton panties. There was a dark stain in the center, where her arousal had leaked out, staining them. His mouth flooded with saliva and his hands ached just about as badly as his cock. He remembered how sweet Ambi tasted. He remembered everything about her, but he had to taste her. He had to taste her like it was the first time. He was so desperate to get to her that he had to take a steadying breath just to slow himself the fuck down.

Instead of splitting Ambi's legs and ripping her panties clean off, Trey forced himself to go slow. To part her legs gently, to trail hot kisses over her delicate satin skin, up her calf, over her knee, up her trembling thighs. He kissed his way to his prize before he hesitated.

Ambi's hands tangled in his hair, tugging him into her so that his hot, rapid breaths exploded all over her panty covered sex.

"It's been five years, Trey. What the hell are you waiting for?" Her hips jacked up into his face, a not so subtle suggestion.

He nearly laughed and wept at the same time. He bit the inside of his cheek to keep from doing either. It was a very good possibility that all he was going to be able to do was this since he was two seconds away from coming all over Ambi's creamy thighs, but yeah. He wasn't about to tell her that and not just because it wasn't sexy. It was also too fast. That's not what she had in mind when she told him to hurry it the hell up.

"I want to take my time with you," he groaned. "Savor you. Make this special. It's been a long time, Ambi. Too long."

"I don't want you to go slow. Just... just get your mouth on me already."

It was a good thing Ambi's eyes were closed because he was grinning like a fool. He ducked his head, running his hand along the seam of her panties, his thumb dancing between cotton and her overheated skin. She whimpered and tried to turn into his touch, tried to position his hand right where she needed it most, but he wasn't going to give in to her. Yet.

Instead, he lowered his mouth to her sex and ran his tongue along the stain there, sucking her panties into his mouth, tasting her and wetting them further. Ambi thrashed below him. Her nails raked against his scalp. She was ferocious, and god, he loved it. He wanted to do battle with her. He wanted to see the ferocious, pent up, angry, wonton side that she'd never showed him.

"What do you want, Ambi? My mouth on you?"

"Yes," she begged. "Yes. Put your mouth on me."

"Even if it's a filthy mouth?"

"Especially if it's a filthy mouth, you dork."

Trey gave her what she wanted. He licked and suckled her through her panties, the fabric so wet that they clung to her sex, outlining every single gorgeous detail. She'd always preferred getting waxed and she was smooth, gorgeous, and glorious. She tasted sweet and raw, exactly as he remembered. She flooded her panties, soaking through the fabric as he drove her wild.

She thrashed against the floor, opening herself to him, pushing her pelvis into his face. When he thrust a finger underneath her panties, she was scalding hot, slick and soaked. He trailed his finger over her blazing hot folds while she just about ripped his hair out. When he slipped a finger inside, she went wild. He groaned against her soaked panties. She was so tight. So fucking tight.

If her rapid breathing and the increased tempo of her moans and her half-stammered please were any indications, she was also very, very close.

She wasn't going to beg him. She'd never begged for him to give her pleasure. He wanted to hear the please fall from her lips. His name. Anything. She kept her mouth resolutely shut, refusing to give up control completely and he didn't fault her. He hoped he had time to wear down her defenses. To hear his name falling from her sugar-coated lips.

He thrust his finger inside of her again and at the same time, positioned his mouth over her clit. He sucked her, through her panties and all, rolling his tongue over the tight bud. It was all it took. She shattered beneath him, bucking her hips and writhing as the climax took hold and washed over her. He kept going, thrusting his finger deep inside of her and suckling her clit, prolonging her pleasure.

He held out as long as he could, then he reared up over her, claiming her mouth and kissing her brutally. He kissed her so hard that their teeth clanged together, but they didn't stop. Ambi whimpered and ground against him, chasing another climax close on the heels of the first. He wanted to give that to her. He ground his pelvis against her panty clad heat, his cock begging to be let inside. He didn't have a condom and he knew that was a no-fucking-go, for a ton of obvious reasons. Even if Ambi was on the pill, there was no way he was going in bareback. That was too intimate, too fast, too soon.

He wanted to keep creating that friction, dry-wet humping her like a teenage kid, but his control slipped. One second he had it together, the next, he lost it. He kissed the shit out of her, their bodies heaving together, drinking in what little oxygen she had left to give, marveling over how perfect they still fit together- maybe even more perfect than they had before- and the next there was a black screen filled up with bright flashing lights behind his eyes and he was coming, in thick, hot spurts all over Ambi's panties, her stomach, her thighs.

Trey jerked back as soon as it happened. He stared down at Ambi, at what he'd just done. It was dirty and it was so ridiculously hot. He still felt like he should apologize though since he hadn't meant to get that carried away and he definitely hadn't asked her permission to take things that far.

Before he could get the words out, she froze. Her eyes fluttered open and she glanced down at her stomach. The next instant, every muscle in her body stiffened, like she was slowly turning to stone, one muscle at a time.

"Ambi, I-"

"Just get off me." She shoved at him, which would have been a butterfly trying to move a polar bear, but he got the picture and rolled away before her wildly swinging hands could connect with any of his more vital parts.

He complied, scrambling away. He glanced around wildly, spotted the blanket that he'd been covered up with, and scrambled to get it.

"Not the blanket!" Ambi ground out. She sat up and stormed off down the hall, slamming the bathroom door shut behind her.

Trey stood there like an idiot. Completely. Naked.

He figured he had better not be standing that way by the time Ambi emerged. Who knew what she'd be coming out of the bathroom with? She probably kept objects like curling irons and scissors in there and god knew what else that she could use as a weapon.

He went straight to the dryer and opened the door. His clothes were pretty much dry, though he did basically scald himself putting his pants on with the hot zipper. Thank god his boxers provided enough of a shield that his man bits didn't take the brunt of the heat.

Thankfully, he was doing up the last button on his shirt when Ambi emerged from the bathroom. She had a fluffy pink robe wrapped around herself, one he remembered seeing on the back of the bathroom door. Her eyes were tear-filled, even after she swiped at them with the back of her hand. He hated her tears. He didn't want her to cry. Her wobbling lips felt like a knife straight to his stomach.

"Ambi- I- seriously. I didn't mean for that to happen. I- it- please. I'm sorry."

She shook her head, her already mussed hair flying wildly like a black velvet curtain all around her. "It wasn't that," she sighed. She sounded tired. So. Fucking. Tired. "It's everything. This- this never should have happened."

"No- it- it should have. I- Ambi, we were good together. We could be good again. Please. Just give me a chance to prove it to you."

She shook her head again and his hopes sunk lower and lower with every movement. Her eyes filled up with tears again, but she blinked rapidly, refusing to let them fall.

"The biggest mistake of my life wasn't getting dumped by you. It was letting you think we could ever do this again. We can't. *That* was the biggest mistake of my life. Right there."

"Ambi-"

She put up her hand, silencing him. "No. Just go. Now."

"Come on. At least sit down and let's talk-"

"Right now!" She stamped her bare foot for emphasis.

It was pretty obvious that anything he had to say was just going to make everything worse. He had to try. One more time. He couldn't walk out like this. He'd been stupid enough to let her go before. He wasn't ready to make that mistake again.

"I really am sorry. We're- what we- I still l-"

There was no way she was letting him get that out. Her eyes widened to the point where they looked like they were going to pop out. Her hands balled into fists at her sides.

"You need to go downstairs now. Wait there until the storm is over. I don't care if it takes until morning. You can sleep in the damn desk chair or go out and brave the storm if you want, but you can't be here. Not in my apartment. Not anywhere near me."

Her throat bobbed viciously as she swallowed. He watched it all, her face, for any signs that she might yield, but she was closed off. A blank wall that he couldn't bull-doze without bulldozing everything that they'd built back up.

"We- the job..."

"I'll still do the job." Her chin angled up. "You don't have to even ask me that. Now, just, please... go."

Trey knew he had no choice. Not at the moment. If he wanted to lose this battle and still win the war, he had to do as she asked. So, he did. He turned and left her just like he'd left her five years ago. In pain, angry, nearly broken.

He vowed that he'd keep fighting. That he could fix things, but the truth was, he was no longer sure. He wasn't sure that he could win Ambi back when she didn't want to be won. He thumped down the steps, back to Ambi's office and parked his ass in her upholstered desk chair. He propped his feet up on her desk and watched the storm still raging outside.

It was time to pull out all the stops. All. Of. Them.

12

AMBERINA

*T*he first thing Ambi looked for the next morning was her phone. Not because she was eager to see who was texting her at the butt crack of dawn, but because she was going to be sure to block their number from her phone so they could never wake her up at five in the morning again.

Of course, the text was from Trey.

Got home safe. Got my car. Everything's good. I have another venue I'd like you to see. Meet me there at nine?

Ambi groaned and threw her head back against the pillow. God. As if last night wasn't enough humiliation. Now she had to submit to Mr. Evil all over again. Of course, he'd mess with her plans to book the hall that he'd agreed on the day before. Thankfully, she hadn't actually done it yet, because of the storm. She gave her head a shake, thrashing against the pillow and probably matting her hair up unmercifully in the process. Mr. Evil had a real nice ring to it. It described Trey perfectly.

Much better than Mr. Eat Me Out Until I'm Glowing Red With Embarrassment And Pleasure And Still Have To Do A

Walk Of Shame In My Own House To Get His Clothes Out Of The Dryer Before I Could Kick Him The Hell Out And Die Of Mortification.

Yes. Mr. Evil was much, much better.

At the thought of what Trey had done to her, Ambi let out another groan. It wasn't overly warm in the room- with the radiators, it never truly was- but suddenly her limbs suffused with heat and she felt achy, almost feverish.

How the hell did Trey even get someone to agree to a meeting first thing in the morning? Was he on a first-name basis with the woman who worked at the venue? Did he call her in the middle of the night?

Something wicked and hot bubbled up her throat. *Jealousy*. She wanted to laugh at herself, but the new level of pathetic she'd just reached wasn't funny at all. It was just that. PA to the T to the T-H-E-T-I-C.

Why couldn't he just make anything simple? Why couldn't he sit back and let her do her job? He'd hired her and paid her a ridiculous amount of money to do the stupid party planning, yet he was the one coming up with alternative venues. Trey's face flooded her mind and with it, the image of her juices smeared all over his chin. Unfortunately, her brain also conjured up images of the sunning he'd given her... and the moon. He had a really good moon. He had an even nicer sun.

God. No. Fudgeballs. Buttstinker. Why her? Aren't there any other women out there for Trey to torment?

Why her? Why her indeed. He'd sat at the table, smug as he fricking well pleased, to tell her that he was just waiting for the right time to get back with her because she was so pathetic there was no way she would have moved on with anyone else.

This time, she imagined Trey's naked moon staring her

full-on, but she was chasing after him with an angry expression on her face and a very deadly, very zappy, very painful cattle prod. It would be no less than he deserved. What he did not deserve was mercy. What he did not deserve was to be proven right. Annnnd that's exactly what she did by spreading her legs for him.

Ambi gripped her phone until the case dug into the tender flesh of her palm. She felt like a caged animal. A wild bird who had just had its wings clipped so that it could never go back to enjoying life as it knew it before.

She knew she had to respond. She'd keep it professional. Clean. She wouldn't let Trey back her into a corner. She'd make it clear by her abruptness, curtness, and coldness that what happened the night before was a mistake of the most epic proportions.

Fine. Nine. Text me the address.

She didn't ask if the streets were cleared. She didn't doubt that the plows would have been working double time and if things didn't look great when she actually got out of bed and looked out, she'd call for a cab.

Of course, Trey did. Her phone pinged with it a second later. Just the address. Nothing else. No follow up. No apology. No freaking nothing. *Great*.

How could she let him do this to her? He had all the power. He held all the cards. She let him get away with it. She gave him the power. She surrendered her cards. She'd let him go down on her and she'd come. And he knew it. And then he'd freaking come too. Obviously.

Ambi threw her phone back on the nightstand and rolled out of bed. What she needed was a cold shower. Which she could never bring herself to actually take, so what she'd do was have a hot shower, wash any traces of Trey off of her, get out, get dressed, put on her big girl panties, make herself a cup of tea and go show Trey that he didn't own her. He might be able to pull biologically exciting reactions from her traitorous body, but the real things didn't and wouldn't ever belong to him. Her heart would never be his. Her spirit would never be broken.

If only things weren't so confusing. If only her body wasn't so reactionary and instinctual. If only it didn't betray her at every turn. Her heart was hers. She needed it to be. Which was why she hated the burning ache in the center of her chest with a passion that she usually reserved for turnip, liver, and traffic jams.

Trey didn't mean anything. He was wrong. She'd moved on. She'd moved on like she said. With herself. With her business. With her family and friends. She was fulfilled and she was happy and there were absolutely no gaps in her armor or cracks in her walls. It only took a short time to form a habit. She'd make a habit of believing it until it was the truth.

13

TREY

*A*mbi strolled through the set of double glass doors that fronted the hall much like the storm that had crippled the city the day before. With deadly precision and brutal cold. Not an ounce of her sleek, shiny black hair was out of place. Her entire freaking outfit- a grey blazer and grey pants which were covered up with a stylish red jacket that flared out at the waist- was immaculate. She'd paired everything with incredibly unsuitable for the weather, black stilettos that instantly made Trey hard as a fucking rock, since he imagined her naked, with nothing else on but those four or five-inch heels.

Her makeup was perfection, her face schooled into a look of unaffected, easy charm that he knew immediately she didn't feel. Her eyes betrayed her. They were seething pools of wrath.

"This place, Trey, really?" Ambi asked sweetly, with enough sugar to give him diabetes. She slid her black leather gloves from her hands and tucked them into her black tote. "I think we both know that your father would shit bricks if the party was here."

Hmm. Two can play at this. Ambi was acting like she had no idea what the real significance behind the hall was when really, he knew she had a memory like an elephant. There was no way she wouldn't have recognized it, even though it had been a long time and they'd both been more than slightly drunk.

"Give me three good reasons this place wouldn't work?"

Ambi glanced around, taking in the ancient fixtures and outdated trimmings. From floor to ceiling, the place really was old and rotted. The hall was built in the sixties and wasn't modern in that good kind of retro way. It was ugly, with shit brown and puke yellow-green as its prominent color scheme. And that was just the entrance. The main part of the hall, one big room, was made of cinder blocks painted white and had a hardwood floor that resembled a really shitty elementary school gym. It was complete with a stage painted- you guessed it, shit brown and a set of- you also guessed it- puke yellow-green curtains that draped across.

He'd already gone in and inspected everything. The woman in charge of opening up the hall and taking the bookings, Doris, who was likely pushing one hundred and fifty, gave him the key and told him to take his time and call her on her landline when he was done. She'd really said that. About the landline. She was far, far too trusting, but then again, he'd offered to become a bronze sponsor of the place, which meant donating ten thousand dollars, if she could meet him before nine to let him in and give him an hour alone in the place. He'd also given her his credit card number and a promise that he wouldn't burn the place down.

Trey stalked over and locked the front door behind Ambi. She watched him, her brows arrowed in, her eyes folded into narrow slits of suspicion.

"Sorry. The lady who takes the bookings had another appointment. She gave me the key and instructed me to lock the door and not let anyone else in while she was gone. Just protecting her interests and all."

Ambi muttered something under her breath and stalked off. *Oh yeah.* There was no way she *didn't* remember what had gone down at that hall back in college.

"This place is absolutely not going to work!" Ambi raged the second she walked into the main part of the hall. Her voice echoed through the empty place. "It looks like a bad high school reunion would happen here. Not a high-class office party. You would ruin my business for sure if I let you hold it here."

He entered the hall behind her, and when she whirled, the rage from her eyes had boiled over to her face. Her nostrils flared and she almost stamped her foot. She caught herself at the last second and instead, dropped her tote to the floor by her feet and crossed her arms.

"Seriously. What was wrong with the venue yesterday? It's classy. It's nice. It's tasteful. It screams money. All the things that your father likes and his company stands for."

"I get a say in it. That's what's wrong with it. I didn't like it. I like this place. It will work fine."

The look of panic that flashed across Ambi's face nearly made him laugh, but that would have ruined everything.

"Are you- are you actually serious? If you are, I'm going to fight you on this one. Tooth and nail. This isn't even big enough to properly host everything and I guarantee you that the place doesn't offer catering. You'll have to have food brought in. Do you know how much work that is? It's another thing I'd have to book and right now, it's looking grim for the entertainment. Catering would be a disaster.

Short of getting some dubious food truck, you'd probably be right out of luck."

"What's wrong with dubious food truck food?"

"Argh!" Ambi finally lost it and did stomp her foot. "You can't! Trey! This is my name on the line here. No one would like this. No one!"

"I paid you to plan this. If I want it here, we're having it here."

"You paid me to plan it. Did you just hear yourself? Me. Plan it. Paid me. I say that this is not the venue. If you want it, I'll give you the money back minus what I already spent on the cake and we- can- uh- call it a day."

"Why are you starting to stutter, Ambi? Are you thinking about that cake?" Trey couldn't help it. He was asshole number one, but he was also sporting a hard-on the length of his arm and he needed, like he'd needed the night before, to push Ambi into seeing something and admitting something that she didn't want to either see or admit. "Or maybe you were thinking about last night."

That did it. Trey knew right away he'd pushed Ambi too far.

"God!" She yelled as she picked up her tote and stalked across the hall. She didn't exit out the way she'd come since he was standing in the doorway and she would have had to walk past him.

She went in the other direction. To the doors at the back of the place that were clearly labeled with a glowing exit sign overhead. Ambi threw open the door and charged down the hallway that ran past the main area to the back exit doors. The click, click, click of her heels resounded through the place with anything but finality. On the way down that hall were the bathrooms and a few select other rooms.

It was too perfect.

Which led Trey to believe, as he chased after Ambi, that she really didn't remember, or recognize the hall. They were both pretty drunk that night, but seriously? How could she not remember? The place looked exactly the same.

Trey caught up with Ambi just as she was rounding the corner that led past the washrooms and the rooms that had the janitorial supplies. The few offices for the place were on the other side of the building, down the hall that branched off at the entrance.

They were far from that now. They were the only ones in the building. He had about forty-five minutes left of the hour he'd been promised.

He wasn't going to waste it.

"Ambi!" Trey reached blindly for her hand and missed, but he caught the hem of her coat. He tugged hard and she let out a shriek as she went tumbling back.

He'd caught her off guard. She didn't expect him to tug her back, that much was obvious. She stumbled, rocking on her sky-high heels. Her tote went flying, hitting the cement with a dull smack. Ambi let out a second, less dignified, slightly louder shriek as she tumbled backward. The horrified sound echoed off the walls and ricocheted off the floor.

Trey opened his arms and caught her. She didn't hit the floor. She hit his chest. Hard. Her shoulder bumped his throat and her flailing hand hit him square in the face. Her entire body melded along the length of his. And he was pressed right up against the delicious curve of her bottom.

"Trey!" She flailed out as she struggled to break free.

There was no way he was letting her go. Instead, he scooped her up into his arms and carried her the few feet to their final destination. She thrashed against him, protesting the entire way, calling him a pig and an asshole and telling him he was as ugly as the back end of a cow with the runs. That one was quite inventive, he had to admit. He mentally cataloged it away for future use.

He didn't set her down until he threw open the first door on the right and plunged them both into darkness. He let her go then, when she had nowhere to go, since he carefully stepped in front of the metal door and flicked on the light- a bare bulb that plunged the small, dank space with the rows of vertical shelves stocked with cleaning supplies, the mop basin on the floor, and all the mops and wheeled buckets, back into shiny yellowed life.

Recognition lit up Ambi's face in an instant. No, not recognition. *Resignation*. She'd known where they were the entire time and she hadn't once cracked. There wasn't even a hairline fracture in that mask of hers.

"Welcome back," Trey purred.

Her eyes widened until they nearly popped from the sockets. Her nostrils flared like she could scent more than just the smell of cleaning chemicals and old mops.

"Welcome back to what?" she seethed, even though he knew full well that she knew. "This place looks like a dump. You stuffed me in some janitor's closet. Congratulations."

The light was there in her eyes and she couldn't smother that the way she shut everything else down. She glanced around and he waited for that split second of fear that would tell him that he should let her out. That despite everything, she wasn't lying and didn't actually want him. He would never, ever force her to do anything that she wasn't willing to do.

She didn't rail at him and tell him to let her out. She didn't tell him that she'd rather eat poop than get close to his dick ever again. She didn't tell him that she hella-regretted those orgasms from the night before.

No. Instead she sucked her bow lip into her mouth and munched on it until he figured the tender skin cracked and flooded her mouth with the taste of copper. She finally released it then, red and swollen.

Trey realized then that he had a problem since he just about came in his pants just from watching her do that much. She was like a drug. Heady. Addicting. Something he couldn't quit. Something he didn't want to quit. She might be just as dangerous and toxic. He wasn't quite sure if either of them were going to get out of whatever they were doing unscathed.

"Welcome back to the first place we ever made love."

As Ambi's eyes darkened and her lips thinned out, he wasn't even sure he'd make it out of the janitor closet alive.

14

AMBERINA

She knew. She knew about the hall. She hadn't recognized the address, but she knew the place as soon as she got close. By the time she pulled up, she was a hot mess on the inside. She knew why Trey picked it. She knew why he'd brought her there. She knew exactly what his game plan was. Except her game plan was not to let him in. Not to show him that she cared. Not to give anything away. Her game was that her poker face needed to be kicked up into overdrive AfrickingSAP.

She'd almost made it out. Out into the fresh air and her car, where she could have yet another meltdown. Out where she could scream her lungs out right after dragging in gulps of air into her burning, painful lungs since she hadn't taken a full breath the entire time in the hall. Out into the fresh, cold air that would clear her head of the memories shimmering and floating on the surface like oil on water.

She'd just about made it.

And then Trey, like he'd made a habit of doing, pulled her back.

Pulled her back and plunged her right back into a past

she didn't want to remember because it was shared with him. She wanted to keep moving forward. Without him. Without needing him or wanting him. Without the memories assaulting her.

He made that impossible.

He was blocking the door. They were in the same freaking closet they'd ducked into back in college when they'd gone to a friend's wedding. The friend had been Trey's. She barely knew Trey and didn't know his friend, but he'd asked her to go and she'd agreed. The wedding was horribly boring. The hall was just as bland back then. The whole thing really was like a bad high school reunion. The fifty-year kind, not the fifteen or twenty. Everyone under the age of eighty had been bored out of their tree and the only reason everyone over eighty wasn't bored was because they all left after the dinner to go to bed.

So pretty much everyone at the wedding proceeded to get smashed. It got a little out of control. Ambi remembered Trey leading her out of the place, down the back way to finally get the hell out of there. They were both more than buzzed. The plan was to get out into the parking lot and call for a cab or walk until they found one.

Instead, they'd found the janitor's closet.

Annnnd the rest was history.

Not the good kind of history either.

The kind of history that she couldn't get past, because instead of storming the door, kicking Trey in the balls until he dropped and she could get past him and then spitting on him as he was down, Ambi couldn't move. She couldn't move a muscle.

Her mouth opened. Worked. Closed. Worked again. Nothing came out. Her jaw just flapped stupidly, like a flag on a windy day. Except she was sure that even a flag would have made some noise. She stood there speechless. Absolutely. Struck. Stupid.

"I hate you." There. At least that was something to say. She wanted to congratulate herself on her achievement.

"Do you though?" Trey asked cockily. "Because to me, it seems an awful lot like you actually don't. Like you're just saying that. To me. To yourself. Except you're not convincing anyone. Not me. Not you."

"What do you want?" Okay, that wasn't so bold. It came out plaintive sounding and pathetic, a little whiny even. No back pats for reaching new pathetic lows.

Trey blinked at her with those eyes she freaking used to love so much. God, his eyes. She hated his eyes because she couldn't stop being enthralled with them. They were there in her mind. She could never banish them. She knew the exact color and pattern. All the flecks and dots.

"That's obvious, I think. I want *you*."

"You- you..." *Come on, Ambi, you can do it. You can spit it out.* "You can't have me." *There. Was that so hard? More back pats for you.*

"Why not? I can clearly see that you want me too. I know we have a past. I know I was a dickhead in it, but that's done now. If you give me another chance-"

"No. No more chances. I can't afford to keep giving chances over and over. I shouldn't have to give it either. It should be earned. Tricking me into this and dragging me back into this room, hoping to score and get lucky isn't going to work."

"Well..." Trey cleared his throat. "I know that your brand of humor isn't like other people's and neither is your brand of romance. I could try to wine and dine you, impress you by whisking you away to Spain or something on a private jet, throw money at you, throw expensive jewelry and designer shit around, but I know you don't care about any of that. You're just you, Ambi. You loved me even when I had no money and you didn't know that I'd ever have any. You saw me. You saw me for who I was. I asked you to that wedding and it sucked, but that night, in this very janitor's room, was one of the best days of my life. I didn't bring you here today hoping that I'd get lucky. I brought you here because I wanted you to remember. I wanted you to know that I never forgot. I haven't forgotten a minute of it. I don't want a chance just to get in your pants, Ambi. I want the chance to prove to you that I deserve another chance. I want to love you properly this time. I promise that I would never hurt you again. I would never abandon you. I would never fuck it all up again."

Ambi stood her ground, but she could literally feel her resolve weakening as the seconds ticked by. She didn't want to give Trey another chance. Not when he'd hurt her so badly the first time. She didn't want to let her guard down and put herself out there. She didn't want to risk her fragile, wounded heart. She didn't want to, but she knew that she already was. She was doing all of those things. She'd never actually stopped. It wasn't just deep down, that knowledge, shoved to the back of her mind and the bottom of her heart. It was at the forefront, a current that was sweeping her away, a current she was drowning in.

She tried to shake her head, but everything was frozen. She was paralyzed except for the sting welling at the bridge of her nose and burning at the backs of her eyes. She was mortified. She didn't want to break down and cry. She didn't want to show an ounce of weakness or give Trey that part of herself. Her brain and her body were clearly at odds. Her head told her no. Her heart was too scared to give an answer. Her body though, was the worst traitor. She couldn't stop loving Trey. She couldn't stop wanting him, especially not after what happened at her apartment. She'd been perilously close to losing control and she'd had to put a stop to it.

No matter what way a person spun it, coming in second place next to money, inheritance, a thriving company, private jets, big houses, fast cars, and oh yeah, more money, really sucked. Then again, everyone made mistakes. Everyone.

She couldn't blink the tears away. They came, scalding and fat, tracing their way down her cheeks. Once they started, they couldn't be contained. They flowed in twin rivers, dribbling off her chin and splashing onto the dirty concrete floor below.

Trey was there. He was there, his big hands cupping her cheeks, so warm and tender. She wanted to push him away, but she couldn't quite find the strength. He leaned in, his delicious scent cloaking her like a comfortable blanket. At the feel of his tongue on her jaw, she froze. He licked away the stream of tears, starting at her jaw, up her cheek, all the way to her lashes. He placed a delicate kiss on her closed eye. It was like a whisper of a butterfly wing. She let out a shuddery sob as he trailed hot kisses over her nose, onto her other cheek. He kissed away her tears before he dropped his lips to hers.

She groaned into the kiss. He was sweet passion and painful regret. His lips were salty from her tears, but she sipped at them anyway, drinking from the forbidden chalice.

Trey's hands smoothed over her shoulders and traveled down over her jacket. Her hands were moving too, tracing a similar pattern over his coat. Her fingers found buttons at the same time his did. Their tongues tangled as her jacket

fell from her shoulders and dropped to the floor. Trey
sucked her bottom lip into his mouth as he went to work on
her pants. She moaned as her finger fumbled with the
button of his pants. They kept kissing each other, mindless
with desire and heady pleasure until suddenly, their clothes
were in a heap on the floor and her feet were no longer on
said floor. They were wrapped around Trey's very toned,
very muscular, very *naked* waist. He spun then, ramming her
up against the metal door. The thing was absolutely freezing, and she let out a little yelp.

"You okay?" Trey's hands tightened on her waist.

"It's just cold."

"I promise it won't be for long."

The implication of what they were about to do washed
through her. It happened so fast. One second, they were
wearing clothes and she hated Trey, then bam, she was
naked, and she wasn't sure that she hated him at all. In fact,
what she felt wasn't even close to it.

"You are on the pill, Ambi?" Trey asked.

His cock throbbed against her stomach, long and thick.
She glanced down because she couldn't help herself and the
sight of it, the tip engorged and swollen an angry red, made
her head spin. It also made her womb clench up, her
stomach ball into a mix of knots, her thighs tremble, and the
space between them throb.

"I- you know- you know that I am."

"I don't know anything." Trey insisted. He dropped his
head and nuzzled her neck, trailing his hot tongue near her
earlobe.

"Yes, well, I am. Still have the same- er- problems. It
helps a lot." From the time she could remember getting her
cycle, the cramps had been unbearable. She'd actually been
on the pill since she was fifteen. It was the only thing that

toned down the excruciating pain. She felt her face heat up. "Of course, you wouldn't know that. I- it's been-"

"Too long." Trey sucked her earlobe between his teeth, and she groaned.

"Still. If we're- if we're doing this-" She still couldn't really believe that they were. Doing it. About to. In the same spot where they'd first done it back in college. Except this time, she wasn't at all inebriated and neither was Trey. He'd planned the whole thing. Maybe there was a romantic bone in his body after all. And yeah. Not *that* bone.

"I'll pull out." Trey's hot breath blasted all over her ear and the side of her face. She shivered violently. His cock kicked between them. Obviously, he liked the idea as much as she did. As much as she *shouldn't*.

Fucking. Snowstorm.

If it wasn't for that storm, Trey never would have ended up at her apartment. He never would have been there. He would never have gotten naked. She would never have gotten partially naked. His tongue would never have sucked on her lady bits. Through her freaking panties. His fingers would never have ended up inside of her. He would never have driven her wild, reminded her of what she'd been missing with that little sampler, and leave her all restless and wanting more.

She did remember how well they used to fit. She remembered how Trey could make her feel like anything was possible when she was in his arms. How those arms were really the only place she'd ever truly wanted to be.

Trey crushed his mouth to hers, bruising her lips. Was it so wrong to give in? Was it so terribly wrong to give him a second chance?

"Are you sure?" Trey asked, pulling back, panting. "Because I seriously need to know now, Ambi, if you don't want this. I feel like your body is telling me that you do, but your head is saying something different. Only you can hear that though. You have to tell me. I don't want to rush you. I don't- I just don't want to hurt you." There was such anguish in Trey's voice that it bit straight into Ambi's soul. It sealed the deal for her.

This was Trey. The Trey she loved. The Trey she'd never stopped loving. She was safe with him. She was going to take that leap. The leap into that scary, unknown abyss and trust that he'd catch her before she fell. All she could do was trust. It wasn't enough all those years ago, but maybe, just maybe, they were different people who'd done a whole lot of growing up and it could be enough in the present.

"Yes." She looked right into Trey's gorgeous eyes. "Yes, Trey, I'm sure."

15

AMBERINA

*T*rey's lips were on hers the second the words dropped from her mouth. His tongue parted the seam of her lips and his taste- the masculine tang of him, mixed with the faded sweetness of rich coffee and a hint of cinnamon, gum maybe- flooded her mouth.

They were still pretty much clothed from the waist up. Trey's shirt gaped open though, and she ran her hands under the fabric, digging her fingers into the warm, veiny muscle of his shoulders. He was scalding beneath her fingertips. His hands shifted on her waist, moving lower to support her. Her back rammed up hard against the steel door again and this time, he was right. It wasn't so cold. She curled her legs, shamelessly locking them around Trey's hips and digging her heels into his ass.

He had a really nice ass. So ridiculously tight that her heels, which she was using as a weapon to keep herself in place against the door, probably didn't even leave a mark.

Trey tore his mouth away, and trailed hot kisses over her cheek, all the way to her ear. She shivered when his warm breath burst over her tender skin.

"Then I'm sure."

He used one hand to guide his cock lower, right to her entrance. He paused, waiting for her to back down even at the last second. Ambi threw her head back against the door and slammed her eyes shut. He'd warmed her up yesterday. Got the foreplay out of the way and turned her into a red-hot inferno of lust and need that was going to erupt if he didn't just get the hell inside of her.

She ground her hips into Trey's and dug her heels harder into his ass, urging him forward. Still, he held back. He was right there, burning and throbbing and in that moment, she lost her mind.

"Please, Trey- please. I want you. I need this." She'd never said those words before. Not to anyone. She'd once told him that she thought begging was in bad taste. She didn't actually know why she'd never said it, because whispering that plea against his ear was one of the most honest things she'd done in a very long time.

There wasn't any holding back or hesitation after that. Trey plunged inside of her, filling her and stretching her painfully. He was huge, but she took all of him. Trey dropped his head and ate her moan of pleasure before it could escape. He swallowed it and kissed her furiously as he began to move inside of her. It was heaven. She was dead and in heaven. She'd forgotten or she'd forced herself to forget, how amazing it felt. How they fit so perfectly.

Trey was careful at first, letting her get used to his thickness and length before he really thrust. The first one hurt, but the pain was agonizingly sweet. The second was utter bliss. The third, it was transcendent.

All she could do was clutch Trey's shoulders and dig her heels in and hang on. She knew she was spiraling down and out of control. But it felt like she was floating away too.

His thrusts picked up in intensity and she rocked with him. Grinding ferociously. She wanted all of him. More. Harder. Faster. Slower. It didn't matter. She just never wanted it to end.

Her spine and head banged against the door as Trey's thrusts grew harder. Wilder. More out of control and frenzied. He plunged in and out of her, filling her full every single time he left her maddeningly empty. It was insanity. Pure pleasure and radiant bliss. Every hard stroke brought her closer to unraveling that knot of heat deep in her stomach.

Trey kept going, kept her deliciously full, hitting all the spots, even a few that she wasn't aware existed. She writhed against him, taking even as he gave. Finally, after a few more incredible moments of chasing her pleasure, she came undone. She shattered and unraveled, throwing her head back against the door and crying out as the pleasure claimed every single muscle and bone. She writhed and groaned and rocked shamelessly as the waves crashed over her.

Trey's thrusts became more erratic. She could literally feel her muscles clenching and working with the aftershocks of her climax. She knew he was close by the way his breaths rasped in and out of his lungs, by the shudders wracking his body and the erratic thrusts. He'd said he was going to pull out. She didn't want him to. She knew that it was pretty damn intimate to take him like she was, bareback, no condom. She trusted the pill implicitly. She'd been on it for so long and never had a scare. That wasn't why he'd said he'd pull out. It was that... coming inside of her was crazy intimate. It was way too intimate, way too fast, but suddenly she didn't want him to leave.

"Come, Trey," she groaned against his ear. "Don't pull out. I want to feel you. All of you."

"Fuck, Ambi...." Trey's hips went wild, pinning her to the door as he churned inside of her. He came violently, his thrusts rocking them so hard that she was sure her spine was going to be bruised from the hard steel at her back or that they might actually break the door down. His groan filled up the tiny room, echoing between them. He seated himself deep and she felt the heat flood her from inside.

She clung to him, to his sweat-soaked skin, her face next to his, nestled against his granite jawline. They came down together, shuddering and breaking until the pleasure had subsided and they were left with the afterglow. And the aftermath.

Trey slowly let her back down to the floor and reality came crashing back. He passed her the discarded panties and the rest of her clothes, which she hastily pulled on while he did the same. When they were fully dressed, sans winter outerwear, they finally had to face each other.

"Trey," she breathed. "What did we just do? We- we shouldn't have- it was- too fast."

"I promise I'll last longer next time." Trey flashed her a wicked grin and Ambi groaned in frustration. Of course, he'd purposely misunderstand her.

"You know what I mean. God. This is a huge mess. I- we..." She glanced around. She was in a janitor's closet, for goodness sakes. With Trey. She still hadn't sorted out her feelings for him. She didn't even know if she wanted to admit that she did have feelings. Everything a huge mess. It was time to put on her big girl panties and act with an ounce of professionalism again. "We can't do this until after the Christmas party." She waved her hand, indicating the space between them. "I mean, whatever this is. Seriously. I have a job to do. I want to do it. We need to just- uh- take a step back until I can figure out how to do that properly."

Trey's jaw ticked, but he eventually nodded. "Alright. Agreed. I'll leave you alone until after the party, but after that, Ambi, I make no promises."

The rush of heat that swept through her shouldn't have been half as thrilling as it was. She had a serious problem. A big, six-foot something problem with dazzling eyes and a charming smile. An entire package of mayhem that had once again managed to uproot her entire life and turn her world on its end.

"We are not having the party here. Ever. I'm picking the last venue. I'll send menus over this afternoon."

"Ambi-"

She put up her hand, cutting him off. "I'll have all the other details taken care of. Please, Trey, you have to give me a break here. Until after the party."

"Fine. It's only in a few weeks. I guess I can cool off and let you do your job. You're coming, by the way."

"C-coming?" It sounded like too much of an innuendo not to be, and she felt stupid when he clarified.

"Yeah. To the party."

"What? N-no. I- I don't do that. I just plan it. I'll have everything running smoothly and by that time, I'll hand it over to you."

"No way." Trey shook his head. "That's a new stipulation. You have to be there."

"I don't have anything to wear." Right. As if that was going to deter him, but it was the best she could come up with at the moment, short of using the old hat, she had to stay home and wash her hair excuse. Did anyone still use that? With hair like hers, it could seriously pass for truth. It did usually take her the better part of an hour to deal with it.

Trey just smiled and winked at her and she knew she lost. She hadn't just lost the argument. She'd lost the battle, lost the war, lost herself.

"I'll buy you one. See you there, Ambi."

16

TREY

*T*he Christmas party was everything Ambi promised and more. Not that she'd given him a said list of promises, but he knew her, and he knew her work ethic and he knew that any party she planned would be nothing short of amazing.

It went off without a hitch. The venue was gorgeous, the dinner amazing, the entertainment top-notch.

The only thing missing was Ambi herself. Which was par for the course, given that she'd managed to evade him since that day in the janitor's closet.

She'd promised him that she'd come. Trey spent most of the night looking for her, trying to catch a glimpse of her sparkling eyes or her raven black hair. As he said he would, he'd bought her a golden-hued dress that was probably too fancy for an office Christmas party and had it delivered to her place. She'd signed for it, so he knew she'd received it.

Finally, as the band was starting up and people began to mingle, get even drunker, and do stupid things like attempt to bust a move on the large dance floor, Trey caught a flash of gold. Intrigued, he wandered up the set of stairs to the second floor of the ballroom that overlooked everything going on below. Most people didn't actually know they were allowed up there, so the place was pretty quiet.

There were only two people up there that he could see.

Ambi, dressed in the dazzling gold gown. She was a vision in the tight-fitting dress. It was cut daringly low in the front and the back and hugged her curves like it was made for her. Her raven hair was piled into a thick mass of curls at the base of her neck. Her makeup was sparse, but as usual, it only illuminated her natural beauty.

The second person, he realized, hovering near Ambi like a shadow, was his father.

A jolt of panic curdled his stomach and Trey burst off the stairs and stalked towards Ambi. His father reached out and shook her hand, all business as usual, but dropped it a few seconds later, like she had a contagious disease.

He glanced up when he saw Trey coming, but Dale spoke to Ambi, not him. "Amberina, what a surprise. It's a pleasure to see you again." His tone indicated that by pleasure, he meant the exact opposite.

Trey hurried to interject. He sensed the imminent disaster looming in the air. This was not how he imagined the party going. He imagined finding Ambi the minute he walked in, romancing her with a few drinks, sitting down to dinner with her, then slow dancing her right into his bed by the end of the evening.

Not only had she managed to evade him for the entire evening, now his father showed up to ruin everything.

"I should have known that Trey would hire you, given your current profession. You've done an excellent job, I must say." Dale glanced his way. "If you have any designs on a future though, I would leave it at the party, my dear."

Ambi's face turned a brilliant shade of scarlet. Trey

gulped hard. How could his father stand there and say something like that? Outright threaten her. What did that even mean, anyway? How far was he willing to take it to keep them apart?

"Uh- Dale- you should probably head down. You have to give a speech in ten minutes." Trey's eyes flicked to his father. He never called him dad when anyone else was within hearing distance. He barely called him dad at all. It felt like a long time since Dale had actually acted like a father.

Of course, his father wanted to save face. He was too diplomatic to admit that there was no speech planned. Instead, he turned to Trey and decided to completely reduce him to ash on the spot.

"If you're going to throw away everything, we've worked so hard for, do it for the right reasons. Do it because you're thinking straight and not because you're being duped by a pretty face. Beauty doesn't last. A name and a legacy, that lasts forever. Don't taint yours by being stupid."

"Um... I'm kind of right here," Ambi mumbled. If it was possible, the red tinting her cheeks deepened to an even darker shade of scarlet. She was wearing an expression somewhere between hurt and disbelief that Dale would again, so casually and blatantly assume that she was only there for the money.

He realized his own face was probably also a brilliant shade of red. "I *am* thinking clearly."

"She won't take you without the money. She's only here because of what you can give her," Dale spluttered.

"That true?" Trey's brow shot up. "Ambi? Did you know my family had money when you started dating me back in college?"

"N-no," she stammered. She clearly didn't want to be

involved in the discussion. She'd somehow found herself trapped between father and son, dragged into a conversation that should never be taking place. It was happening, even if she didn't want to participate.

"There's always the possibility that it's not the entire truth," Dale pressed.

"It doesn't matter!" Trey stepped up to shield Ambi from his father's harsh gaze. "We are not having this discussion right now."

"You do that then son. You make whatever decision you want. Just make sure it's the right one." Dale didn't wait around. He let those ominous words swirling in the air as he turned and stalked off, descending the stairs quickly to once again become king of the empire he'd created. He might as well have told Trey that if he picked Ambi, he'd be dead to him. Cut off. Finished. That was the impression he left, lingering between them like a terrible stench.

Ambi turned and walked to the railing. She stood there, her shoulders straight, her bearing regal, but her knuckles stark white. Trey stepped up beside her. He leaned into her periphery. He watched her blink rapidly. She was so perfect, so gentle, so *everything*. He wanted to put the pad of his thumb underneath her eyelashes to wipe away the tears before they spilled, but he didn't dare touch her.

"I can't do this," she breathed. She turned to him slowly, her eyes pools of misty anguish. "You're perfect, Trey. Really. All that you ever were, are, will be… it doesn't belong to me. Six months in college and a few stolen moments over the past few weeks isn't enough for me to demand all of you. If you're not happy at your job and you don't give a shit about the money, that's one thing. Breaking with all that's left of your family is another. That would be a mistake and I can't let you make it. I don't want you to regret me. Ever."

No. No, no, no, no! He couldn't let her do it. He couldn't let her walk away from him again. "What do you mean you can't do this? You *can* do this. You can do anything, Ambi. He'll come around. He was just being ridiculous. My father flies off the handle all the time."

"No. No, not about this. I don't think he will, Trey."

"Don't say that! You don't know. With time..."

She finally turned to look at him, even though it had to hurt. It hurt him. It hurt everywhere. His chest. His stomach. His legs, his feet, his hands, his head. Most of all, it hurt his heart.

"We're different people." Ambi started in on the usual break up shit, but one look at his face and her voice thinned out. "It never would work. Ever. It's not you. It's not even me. It's just this. All of it. Our lives. Our worlds. They don't belong together. We're like two opposing forces. Like hot and cold air and when we mix, all we create is this massive tornado of destruction. I can't let you throw away your relationship with your dad. He's the only parent you have left. I know you'd regret it. If you lost what little family you have, just to be with me. It isn't right, Trey. It's never going to be right. Hurting people to be with me is never going to make you happy and it's not going to make me happy either. We'll just end up a sullen mess."

Trey's felt his face harden. He was fighting it, doing battle against the destruction he was bringing down on both of them. He was shattering. So was she. They were watching each other do it, doing it to themselves, trading stab wounds with their words, and neither of them could stop the bleed out.

Wounds could be stitched, but it was true. Throwing away his family would be like nicking an artery and bleeding out. Ambi was too good to let him do that. Fast or slow, it would be agonizing and painful and she just couldn't do that to him.

"I love my mom," Ambi breathed. "She's all I have left. It's always been just us. I could never give her up. I know it's just you and your dad. I know you don't have the best relationship. I know that he works too much and you feel like he hasn't been there for you and that he feels like he lost all the good things in life when your mom died, but you still have each other. You just need to figure out a way to get through to him. Repairing that is far more important than us being together. We don't even know that it would work. Given that half of marriages fail and that's just stats- god knows about the rest of the mess for everyone else, the odds aren't good. I wouldn't hedge your bets on us."

"That's not what I'd be doing." Trey's jaw ticked. Ambi noticed, but he couldn't make it stop. "Life isn't about bets. It's not about rolling the dice. It's about making a decision and sticking with it. Growing and changing with someone else. Putting in the time and the effort."

She swallowed thickly. She obviously didn't expect him to be so persistent and that cut. He hadn't fought for her before. He needed to now. She obviously wanted to save him from himself.

"Trey, real life relationships are messy. They're not about quoting self-help books and thinking that's going to work. It's not. We are not meant to be together. We never were. We wouldn't work out. Our emotions are all over the place. We don't fit together."

"I can think of more than a few ways that we fit together," Trey edged.

"That's not funny."

"It wasn't supposed to be. I didn't just mean physically. We work. We've always worked."

She raised her head. She looked him in the eye as she dug her knife in deep. Her words were the only weapon she had left.

"Trey, you're the sun. You're also the shadow. It feels like when you look at me that you bathe my heart in this golden light. You taught me what it was to feel. To really fall. You were the first guy I ever loved. Hanging on to some romantic, nostalgic memory though- that isn't love. It isn't anything but a fantasy and that's all we're ever going to be. Just because our bodies fit together and we might fit in- in other ways, doesn't mean it's enough."

"It's always been there for us. That magic. You can't tell me that you don't feel it." He was growing more desperate by the second and he knew he sounded like it, but that wasn't going to make him stop. He'd fight to the death for her this time.

"That's the thing, Trey. I *don't* believe in magic."

Apparently, he'd fight to the death and die trying. That's what it felt like. Like he was dying a slow, painful, terrible death as Ambi left him at the railing. His lips pressed into a thin, hard line. His jaw clenched up tight. His knuckles gripped the rail so tight that there was no color left in them at all. She left him bleeding out all over the floor. He wanted to fight for her, but she didn't want him to. She left him like he'd left her all those years ago. With his heart ripped out, lying in tatters at his feet.

17

TREY

*I*t might be childish, but Trey *did* believe in magic. He knew that most of it was fake, but there had to be some of it that was inexplicable. Some skills that took a lifetime to master. Some things that just transcended belief.

He wasn't done trying. He wasn't giving up. It wasn't in his nature to just crawl up in a ball and die. He'd done that once already and he'd spent the better part of five years regretting it. He wasn't going down with the ship again. In fact, the ship wasn't going down at all.

Which was why he paid John from their HR department twenty bucks to use his personal phone to book a fake appointment with Ambi. She did keep office hours, but every single time he went by her building for four days straight, the door was locked. He decided he couldn't leave it any longer and he sure as hell wasn't going to leave it up to chance. Maybe she was avoiding him. Maybe she knew that he'd come by and beg her like some pathetic fool, so she locked her doors to dissuade him.

He almost started to believe that she'd packed up and

moved overnight. Panic welled up at that thought, nearly choking him. He couldn't let her go. He'd hire every single PI in the freaking state to find her if she'd truly disappeared. Any state. Wherever. Whatever it took, he'd find her and get her to listen.

Thankfully, he didn't have to resort to that. Yet. John was able to set up an appointment for that afternoon at four.

Trey spent the next four hours pacing around in his office, wearing down the carpet in a six-foot square pattern. He'd been in a couple of plays in high school and he remembered pacing back and forth like this, reciting lines. He mumbled to himself the same way, except it wasn't pre-written garbage he was spouting. If he flopped, it wouldn't be an embarrassing moment in front of a small audience. He couldn't laugh it off later. This was it. This might be his last shot at getting Ambi back.

Thankfully, at four, when he tried Ambi's front office door, the heavy glass gave under his hand and it pulled open. She really was there.

His heart kicked up from its already rapid skittering into an alarmingly painful pattern. He slammed a hand over the spot, trying to prevent an ambulance ride. Dying of a heart attack before he even stepped foot into the building wasn't an option.

The bell above the door tinkled announcing his arrival. He heard a chair scrape back in the next room and he froze for just a second before he turned and slid the deadbolt in place on the door. Yeah. There was no freaking way someone else was coming in there while he made his grand speech.

Or, at least, he hoped he got to make it.

Ambi rounded the corner and as soon as she saw him, the pleasant look on her face, ready to welcome and greet her appointment, changed into a pissed-off looking frown. Her eyes narrowed into two slits and her hands actually balled into fists at her sides.

"Oh no. Not you. I have an appointment right away. You're going to have to leave."

Trey leaned up against the front door he'd locked, trying for non-threatening and casual, but in a suit, he wasn't quite sure that he actually succeeded. He cursed himself for not having thought to change first.

"I-" His voice came out rusty, so he cleared his throat. "I'm your appointment, actually."

Ambi's already pissed off expression soured into something close to one that said she'd just stepped, barefoot, into a warm, nasty, stinky, gooey pile of dog shit. Like it was squishing up between her toes and flooding around her delicate arches. Like she'd just sunk up to her ankles in an enormous pile.

"No. You didn't! You got someone else to call to be sure I'd be here?" Her eyes rolled in their sockets. "You are such an asshole."

Trey nodded. "Yeah. No disagreement there. I am an asshole. Or, I was. I was back then, Ambi, but I came here because I have something to say that you need to listen to. I-I can't- what happened at the Christmas party- I..." *Nice. Super smooth delivery there. This is going so fucking perfect.* Truthfully, it was going exactly how he thought it would go and that was the bad part. He didn't want to turn into a stammering, bumbling idiot who couldn't get the right words out when he needed them most.

"Trey-" Ambi sighed, cutting him off before he could get anything else out. "What happened at the party wasn't anything I didn't already expect. It wasn't even anything new. We've been through all this."

"Ambi, no, you need to listen-"

"No. Trey. You need to listen." Her frown dropped away, replaced with something far more resolute. Far scarier. Far worse. It was so glaringly obvious that she'd already made up her mind.

"Please. You have to give me another chance. It will be different this time. I promise. Everything will be different. We're not the same people we were. I'm not the same person. I'm not afraid to fight for you. To fight my father. I made the wrong choice last time. I was an idiot. I was scared and lost. I'm not making that mistake again. I'm not letting you go. I'll leave the company. I'll never speak to my father again if that's what it takes. I promise I'll do what I have to do. I have my own money this time. We can start our own company, or I can support you in this one. We can move somewhere else. Go anywhere. Do anything. We can even take your mom since I know you'd never leave without her. Please, Ambi. I'm here this time. For real. For good. I need you to see that."

"I do, Trey." Her voice sounded little and lost and her face was a carefully composed mask.

He couldn't hope to read her. She was closing herself off, or she already had. Some people might accuse Trey of being pretty emotionally stunted, or at least, emotionally stupid, but even he could see that she'd already made a decision and it wasn't in his favor.

"I do see that," she continued, her words drenched in finality and sadness. At least if she was going to break his heart, she felt bad about it. "There isn't any future for us unless your dad changes his mind and that's obviously never going to happen. I spent so many years hating you for choosing the money instead of me that I never fully realized that you never chose the money. You chose your family. The only family you had left. Your dad. I used that resentment as a way to deal with my own hurt and anger and let myself off the hook. I'm a big girl now. I've spent years thinking about it. Family is the most important thing in the world, Trey. I can't let you choose between me and yours."

"But- Ambi-"

"It's alright, Trey. We're going to be okay. I've spent years learning how to make myself happy and so have you, whether you know it or not. We had a good time in college. Honestly, these past few weeks were fun too. Frustrating and crazy and- and everything, but I'm a big girl. We're both adults now. We're not some college kids too naïve to realize how the world really works. We'll be okay. We'll move on. I'm not saying find other people, but we both know how to survive in the world, so we'll keep on doing that. Your dad isn't going to change his mind. I can never be with you knowing that I tore you away from your family. He might not like me, but he's still your dad. You're his son. I don't want to take that away from him. He's already lost a lot. Losing you would break him."

Trey was floored. He'd never thought about his father in that light before. His dad had always been a powerful man. A man who built up a thriving company from almost nothing. A man who exuded confidence, and later, wealth. A hard man who didn't talk about his feelings often. He was fierce and passionate about the things he wanted in life and he'd passed that down to Trey. He'd never thought about his dad as someone vulnerable and breakable beneath that rigid exterior.

"He'll change his mind." Even as the words came out, there wasn't much conviction behind them. He knew his father better than that. Apparently, though they'd met only twice before, so did she. She snorted, but it was a soft snort, not the mocking kind. More like the sad laughter kind. "I'm not letting this be a goodbye," Trey ground out. "He'll change his mind. I'll get him to understand. I'm not letting you get away again."

"Alright." She ducked her head, her voice so soft that he almost missed that one word.

"Alright?"

"Yeah. Alright. If he changes his mind, really changes his mind, come find me. You know where I am. I'm not holding out hope though, Trey. I can't promise that I'll still be single in another five years."

"I get it, Ambi. I do. I know I wasted a lot of time. I'm not planning on letting it happen again. It's not going to take me five years to get my head on straight. I promise."

"It's okay, Trey. Really. You can't force this. You just have to let it happen. I'm just saying. I don't think it will ever happen. I don't have any expectations. I think we just need to get on with our lives and keep learning what it takes to make ourselves happy. If you should happen to meet someone in that time, I'm okay with that." Ambi's lips wavered at the end, but she clamped her top teeth down into her bottom one to keep it from wobbling.

It was pretty damn evident that she was so far from being okay with what she was saying, but she was making an effort. For him. She was letting him go, not because she thought she should, but because she didn't want to hurt anyone. Not him. Not his dad. She was doing what she truly believed was the right thing. Hurting herself to keep his family together.

It was noble.

It was honorable.

It didn't matter that he didn't want her to be either of those things. When she made up her mind, she was unshakable. She was a much better person, definitely a bigger person than he was and would probably ever be. That was part of the reason he loved her so much. Because she was fiercely intelligent, completely loyal, kind and compassionate to a fault. She was goodness and so much freaking light. He wished that she had an ounce of darkness in her soul. Just a little selfishness. Just enough that she'd tell him to stay, no matter the consequences.

She didn't though. Instead, she stood tall and regal, her hands still bunched at her sides, her neck straight and proud, her chin tilted up. She was glorious, a queen among women. The only woman he'd ever loved and the only one he ever would.

"He'll change his mind. I promise."

She didn't nod. She didn't say she hoped so. She didn't say anything. She just blinked at him slowly, her eyes filled up with pain she couldn't tamp down and hide away.

He let himself out. Without a goodbye, because he didn't want to say those words. Good. Bye. Such simple words, loaded with so much meaning. It wasn't goodbye. It couldn't be.

Because he was beyond certain that he couldn't live without Ambi. Losing her would be a mortal wound, one he'd never recover from. So, no. Goodbye was not an option.

18

TREY

*E*ven though it was past six and dark, his father was still exactly where Trey expected to find him-tucked behind the massive oak desk in his office. It wasn't made up of particle board or pressed wood. That desk was the real deal. Passed down in their family through generations. His father didn't keep the desk at home, in a home office. No, he brought that bastard all the way downtown and had a moving crew haul it up. How they got it through the doorways and into his father's office, Trey had no idea.

Turned out, miracles did indeed happen. Or just really good feats of engineering.

Dale glanced up as soon as Trey entered. He pushed open the glass door without knocking. It wasn't his usual MO. He couldn't remember the last time he hadn't knocked before entering his father's domain. Even as a kid, his mom taught him to raise his little fist in greeting or warning, before he entered another person's somewhat private space.

"We need to talk." He didn't bother with preamble before he shuffled across the vast distance of empty office space- the place was absolutely huge. It was the largest office in the building and Dale had pretty much chosen to leave most of it empty, almost like a big fuck you to everyone else in the place who struggled and clamored for more space.

Trey sunk down in the black modern office chair across from his father's desk. It was so incongruous with the antique piece that he almost laughed at the fact that he'd never noticed it before. He felt like when it came to everything about his life, he was seeing clearly, eyes wide open, for the first time in his life.

"I figured you'd be by sooner or later." Dale set down the expensive fountain pen he used. It was a gift from Trey's mom and Dale used the thing almost exclusively when he wasn't working on his laptop. His dad was old-fashioned in the way that he still liked to send handwritten cards at Christmas, not emails like he was doing just now.

That caught Trey off guard. He watched as Dale folded his hands on the ancient desk top. He actually raised his head, giving Trey his full attention.

"You fought tooth and nail to marry mom. Her dad didn't think you were good enough for her. You wouldn't give up. You had nothing, but you promised him that you'd look after her. That you'd give her a good life, and most of all, that you'd never stop loving her. That you'd cherish her above everything else. And you did. I didn't really know it at the time, but I was a lucky kid, growing up, to get to see two people who loved each other like you and mom. You were happy. Both of you. You never stopped loving each other. She was your entire world." Trey cleared his throat. His father stared at him impassively, but Dale had years of perfecting the perfect stern look. It was the same look he liked to give problematic clients, disgruntled employees, and his wayward son. "Why won't you give me the same chance to have that?"

His father did something he didn't expect. Dale laughed. He chuckled under his breath and leaned back just a little. "I didn't realize I was stopping you."

Trey knew he probably looked like a fool at the moment, a mix of shock and disbelief twisting his face. He'd come prepared for battle. Not- not whatever this was.

"How can you say that? You were the one who told me to choose between Ambi and my inheritance in college. You told me it was break up with her or lose everything."

Dale shifted in his seat. He kept his face impassive and bland. "I did give you that choice, yes."

"You told me to make the right decision. Not to disappoint mom."

"No. I told you to make the decision that would have made your mother proud. I never told you what that was."

"You made it obvious!"

Dale rearranged his hands on the desktop. Trey's eyes were drawn to them. Those hands. Strong hands. Hands that had picked him up when he'd fallen as a kid. Hands that healed his scraped knees and elbows. Hands that guided him on his bike for the first time, hands that taught him to fly fish- which he and his dad did every single summer. Hands that taught. Guided. Loved. Hands that were there to instruct.

His father taught him that nothing in life was final. Anything could be achieved through hard work and dedication. Trey used to think it was an old-school mentality that wasn't quite true, but now he wasn't so sure. His dad tried to give him the most important thing in the world. Values. He tried to teach him what was important in life. Somewhere along the way, had he misunderstood?

Dale wasn't snarling at him at the moment. He wasn't giving him a list of ultimatums. He was just sitting there, staring at his hands like he was waiting for Trey to make up his own mind about what was happening. About what had happened in the past.

"I came here because I wanted to tell you that I'm not giving up on Ambi. Not this time. I've spent the past five years living with the weight of my regrets. I don't want to sell insurance. I never have. I wanted to do something creative with my life, not be chained to a desk day in and day out. I want to go down a different path. I've saved and invested all the money that I earned and that you gave me. I've been careful. I've made a name for myself and I've made a good living and I thank you for providing me with that. For setting the foundation and helping me build up the walls along the way. You and mom. You taught me everything. You gave me every opportunity in the world. I just- I don't want to do this anymore. I don't want to work here. I actually hate working here. I always have."

"I never would have stopped you from leaving."

That was news to Trey. He stared at his father like he was a complete stranger. Dale raised his head and stared back. They had the same hairline, jawline, nose, and eyes. It was like looking into a mirror.

"I want you to be on board with it. Whatever I choose to do. I'm not just leaving here, I'm going after Ambi. I'm going to do what it takes to win her back because I love her. She's the love of my life. She's my everything. I've spent years thinking about how I could make it right. Years. Years planning. Planning how to get her back. How to have a life with her. How not to fuck it all up again. I'm not giving up this time. This time is my time. It's our time. I just wanted to say that you- that you can't stop me from doing this. I want you to be on board with it, because Ambi is it for me. I love her, or at least, I want to learn how to love her, like you loved mom. Timeless. With my entire being."

When Trey was finished, he leaned back, drained, like the words pulled the last ounce of strength he had left from him. In reality, they did. He felt empty. Hollowed out.

He expected his father to explode out of his chair, rail, rant, and rage. To tell Trey that there was no way in hell he was leaving. That he'd be ruined if he did. That he'd never speak to him again. That Ambi was just after his money. That he was in puppy love and it wasn't real, and he was making the worst mistake of his life.

Instead, Dale shocked him again by smiling. Not a sardonic, sadistic smile, but a real, honest, genuine smile that spread across his face. He followed that up with another soft chuckle.

Trey raked a hand through his hair, mussing it all over the place. "What the hell is so funny about all of that? You'll have to tell me because I seriously don't think it's a joke."

"It's funny to me that you're just seeing this now. I'm glad you finally got here. It's been a long road."

"What are you *talking* about?" Trey was growing exasperated. He felt like he was in the middle of a maze with no hope of ever finding his way out.

"All I ever wanted was for you to be happy. I'm sorry that you misunderstood everything I said and tried to do. I made a promise to your mother. That I would always take care of you. You're my son and naturally, I want what's best for you, but it goes beyond that. I promised her that I would help you find your way. Five years ago, I gave you a choice. Pick the girl you'd been dating for all of six months or lose your inheritance. Honestly, I hoped you'd pick the girl. Instead, you picked the money."

"I would have had nothing!"

"That's not true. I never said choose between her or your family. I told you to make your mother proud of your decision. She would have been proud if you'd have followed your heart. If you would have chosen Amberina, I wouldn't have given you your inheritance. I would have offered you a job here and let you work your way up. I didn't want to hand everything to you on a silver platter. I wanted you to learn the value of it."

"That's a little fucking cheesy, don't you think?" Trey snapped.

"No. Well, if it is, then I'm sorry. I did what I thought I should do. I didn't want to just hand over the money to you. It was a large sum and I wanted you to invest it wisely. Working here, I think, taught you that. It helped you prepare for the world out there. I knew you wouldn't stay here forever. I wanted you to learn a little before you went out there. Learn about yourself. I wanted to give you the tools you needed to build a life. I was trying to look after you. I would have eventually given you the money anyway when I thought you were old enough and mature enough to use it wisely."

"That's not- you can't just... you can't just use reverse psychology on me and tell me that I'm the one who made all the mistakes."

"I'm sorry you see them as mistakes. I don't. You chose a path. You thought it was what you wanted, but you know now, that it's not. Your grandfather made me work for your mother. It was true that he didn't like me. He didn't like that I came from nothing and had no way to support us. They weren't rich, but he wanted to know his daughter was taken care of. She was his treasure. She was worth fighting a thousand lifetimes for her. He made me earn her. Earn her

respect, her trust, and her love. He made sure that I under-
stood what a treasure I was getting and that I wouldn't just
love her, I would truly cherish her over the years. That I'd
never stop. The point is, I wanted you to make your own
path. Work hard and appreciate the value of that. I wanted
you to work hard earning Ambi's love and respect and trust
and if you weren't prepared to do that, then to take some
time to mature and truly understand what it is you want out
of life. Maybe you had to be miserable in order to appreciate
the other side of things."

"You're not a psychologist!" Trey spat. "You can't just
choose those things for me. Do those things and expect me
to think that it was a good idea when I find out that you had
an ulterior motive for commanding me to give up Ambi."

"I never commanded you to give her up. I gave you a
choice. I also never said that I wouldn't support you, whatever that choice was. You read between the lines what you
wanted to read. You never asked me for clarification. You've
never once said you didn't enjoy working here."

"I work here because it was expected."

"I've never expected that of you, Trey. I wanted you to
continue on the legacy here, wanted you to take the
company and make it your own if that's what you wanted,
but if not, that's fine. I want you to be happy. I would never
tell you to stay here and waste your life on something that
you didn't love doing."

"No!" Trey banged his hand on top of the desk. His dad
never flinched once. "You can't just say those things now and
act like it's all my fault. Like all of this was a misunder-
standing."

That time, Dale did flinch. "I'm sorry, Trey. I really am. I
didn't know. I didn't know you were unhappy. I didn't know

you were so serious about Ambi. I wanted you to fight for her and when you didn't, I just thought she was not the right one. I gave you a job here because I thought you wanted to do this. You never once told me otherwise. You never told me how you felt. About anything."

Trey slowly shifted back in the chair. It creaked under his weight, all that fancy square modernness of it not doing a damn thing to help bear the load of his shame and sorrow. The weight of realization. The weight of regret.

His dad was right. He'd never once voiced his feelings. He'd gone through life, doing what he thought was expected. He and his father didn't talk. Not even on their fishing trips. They didn't talk about their feelings. They were men. His dad was old-school. That kind of thing wasn't easy for him and Trey never instigated a conversation about it. It wasn't easy for him either. His mom had always been the go-between for them and without her there to mediate and spell out what the other was feeling, it was like all those lines of communication had been burned and he was just guessing. Was it possible he'd guessed wrong? For so many years?

"There are things I regret, Trey," his dad said, slowly. "I regret that we never talked about this properly. That we're just doing it now. When I saw Ambi at the party a few nights ago, I knew why she was there. I knew it. I just didn't know if you did. I was trying to push you in the right direction. The direction where you finally fought for her. If I'd just come out and asked you if you loved her and gave you my blessing, would that have been easier for you? Would you have been able to communicate to her what you felt for her? Would you have fought so hard for her? Would you have been able to tell me now that you love her and that you aren't happy where you are? Would you ever have left here? I didn't know how to talk to you, Trey. I'm your father and it's the one thing I was never able to do. Talk. Feel openly. That's not my strong suit. I'm sorry about that. For my failings and shortcomings. I was trying to push you into taking that step forward or stepping back for good. Can you see that? Maybe I was wrong..."

"I don't know," Trey shook his head. "It's going to take me some time to process this properly, because yeah, it probably would have been easier for you to tell me that I had your blessing."

"I'm sorry. I didn't know any other way than to make you fight for her like I fought for your mother. To make you realize, for yourself, just how far you were willing to go for her. That you don't just love her, but that you truly cherish her. That you're truly in love. I needed to make sure that you weren't just giving your heart to anyone and that you'd be willing to move heaven and earth for her because that's the only way these things actually work. The only way you'll ever succeed is to have the kind of love that they write stories about. I had it. I never lost it. I still have it, even though your mom isn't here anymore."

"I- dad..." Trey raked his hand through his hair again. He let out a sigh that wasn't so much frustration as it was just a release of everything. Everything he'd held pent up so tight for the past five years.

"And what about her? Does she love you? Does she love you enough to move her own heaven and earth for you?"

Trey finally looked his father in the eye. There was no malice there. No anger. Not even regret, as though he'd purged it all by telling Trey he was sorry and admitting that he'd certainly failed in some respects, as a father, and as a human being. He saw love there, shining in his father's eyes.

Pride as well. His father never told him he was proud of him. He'd never used those words, but Trey could see it. He could see it, for the first time, because he was finally, finally actually looking. He knew he would have seen it before if he'd had his eyes *open*.

It was like he was seeing Dale for the first time. Not as a little kid, but as a fellow adult. As a fellow human being who had fumbled, stumbled, and done the best he could, even if it was messy and open for debate. He'd done what he thought was right. He'd tried to set Trey on the right path, even if Trey saw it as a pretty convoluted way to get there.

"She told me that we couldn't do this without you. That she wouldn't be with me if it meant that I had to give up my family. She knows that you're the only one I have left. That it's just us. It's always been her and her mom and family is everything for her. She told me not to come back if you weren't on board with this."

His father's lips wobbled. "Smart girl. Beautiful too. Definitely worth fighting for as hard as you have."

"I did pick wrong," Trey mumbled. "I get it now. You never told me what to do. You were just trying to help me open my eyes and see. I went through most of my life with them shut like a blind man. I didn't love Ambi enough back in college to fight for her properly. I know that was a mistake. I'm never going to make it again because she's it for me. She's the only one I'll ever want."

Dale grinned. "What are you waiting for then? Give me your damn resignation and go find out what makes you happy. You'll always have a position here if you ever want to come back. And for goodness sake, go out and get the love of your life back."

Trey stood up so fast he just about knocked the chair over. He set out a hand to steady and right it. "Thanks for the advice, dad. One day I'll come back here and thank you for everything. When I can truly mean it."

His father nodded solemnly. He picked up his favorite pen and rolled it between his fingers, almost absentmindedly, except that his father didn't do anything without a reason. "I'm looking forward to it, son. Very much."

19

AMBERINA

"*I* can't believe you recorded everything."

"It was the only way I could think of to get you to believe me. If I'd just told you he was on board, you would have called me a liar. Even if he told you flat out, I don't think you would have believed he hadn't been somehow coerced into it."

Ambi stared at Trey's phone, which sat on the edge of her desk. She was standing on the far end of the room, her arms pretty much wrapped around herself. She couldn't press into her floor to ceiling bookcase any further if she tried. It was one of her favorite parts of her office. The built-in bookcase from the previous owner. She'd filled it up with every single book she owned and there was still a bit of room. Which was good. She loved reading and she couldn't help buying books, even if she had switched over to mostly reading electronically.

Trey stood in the doorway. He'd basically caught her at the office and cornered her so she couldn't dodge past him and get out of the office. She'd retreated to the far end of the room, up against the bookcase, putting as much distance between them as she could, and she'd stayed there, her massive metal desk between them. Trey had slapped his phone down and told her to listen. She didn't want to, but short of plugging her ears like a disobedient toddler, she had no choice.

She'd listened.

She'd listened to the whole twenty-minute recording.

"Does he know? That you recorded it?"

"No. I had my phone in my pocket the entire time. I wanted to record it just for evidence. I needed it. I knew if I came here again claiming that I'd talked to him and he'd agreed just like that, you'd call bullshit. He didn't know I was recording, but he wouldn't be opposed to me sharing it with you. You heard the end. He told me to get my ass in gear and get you back."

Ambi nodded. It felt like a dense fog had flooded the room and was swirling around her in a dense cocoon. Her brain was processing so slow that someone might as well have undone the top of her head and jammed it full of slow-moving molasses. She realized, belatedly, that it was shock. She wasn't just shocked. She was in shock.

"I agree with you," she finally breathed.

Trey had waited until the afternoon when he was probably sure she'd be at the office. He wasn't wearing a suit, which told her that he probably hadn't gone to work that morning. It made sense now, seeing as he basically told his dad he was done there. Instead of his usual suit, he was dressed in a pair of faded jeans, a grey t-shirt, and a black zip up. He looked amazing, as usual. Somehow the casual look suited him better than the expensive formal clothes.

"About what?" Trey's brow arched up. He lounged in the doorway, so maddeningly casual. He didn't seem ruffled at all. Did he always have to be so sure of himself?

"About your dad's methods being questionable at best. I'd call them outright shitty. I don't know why he thought he could accomplish anything by testing you like that. I mean, maybe I do. I don't know. I didn't know that he had to fight for your mom like that. I don't know how he grew up. I don't really know anything about him. I only really know what you've told me, and you didn't understand what he was really trying to do, so maybe I just have the wrong impression."

"No, his methods were pretty shitty. I see where he was coming from, but I'll have to agree to disagree about what he did. I can see his reasoning behind it after he tried to explain, but it's still terrible." Trey sighed. "Either way, Ambi, I lost the past five years. I lost them because they weren't spent with you. I was a shithead. My father was less of a shithead than I thought. Maybe just a different kind of shithead. It doesn't make a difference. I made the wrong choice. I made that choice myself. I don't have anyone to blame for it except myself. I'm owning it now."

"So, you're here. You're here because I said we couldn't do this if your dad wasn't on board and he appears to be, so you're back to ask me for a second chance."

"Yeah. Pretty much." Trey grinned, but it was a reluctant, self-deprecating grin. "I'm back for more punishment. Whatever you want to dish out. I'll stand here and take it because I more than deserve it. If you want to call me an asshole, it's well deserved. A turd, or whatever you were calling me before, I agree. I'm a turd. The smelliest, squishiest, drain clogging epic kind of turd."

"That's disgusting."

"Yes, well, I'm that too. I agree. I'll get on my knees if you want me to, Ambi. I'll beg you for another chance. I'll beg you to forgive me."

Ambi knew that her face was blank so far, but in another few seconds, she was going to crack. Her chest felt like it was going to explode and rain rainbows and glitter and happiness all over the place. She wanted to be cautious. She wanted to tell Trey that she needed time. That she needed space and distance to think. Fortunately for him, she'd spent the past five years doing all of that.

Somewhere, buried not so deep inside of her, were the seeds of love that Trey planted all those years ago. She'd kept them carefully protected in the most barren soil. She hadn't given them water or fertilizer, but they remained. They stayed dormant and she always knew that if given even a glimpse of sunlight or a drop of rain, they'd sprout up and in a matter of minutes they'd be full-grown, blooming and blossoming all over the place.

That first time Trey kissed her when they were cake tasting was the sun.

When he'd ended up at her apartment that night, he was the rain.

He'd pulled her into the same closet where they'd had their first time. Those seeds came busting up to the surface and she could do nothing to hold them back.

She'd thought that Dale pulled out all her precious plants at the Christmas party. She'd lost all hope and was ready to let those plants die.

Then Trey came back. He went to his dad and talked it out. He was here and he was hers if she wanted him. They could try again. They could try and they could be something. He'd fought for her and he was finally here, ready to love her.

If she wanted him to. If she let him.

She should be afraid. She should be filled with doubts and hesitance and reluctance. She shouldn't just give in, but if the past five years had taught her anything, it was that there wasn't time for fears or doubts, hesitance or reluctance. She loved Trey. She knew that beyond the shadowiest shadow of a doubt.

"Did you mean it? That part?"

"Which part?" Trey's voice was so soft. So gentle. So hopeful.

"The parts about me being your everything and your whole world."

"Of course." Trey took a step forward. "I'm sorry I wasted so much time."

"It wasn't wasted," she said. Trey took another step forward and another. "We both needed to grow up and go after what we wanted. We needed to figure out how to make ourselves happy before we could even think about trying to do that for each other. We had to mature."

"Like fine wine?"

"Well, I turned out fine. I think you might have turned into vinegar."

Trey threw back his head and laughed. Truly. Laughed. God, she missed that sound. She missed it almost more than anything else. She couldn't remember the last time she'd actually heard him laugh like that. It was always chuckles here and there. The not so serious, not so real, a little forced even at the best of times, kind of laughter. This was real. This was authentic. This was beautiful.

"Wine or vinegar, pickles or cucumbers, whatever I am, whatever I have, it's yours. This time I'm here, Ambi. I'm all in. I promise that I'm here for good and that I'll never stop fighting for you. I love you. I never stopped. Will you give me a chance? I promise this time, I'll get it right."

She sighed and put her hand to her chin like she had to think about her answer. Trey hesitated. He'd reached her desk and he was only a couple feet from the bookcase. She couldn't go anywhere but forward. It was a good metaphor for life. She didn't want to go back. She wanted to look to the future. To a good future. To a future with the man she loved. To a future with Trey.

She'd never actually allowed herself to hope for it or think about it over the years. She'd always thought about him in safe terms. Past tense. Not future or present tense.

"I never stopped either," she admitted. She had to grin when she watched Trey's lips part. He let out a sigh of relief that he obviously couldn't contain. "I wanted to. I wanted to stop loving you. I really tried, but like a bad STD, you stuck around."

"Thanks. I'll remember that one. You just upped your game from turd to something even viler."

This time, she laughed. "Oh, god, Trey. What I'm trying to say is that I couldn't purge you out. I couldn't, and maybe it was for a good reason. Maybe the reason was that I was never supposed to. I'm going to stop trying to get you out. So, if you want to keep trying to get in, I'm open to it."

"That's a really weird thing to say. I'm not sure if it's outright sexual or if I'm just imagining some really good things right now."

She bit down on her bottom lip. "It wasn't supposed to be, but I can see how it could come across like that…"

"Oh really?" Trey finally crossed the distance from the desk to the bookshelf and in another second, he reached out. He didn't manhandle her into his arms. Just held out his hand and let her curl her small fingers around his much larger ones.

"Really," she said breathlessly.

"We are going to have a really, really good future. Starting right now."

"Even if you're vinegar and I'm wine?"

"Especially if I'm vinegar and you're wine."

"Even if you're a turd?"

"Even if I'm a turd. I promise to be less turd like going forward from this moment."

"That's good," Ambi breathed since Trey opened his arms and tugged her gently into them.

She went the rest of the way until she was pressed up against his chest, her hand still in his, the other resting right above his heart. It was beating. Hard. Kind of like hers was. All messed up and all over the place. She was in that. She was in that wild, racing heartbeat. She inspired it. At least part of it. They were really doing this.

Trey sealed the deal by tipping her chin up gently. "Can this smelly turd give you a kiss?" he asked with a wide, wicked grin. Heat and desire burned in the depths of his eyes, but this time, this time she could see all the love swelling there too. He wasn't hiding it anymore. He wasn't shutting down or locking her out.

"No, but you can give me a kiss. Trey. The love of my life."

"I think I can agree with that. Merry Christmas, Ambi, my love."

"Merry Christmas."

It was going to be. It was going to be a really, really good Christmas. Maybe the best ever. She was going to enjoy the hell out of every single second of it.

EPILOGUE
TREY

*S*ometimes things just made sense. Once in a while, everything turned out alright. Every now and then, happy endings really were a thing

Except they were so far from ending. Their story wasn't over. It felt like it was just beginning, every single day that they woke up together. Every single night when they fell asleep together, wrapped up in each other. It was a new beginning. Another day in their forever ever after.

"Did you buy the turkey?" Ambi ran up to greet him the second he bustled through the front door. They now lived in a large, three-story antique house. It was over a hundred years old and even though it started out as an unlivable death trap, they'd brought it back to life over the years. It was now nearing completion. He couldn't complain about it being a money pit. Ambi loved it too much and her love for it might have worn off on him just a little.

"Yes, yes I got the turkey." He set down the overflowing grocery bags. "And the other hundred things on your list."

Ambi twisted her hands in front of her and bit down nervously on her bottom lip. "It's just that- well- this is the first Thanksgiving that we've actually hosted. Everyone is coming, even Marcella."

"She always knew that we'd end up together. She's baking a special cake just for our anniversary. I can't wait to taste what flavor she's invented now." It just so happened that they'd been married on Thanksgiving three years ago. Of course, Marcella was there. Of course, she'd baked a cake just for them. Pumpkin chai spice. Of course, tasting it was like being ushered through the gates of heaven.

"Your dad and my mom though. God. I just hope that they don't wind up hating each other. That would be really awkward for us to have to police between them. Maybe it's a bad idea to have everyone over. Maybe-"

"It's a great idea." Trey stepped over the overflowing bags with the groceries spilling out onto the floor. He wrapped his arms around Ambi and she melted against him, some of her tension draining away. "And don't worry about them, they'll figure it out."

"It's just- don't you think it's weird? That they're-together?"

He grinned down at his wife as he smoothed some of her raven black hair away from her forehead and tucked it behind her ear. "Nope. Not at all. They were in love from the minute we took them on that trip to Mexico." Instead of going alone after Christmas, he and Dale had joined Ambi and her mom. It shocked everyone, his dad and her mom included, that there was a spark there. Two years later, Dale finally got brave enough to ask her out, and ever since, they'd been going pretty strong.

"This puts a lot of pressure on me. What if I screw up the turkey? What if I undercook it and end up poisoning everyone?"

"I think you'll do just fine. Just ask Marcella's opinion. She'll be here in a couple of hours."

Ambi let out a little screech of horror and began to gather up the groceries. Trey helped her carry everything to the kitchen and set it on the counter.

"Don't worry. You can always blame anything that flops on me. Everyone knows I'm a terrible cook."

"That's not funny." Ambi shot him a death glare.

"It's a little funny."

"So not."

"Yeah, it kind of is."

Ambi stuck her tongue out at him and began loading the fridge up with vegetables. He set out the dry goods, the box of stuffing, the cranberry sauce, the bag of potatoes, cans of corn. They'd have enough food to last a century.

"You know what isn't funny?"

Ambi whirled. "I can only guess."

"How much I love you."

Her lips wobbled into a smile and she couldn't hide the sheen in her eyes. She ducked her head, shaking it as she continued unpacking. "You always know just what to say, don't you?" she quipped, but he could hear the smile in her voice, even if he couldn't see her face.

"I think so. I got you to marry me, didn't I?"

"Some days, I wonder why," she remarked dryly as she slid a container of milk into the one open space still available in the overstuffed fridge.

"Because I'm amazing," Trey deadpanned.

She turned, hands on her hips, but she couldn't keep a straight face. She had to giggle. "Geez. And so humble too. How did I ever get so lucky?"

"Luck has nothing to do with it." Trey sauntered over and pulled Ambi into his arms. He placed a searing kiss on her lips and for a minute, she forgot all about their stressful Thanksgiving dinner that was still hours away and melted into him, kissing him back. He wanted to ask her if he could take her upstairs, or maybe just on the kitchen counter, but he knew better than to press his luck. "Like I said," he murmured against her lips. "I'm just that awesome."

"Okay, Mr. Awesome. How about peeling potatoes for me then?"

Trey released her, but when she turned, he gave her a gentle pat on her ass that had her turning and rolling her eyes at him.

"I'll do whatever you command of me, my love. My darling. My incredible, amazing, beautiful, talented and perfect wife. I'll even bend the knees right here right now if you ask me to."

"Oh brother." Ambi slid open the drawer and threw the peeler at him. He caught it easily. "Get peeling."

"Okay. I really do love you, though, Ambi. Undercooked, overcooked, anycooked turkey and all."

She rolled her eyes again, but when she turned, he knew she was still grinning. That was the way they went through life. Together. Sometimes annoying each other so much but loving the hell out of each other and laughing their way through it.

"I love you too, you cheeseball. Always."

"Forever and always?"

"Yeah. Forever and always."

Well. At least he'd graduated from anything that had to do with turds. Cheese was delicious. Exotic. Expensive. A definite improvement. He'd take it.

The End.

KISSED BY THE BOSS

BOOK 2

BOOK DESCRIPTION

Drinks + Christmas Party + Lost eye contacts = **Flaming Hot Kiss**
Except I have no idea who was on the receiving end.
I didn't even see (extreme short-sightedness problems big time).
But it was definitely someone from the office.

New week, new day at work,
Annnnd my lips are still tingling whenever I think about it.
But it's not like I can kiss every guy in the office,
And see who would turn out to be the charming prince of that night.

Not that I don't already have enough on my plate as it is.
What's with all the shooting glares my hotshot player of a boss keeps directing at me.

Why was he suddenly acting so out of character?
What was he so mad about?
Did I do something?
Clip his documents in the wrong order probably?

1

CALLIE

There were just some things in life that were better off not done. Office Christmas parties were near the top of Callie Canahan's list. Unfortunately, her best friend, who was also her roommate, wasn't of the same mindset.

"Come on! You can't skip out. It will be fun!" Chantara stuck out a lip in a pretty pout. Everything Chantara did was pretty. She was the kind of woman who would look beautiful in a sack. Or a paper bag. Whatever people always talked about.

"Fun as in... super boring? I just started there. I don't know anyone. I shouldn't even have the right to come."

"You've been there for over a month. That certainly qualifies you. Even if you didn't work there, I could still bring you as my guest. Which would be far better than anyone I've brought in the past. Last year, Troy drank like sixteen free whiskeys and that was the end of the night for us. It's lucky I didn't get fired."

"It was more than just the end of the night. You dumped him and left him in the cab outside the apartment and he'd lost his wallet, so the cab driver wouldn't take him any further. He kept ringing the buzzer until I got the story out of you and went down and gave him twenty bucks."

"Ugh, that was a bad night."

"One of the worst."

"Ha! Not nearly." Chantara's dark eyes glittered with amusement.

She gave a toss of thick black hair over her shoulders. She currently had on a matching pajama set, a pink tank and fuzzy pink bottoms with little bunnies all over them. They were absolutely adorable. But not nearly as adorable as Chantara looked in them. Callie was vaguely jealous. If she'd worn those pajamas, they would have made her look like a five-year-old girl. She didn't have the lush curves that Chantara did. She was tall and also slightly on the stick-kind-of-body side.

Once, in high school, they'd been discussing body types, the whole apple and pear thing. She wasn't either of those. More like celery. Or banana. Or... or carrot- a real thin, long one.

"You're right. Not nearly. I remember a few nights back in college..."

"Don't go there," Chantara groaned.

"Then there was the night you got so drunk at that bar you were dancing on the rooftops of cars."

"No! You are forbidden to talk about that!"

Callie giggled and it wasn't long before she and Chantara dissolved into giggles. Chantara wiped a few tears from her cheeks.

"You know, I thought at twenty-seven we'd be with people and in real houses and not a dumpy apartment, still using each other for wingmen and company."

"I'll always use you as my wingman," Callie said soberly. "And for company. Boyfriend or no boyfriend."

"Didn't you think though, that at this age you'd be married or something? Like, back in the day? When you were a teenager?"

Callie sighed. "I guess so, but now, twenty-seven seems really young. Aren't they saying forty is the new twenty? And we have a long way to go before that."

"Oh god, I hope so. I hope it goes slow. They also say men age like fine wine and women age like cheese."

Callie snorted. "That is terrible! Who said that?"

"I can't remember."

"They should not be allowed to say things like that. Seriously. So awful!"

Chantara giggled again and swiped at her eyes one last time. She took a deep breath and Callie could tell by the focus in her best friend's eyes that she hadn't been completely distracted.

"You're trying to change the subject here."

"I really wasn't. I was just protesting. I don't want to go to the Christmas party. I don't have anything to wear. It's going to be boring. They're always boring. Just crappy speeches about all this corporate stuff that I can't stand. I have to listen to that and put up with it all day. I don't want to hear it by night too."

"But it's free and last year, it might have been boring, but the food was soooo good."

"It was so boring that your date got shit faced and nearly got you fired."

"I didn't almost get fired. Everyone knew that Troy drank too much and it wasn't my fault. I wasn't even drunk. I had one drink. I could control myself. I wasn't responsible for his actions. If he'd wrecked anything, now that might have been another story."

"Good thing he wasn't destructive then."

"You're telling me. I never could have got you the job you love so much."

Callie rolled her eyes. "It's not that I'm not glad for the job. I am. It beats getting out of retail. And god, I hated the Christmas season. It was absolute murder. You would think that if I had a degree, I would actually get to use it."

"You might have if you had a degree in business."

"Stop." Callie got off the edge of Chantara's bed. "I don't want another lecture on how English degrees are useless. People get jobs in big corporations all the time with English degrees. Like in Communications and what not."

"But those jobs are hard to get."

"Well you don't even need to have a business degree to get an admin job."

"You don't have to," Chantara admitted. "But it definitely helps. And I'm not just any admin. I support one of our VP's."

"And I just get to support a Directing Manager. How boring." Callie giggled despite herself.

"Matthew Hilbert isn't just a DM. You're damn lucky you're his PA. The guy is a god. Or so I've heard. But he's not my type."

"I know. He's too clean. Clean shaved, short hair. He doesn't look like your type, but he sure acts like it."

"No!" Chantara jumped up. "Don't say that." She put her hands on her hips in mock anger. "It's only because you're my best friend that I'll let you get away with saying horrible shit like that about the guys that I date. They don't have the same reputation. I like bad boys, not players."

"And Matt Hilbert is definitely as player as it gets. I see

the emails that come in. On my first day he actually sat me down and had a talk about-"

"I know. You told me he said to *discreetly* get rid of the less than savory emails that come in from any of his female companions. And to screen the angry phone calls. Just the *angry* ones though. Oh god, I remember."

Callie couldn't help but let a little dreamy sigh escape. "It can't be helped that he's attractive. Very. Very. Attractive. But he's not my type either. I don't like players. I don't like guys that bounce around from one girl to another. I don't like guys for whom relationships do not mean anything. It's gross. It's just- distasteful. It really ruins the fact that he's super handsome."

"He'll be at the Christmas party."

"Oh, hell no..."

"You can't even be tempted with good food? You were just saying how you wished you had someone cook for you. It's Christmas. You probably aren't going home, so come and get a decent meal at the Christmas party, if for no other reason."

"Yes, but when I said that, I didn't want to have to endure a shit load of speeches and boring presentations and corporate blah, blah, blah to get it."

"I'll lend you earplugs."

"I think people would notice." Callie rolled her eyes.

"Please!" Chantara pulled a puppy dog face. "Don't make me go alone! I can't endure it alone! I'll look pathetic. People will try and drag me up to dance in those awkward, horrible tight little group things they do on the dance floor."

Callie couldn't keep a straight face. She laughed a second later and she knew it was over. Chantara won. Her best friend usually got her way. The temptation of food was a little too much to resist. And the fact that Matt Hilbert would be there, probably in a full-on suit. God, suits were attractive. He wasn't for her though. She wasn't into guys who dined and dashed. In truth, she hadn't been into anyone for a really long time.

Even if the Christmas party was horrible, she didn't have anything better to do or any place better to be. She hadn't gone home for Christmas in years either. Her previous job was too hectic for her to do so. So, with the party, it might actually be the one time she actually got out and did something for Christmas.

Maybe it would help get her through it.

"I still don't really have anything to wear. This thing is going to be fancy."

Chantara shot her one of those mischievous, twinkling eyes, I have a solution for everything, kind of looks. "Don't worry. I've got you covered." She jumped off the bed with renewed enthusiasm, grabbed Callie by the elbow, and steered her straight for the tiny closet. "I bought a dress last week. I was going to wear it, but it's actually a little tight. It will look perfect on you."

Callie knew exactly what dress Chantara was talking about. It was short and black and flirty and far too sexy. A whole lot of not at all Christmas party appropriate. She barely managed to stifle a groan. She already knew they were going to be in trouble. A night out with Chantara usually only ended one way, *office* Christmas party or not.

2

MATT

$\mathcal{M}$atthew Hilbert was the first to admit he might enjoy the nightlife a little too much. Or had. Past tense. He was really trying to get his shit together. He didn't like that he was starting to get a reputation. Truly. He took it to heart. He really did care about what people thought. He just- always seemed to find himself in the worst kind of situations. Which might have been because he chose to put himself in them in the first place.

He was cutting himself off. No more dates, no more parties, no more going out with friends when he knew where it would end up. He was thirty-three. He was starting to feel like he was way too old for that shit. And the drama. Lord, the drama. He knew it was bad when he had to get his PA to screen calls.

Beer with his long-time friend didn't exactly count. They hadn't even gone out. He'd gone to Jason's pad to break the news.

"So, you're really getting serious then?" Jason cracked the top off a beer and passed the chilled bottle over. Beads of condensation dripped on the kitchen floor.

"Yeah. No. I don't know. Not about anyone. I'm just over it. I had to ask my secretary to start screening my calls and emails. It was humiliating."

"That's because you attract the wrong kind of people."

"It's not like I try."

"Look at you, man." Jason chugged back half his bottle and set it down on the counter. The kitchen wasn't clean by any means, but he didn't move to tackle the dishes in the sink. They would probably be there for another week before the guy did anything about them. The countertop wasn't much better. It was scattered with old food wrappers and half-empty bread bag left open, the bread dotted with blue on top. Dirty dishes lined that surface too. "You're too well dressed. That's your problem. People know how to spot it."

"That is not the issue."

"Then grow your beard and hair out. Women hate beards. Gain some weight. Stop going to the gym. Wear dirty clothes. That's a turnoff. And stop driving an expensive car. It's a dead giveaway that you have money."

"Stop."

"Well, seriously. If you wear and have nice things, people are going to hone in on that right away. You seem to be attracted to- uh- not the right sort of person either. I know you're tired of the endless phone calls from people who said they wanted one-night stands. I know that you're sick of being hosed for money and taken advantage of, but you bring it on yourself. You attract that by not going for the right type of person. Women who look like the ones you usually date- they generally just want one thing. To be taken care of. Even if they're nice, you wonder why even after you break up with them, you still get calls for six months about money. That would be why."

"I was just trying to help…"

"And I'm just saying. You're too nice. People sense that. They take advantage of it. You have to stop meeting people in clubs and online. That is never going to work out."

"Where else do you meet anyone?"

"I don't honestly know." Jason was avowedly single. He stayed away from drama. Even if they went to the same places, he never had the luck that Matt did.

"I'm just exhausted. I'm tired of thinking I found someone who actually wants to be with me because they want to share their life with someone, or whatever that even means, and I just get- people who steal credit cards. Girls who ask me for things constantly and if I say no, they leave. People who call and call and call with all those sob stories and when I help out, I find out it's all lies."

"Like I said. It's your own fault. You attract the wrong kind of person. You go for the same kind of girl every single time."

"It doesn't help that my mom keeps asking me when I'm going to finally settle down and give her grandkids."

Jason rolled his eyes. "Ignore it. Moms always say things like that."

"I'm serious. She's been at it for a few years and I can tell she means it. My dad too. When I go over there, I get the same questions every single time. I would ignore it, but it makes me feel like there really is something wrong with me. I used to like just going out and have fun. If that's all they wanted, I was in. I never used to even think about getting serious. That was like the plague. And then when I actually want it-"

"It's nothing but a clusterfuck."

"Right." Matt finally took a sip of his beer. It wasn't warm, even though it was overly warm in the house. It was damn well bordering on tropical how high Jason had it in there. Compliments of November in Denver.

"Maybe you're trying too hard. Just stop."

"That's what I came here to say I was doing. I'm done. I don't care if I spend the rest of my life alone. Seriously, it would be better than how I've been doing so far."

"I agree."

"That's because you always wanted to be a bachelor." Matt drained the rest of his beer. He plopped the empty bottle down on the small amount of bare counter space he could find. "Can I have another?"

Jason nodded towards the fridge. "Help yourself."

Matt did. He let his friend pass him a bottle opener and he cracked the top on a fresh beer. Normally they'd be watching some game by now or playing pool in the basement or working on Jason's house, which was a never-ending money pit, but Jason sensed right away that the conversation was going to be serious as soon a Matt walked through the door. He wasted no time in offering beers and his sage advice.

"I might have- wanted to avoid all the shit that everyone else wades through, but- hey... that's what I've always wanted and it's not going to change given that I'm older or how much my parents bemoan the fact I'm never going to give them a grandkid. They think there is something morally flawed with me. If there is, I blame them. They raised me after all."

"I'm sure your mom appreciated you telling her that."

Jason grinned. "I'm not that dumb. I would never say that to her. I was kidding. They raised me fine. I just see all the shit everyone else goes through- I've seen what you've been through, and I just don't want any part of that."

"It can't all be bad, can it?"

"I think it can. For you, at any rate. I've been lucky enough to find people that just want to keep things casual and they respect the boundaries. I think I find the good ones because they realize I have no extra money to give them. I'm not a nice person either. I don't do anything to help, so they don't expect it in the future."

"That's a lie. You'd give your left nut for me."

Jason raised a brow. "Would I? You seem pretty confident about that. I think I'd like to keep my nuts, thank you very much."

"Yeah, well- anyway. I'm done. I'm taking a break. No more anything for a while."

"Your life sounds like it's going to be really damn boring from here on out."

"It might be, but it can't be worse than what it's been."

"Wholly agreed on that front."

"I can count on you to keep me entertained, can't I? You always seem to have a limitless amount of things to do that don't involve going out."

"No. I just prefer to skip out on the things I don't like to do. Plays and ballets and shopping and musicals and whatever else. Nope. Hell no. I never signed on for that. I'm not about faking it until I make it. I don't want to make whatever it is that is at the end of that shit road. You're better off getting rid of that nice house of yours and buying a fixer-upper. Believe me, they take all your time one way or another. Between fixing them up and working to pay to fix them up, it eats up all your spare minutes."

"I might just have to do that."

"Or get a dog. Or both." Jason shook his head. "I'm sorry, I just can't imagine you not going out anymore. Not doing all that shit that I hate so much."

"It wasn't that bad-"

"No? It sure sounds like it was a blast according to what you're telling me right now. I warned you about that. I told you never to get involved with online shit. I told you to just stop with the dating and the looking and the drama and trying to please people you'll never be able to please because they only want one thing and it isn't what you want to give."

"Yeah, yeah, so you were right. I'm off of it now. I just- I don't know... maybe you're right. I need a project. Or two."

"Hobbies, my man. They're called hobbies." Jason clapped him on the shoulder. "Now grab another beer and we can start laying that floor in the basement. You can tell me all about how you're going to pass your time now that you're a bachelor too."

"I didn't say that exactly."

Jason rolled his eyes. "I know. But I'm going to help you stick to your guns here. Maybe when you learn how to be by yourself, you can attract the right kind of person. Put something good out, get something good, hmm? Makes sense?"

Matt wanted to tell his best friend where to put it, but the hard thing was, he couldn't really argue with the guy's logic. He hadn't been putting out the right energy or even the right intention. It wasn't a wonder that he felt played, cheated, and used. He tried to treat people fairly and thought it wasn't right when his life ended up turning out like a shit pile, but maybe the guy was right. Jason was definitely right about the kind of people Matt dated. He could see that now. He really did attract the same kind of woman every single time. He couldn't be surprised when the results were always the same. There was the whole common denominator as well. *Himself.* He knew already he needed to work on that before Matt so blatantly pointed it out. Which was why he was done. As in zero.

He just had to get the office Christmas party out of the way, but that didn't truly count. It was shaping up to be as boring as all the other years had been. Definitely not nightlife, that was for sure. As soon as that was out of the way and the busy season at work was over and he could actually relax, he'd find some hobbies.

It was just unfortunate that he had no idea where to start.

3

CALLIE

$\mathcal{T}$he hotel where the Christmas party was being hosted was of course, huge. It was one of those fancy hotels, the kind that has never-ending banquet rooms, real marble floors, and huge chandeliers. The lobby had a damn fountain in it.

"Ugh, I told you we shouldn't have come," Callie whispered under her breath just as the speeches were getting underway. She could smell the food that was being set out in the back by the catering staff and her stomach literally groaned. She glanced around, hoping like hell no one heard the noise.

Chantara leaned closer. She did her best to cover a smile as she whispered under her breath. "Okay, sorry, I never said it wasn't going to be boring. I said that you should come and save me from having to endure it alone."

"How am I supposed to save you?" Callie hissed. "I can't believe we spent the entire day getting ready for this."

"Well, you look good." Chantara smiled maddeningly. "The speeches will be done in a few minutes. Just wait."

Nearly an hour later, Callie was still waiting. She was

still waiting, and she was still starving. "It's never-ending," she whined in Chantara's ear.

Her best friend nodded silently. "I know," she whispered back. "It's bad this year. Last year wasn't nearly this long."

"I can smell the food. God, I think I'm going to pass out from it. I should have packed a damn snack in this stupid little clutch."

"The only thing you could pack in that tiny thing is like-astronaut food. Freeze-dried turkey or something."

"Ewww!" Callie wrinkled her nose.

"Oh look! Matt Hilbert just won an award. Too bad you just started working as his PA. If it had been longer, he might have mentioned you in his speech." Chantara grinned devilishly.

Callie took a covert peek at the other six people seated around their table to see if anyone had heard or noticed that they weren't really even paying attention to the program. Everyone else seemed lost in their own world or completely absorbed in what was happening at the front.

"Don't," Callie warned under her breath. "Don't talk about Matt Hilbert."

"Why not? You think he's hot, don't you? He looks nice in that suit. All black. Black shirt and black jacket. Black tie. Good choice. I'm not a fan of white. It looks like people are going to a wedding when they're dressed like that."

"I don't think he's hot," Callie hissed. "Seriously. I don't. I think he's the kind of guy who thinks he's hot."

"Not even a little? Come on. Let's sit here and judge him while he does his speech. There isn't much else to do."

"Judge him?" Callie barely suppressed a giggle.

"Yup. Judge him." Chantara bent her head in so far that some of the pins from her updo nearly stabbed Callie in the side of the face.

"Like, how? He won an award. I don't think there's much to judge. He's dressed nice. He has the body of a god. He's tall with those crazy broad shoulders and he looks like he works out every day all day and drinks protein shakes for every single meal. He has what people would call *chiseled* features. He has a strong jawline, a face that is both way too pretty and far too masculine at the same time. And he's blonde. What the heck could we possibly judge?"

Chantara blinked hard and Callie realized way too late that she'd just given herself away. Big time. "Right... and you don't find all that perfection and chiseledness attractive?"

Callie fought to regain her equilibrium. Another quick glance told her everyone at the table was still oblivious to the fact that they were sitting there not paying attention to the program at all. *Maybe they can't concentrate on anything because they are slowly dying of hunger. Maybe they're being eaten away from the inside out just like I am.* The painful fist in her stomach kept on getting tighter and tighter with every passing moment.

"I don't," she finally whispered back. "Because we work together so first of all, that is completely out of line and off-limits. Secondly, I told you, he's not my type."

"Matt Hilbert is *everyone's* type. Not mine either though. Like I said, I like them way- uh- rougher around the edges."

"Yeah. I know that. And I'm serious about what I said. I'm not interested in Matt Hilbert. Even if he is attractive, that means nothing. Sometimes people's personalities come through and make them unattractive because seriously, deep down, under those fine, flawless layers, they are."

"Yeah, yeah, the whole inner beauty or inner ugliness thing. I get it." Chantara indicated the front eagerly. "Listen, it's over! Jack Bron is coming up to announce dinner! He always comes up every single year to give the instructions. Hallefuckinglujah."

Callie couldn't agree more. Their table had to wait another twenty minutes while the instructions were given, and other tables were allowed to go before them. By the time they got to line up, she was just about at the point where she could have eaten the dinner plate and probably the knife and fork too, maybe the napkins as well.

Chantara stood in line right behind Callie. She decided to be a good bestie and passed over an extra plate and napkin. She turned to hand them over and as she did, she must have blinked funny, because her contact popped right out.

"Oh my god!" Callie nearly wailed. "Chantara! I just lost my contact!"

"What? Which one?"

"Does that matter at the moment? We're not going to find it and even if we do, I wouldn't stick it back in my eyes. We're just about to eat and now I'm not even going to be able to see what we're eating."

"Oh my god. Okay. Stay calm." Chantara's hand closed around Callie's elbow. "We'll just go back to the table and get your glasses. Take the other contact out and you're good, right?"

"No! I completely forgot to bring them."

"What?"

"I only brought that stupid little clutch and it just has my money and phone and ID card."

"Okay, okay." Chantara's hand tightened. "Don't worry." She stepped in front of Callie and pulled her behind her.

"I can't keep just one in. I'm going to get sick to my stomach. I feel completely dizzy already just looking around like this. One eye, I can see nothing out of but blur and blobs and the other is completely in focus."

"You could just walk around with your bad eye closed all night. Or we could try and find the contact and you could wash it in the bathroom sink."

Callie sighed. She felt close to crying. Probably because she was so damn hungry. "There's no chance of that happening now. It's probably been stepped all over and ruined. They're just disposables so it wouldn't have mattered if it wasn't for the fact that I can't freaking see."

"It's okay," Chantara soothed. "I'll just guide you along the buffet. Just keep your bad eye closed and fill up your plate. When we get back to the table, you can take the other one out."

"I won't be able to see what's going on all night."

"You probably won't want to. They are opening up the bar right away. People are just going to get drunk and swap shitty work stories. Because, you know, no one actually has a life outside this place."

"Because corporate meetings and paperwork and business lunches are so exciting."

"I know. It's bad."

"Remind me again why you made me come to this? I didn't want to go, and you forced me. You said you needed a wingman. We could just leave after dinner."

"And miss the one-dollar drinks? Not a chance. This is the one night a year selling insurance actually pays off."

Callie shut her bad eye and helped herself to a scoop of the sweet mashed potatoes. The orange blobs looked delicious at the moment and she didn't even like sweet potatoes. Or yams. Whatever.

"I'm sure it pays off for other people as well. Like the ones who use it."

"You know what I mean. As administrative assistants, we put up with a lot of shit. We do everything around the place and never get any credit. You make it so Matt Hilbert can function on a day to day basis and he gets the award. Never thanked anyone once."

"How do you know? I thought you were as tuned out as I was during his speech."

"Unlike you, I wasn't so busy eyeing up his assets that I couldn't hear what he was saying."

Callie felt her entire body go out. Okay, so Matt Hilbert was freaking gorgeous, but what could she do about it? Nothing. She wouldn't have done anything if she wanted to. It was just strange, realizing that she was actually attracted to another person, even on a base level. She'd been pretty damn done with that kind of thing for the past eighteen months. Ever since her fiancé walked out on her the night before their wedding. It hurt. Obviously. It still did, even if she pretended that it didn't.

"Stop. Show me where the turkey is and the peas and put some salad on my plate and let's get out of here. Is there a dessert table? Tell me there is. We should stop there before we go back to the table to make sure that people don't take all the good stuff before it's gone."

"I don't think anyone's taken anything from there yet."

"Perfect. Let's be rebels. No one will notice us anyway. You said so yourself. Let's go take a damn cheesecake or something. There *had better* be cheesecake."

"Alright, alright," Chantara laughed.

She filled up Callie's plate and Callie followed close at her heels. She let Chantara point out which white lump was actually cheesecake and followed her back to the table. She set her plate down and sick of being completely dizzy, slid her other contact out. She wasn't sure what to do with it after, so she hid it in a fold of her napkin.

"It figures," she complained between a mouthful of sweet potatoes, which were actually amazing.

"What does?" Chantara asked, mouth also full of food.

"That I would lose my stupid contact at the worst moment. I've never lost one before. I honestly didn't even think of bringing my glasses or a second pair."

"Sounds about right. Oh well, don't worry. I'll be your seeing eye dog. We'll have a couple of drinks, complain some more, listen to some bad music, watch some bad dancing, which I will, of course, describe to you in full hilarious detail and then we can leave. Deal?"

Callie started laughing. It was one of those silent, uncontrolled laughs that didn't even allow for breath. She had to brush away a stray tear forming at the corner of her eye after. When she could actually breathe again, she put a hand to her aching stomach.

"Oh god. Alright. It's a deal. Even though I'm starved, and the night has been completely boring so far, you're right. It would have been way worse alone. And the food is good."

"That's just because they made us wait so long for it. An old boot would have been delicious at this point. There are the drinks though. I'm in for that. I haven't had a good gin and tonic in a long time."

"Oh no. Not that. I thought you were talking about a beer here or there."

"No way. I don't drink that swill."

"Okay, coolers then."

"Heck no."

"Punch?"

"Nope."

Callie sighed. "Just make sure they put more tonic than they do gin and we should be fine."

"I'm done with that. There is going to be no more dancing on car roofs. I promise." Chantara put a hand over her heart.

"Serious? I need you now. I can't even see. I'm so damn blind that I am relying on you to navigate the rest of the evening for us. So please, please, please, manage to stay upright."

"Got it." Chantara flashed what Callie thought was a huge grin. Maybe even a thumbs up. She saw a flash of hands and a blur of teeth.

Callie finished up her meal, way too fast, and started in on the cheesecake. Everything was absolutely amazing. It had definitely been worth the wait. Although, maybe Chantara was right. It was the wait that made everything taste that good.

Now that the food was done, she really was looking forward to leaving. She didn't mind having a few drinks, but she was definitely not up for dancing and all that corny Christmas office party spirit that people either faked or produced by some miracle, as genuine. She wasn't into it. It was the whole holiday overall. Ever since she was a teenager, she found Christmas really, really hard.

Don't think about it. Don't go there. She promised herself she was going to have a fun evening with Chantara. Her best friend had been there for her through thick or thin and it could be one of their increasingly rare girl's nights out kind of a deal. Except she really hoped Chantara meant what she said. If her friend chose to get up and dance on cars or into the street, Callie wouldn't see it coming.

She heaved a sigh, actually hoping that Chantara would go get them a drink sooner rather than later. Her thoughts were beginning to churn back to things she'd rather not think about. She could use a good stiff gin to chase them back to oblivion. *Just for one night. Just one night. I wanted this to be fun. Just one night without thoughts of Ben or my family or… or anything else.*

If only she hadn't lost her contacts. She could have distracted herself by studying, discreetly, of course, the fine features, even finer form, and sea blue eyes that belonged to Matt Hilbert. No matter what she said or thought, it would have been a good distraction.

4

MATT

*J*ust as he thought, the Christmas party was as bone dry boring as it had been all the previous years. He wasn't sure why he thought this one was going to be any different. It turned out that people who were boring during the day at work were just as boring at night. Unless they got a few too many drinks. Then sometimes, it was entertaining.

As it was, it was nearly eleven and no one that he noticed was making a drunken spectacle of themselves. He was almost disappointed. *It's probably far too early.*

But it just made the evening dry. Real dry. Desert level dry. At least the food was good. That was a bonus. The party the year before was held at a different hotel and the food had been absolutely terrible.

The DJ was just starting up the tunes when Matt stood up. He decided that enough was enough. He'd had enough pleasant chit chat to last him the night. Of course, there had also been the occasional conversation about work snuck in there. He hated that. He would like, for once, to just have a fucking night off and not talk about insurance.

He left his award on the table. God, it could stay there for all he cared. He didn't mind his job. He didn't even mind the company. He just hated being singled out. He didn't even know he'd done so well with his sales. Well, really, his department had. He just managed the whole thing. He must have done something right. There was a good chance that Richard, his boss, probably had informed him of the fact at some time or other but he'd probably just tuned right out. He tended to do that most days.

A drink. I need a drink. As in, like, a triple. Or maybe just straight up whiskey. Would they serve that to me here? Probably not.

It would look bad to be seen pounding back drink after drink or carrying too many to the table at once, so maybe he could convince the bartender to give him two doubles. He'd nurse those for all of ten minutes and get two more. That would help him endure another hour before he could feel like he hadn't left too early. Midnight seemed appropriate. And he'd take the damn award with him. Maybe he'd get lucky and forget it in the cab on the way home.

Fortunately for him, the evening went uphill from there. Thanks to the bartender's free pouring, the one-dollar drinks and the DJ who shit the bed and forgot some piece of equipment to actually make everything work together, people were getting inventive. The drunk kind of inventive.

Cayden Wall from their marketing department charged to the table where Matt was currently nursing his sixth double. Or was it eight? He wasn't even sure. The edge he'd felt at the beginning of the evening was long gone. He was actually beginning to forget the string of disastrous dates and all of his recent relationships that hadn't worked out. He was in a nice numb state when Cayden's curly haired head swam into view.

"You have to come see this, man."

Matt blinked. He actually looked behind him just to double check that Cayden really was talking to him. The guy probably hadn't said more than two words to Matt the entire four years the guy was with the company. They'd started around the same time. Matt remembered when Cayden was hired. Judging from the way Cayden's shirt had come untucked and his tie was hanging askew, he'd had a few doubles himself. Or way more singles. Either way, the guy had that bleary-eyed look of someone who had imbibed a little too much. A lot of the people still remaining in the room were getting that look.

"What's that?" Matt finally asked. His own voice was still surprisingly even.

"They're hanging mistletoe out in the hall. People are grabbing each other left and right and puckering up."

"Are you serious?" Matt sat up a little straighter.

"Yeah. Dead serious." Cayden grinned like they were old friends. "You should come see. It's pretty hilarious. Mrs. Dews just kissed Ron from sales. I think she's going to be seventy-something next week."

"Ron? Isn't the guy barely past twenty?"

"Yeah. The one and the same."

Matt slammed back the rest of his drink and stood. Someone should put an end to whatever drunken foolery was going on in the hall before someone started recording. It made Matt feel like he was a hundred fucking years old.

By the time he made it through the room, dodged a few well-meaning stragglers wanting a few minutes of conversation about this and that, someone who offered him another drink ticket, like he needed it, the frazzled DJ running around with a cell trying to figure out if someone could get to his place and pick up some cord or other, a group of women in their fifties and sixties trying to dance- music or no music, servers actually putting out midnight lunch and those trying to get plates, there were only a few people remaining in the hall. In short, the whole thing had pretty much turned into a giant shit show.

The folks that were there were already shrugging into their jackets and staggering down to rooms booked or cabs waiting. At least he fucking hoped it was cabs that they were heading to. Matt glanced behind him. Somewhere along the way, he'd lost Cayden. Go figure.

Sure enough, there was an errant spring of plastic mistletoe dangling from the top of the hall's doorframe. He reached up to pull it down and right as his fingers closed in above his head, someone slammed into him hard from behind.

Matt struggled to stay upright. He flew forward a few steps and managed to catch himself before he fell flat on his face. He whirled, ready to lay a strip into someone, a nice strip since it was a corporate thing and all. His eyes widened when he saw his secretary, Callie, of all people, fumbling around. She was drunk. Real drunk. As in, couldn't stay upright drunk.

She had her hands out in front of her like she was feeling for something, probably the air. No, more likely the wall, so she could brace herself. She caught the toe of her shoe in the carpet and nearly fell flat on her face.

Matt couldn't take it. He rushed forward and put out one arm, which she grasped with the death grip of someone who was drowning.

"Oh... I'm so sorry," she stammered. She didn't sound drunk, but those eyes of hers were so unfocused, she definitely looked it.

"I..."

Matt didn't know what to say. He didn't know what to do about the whole situation. Find a cab and put Callie in it? Would she be sober enough to tell the driver where she lived? Find her friend, one of the other girls who did admin, the one he saw at Callie's desk throughout the day? Did she have a room booked at the hotel?

Just as he was trying to make up his mind, he breathed in and got a heady noseful of floral-scented perfume. It wasn't the horribly gross kind and she hadn't bathed in it. It was subtle, which probably meant it was expensive. The office was a scent free environment and he'd never smelled anything on her before.

He took a brief second to glance down into her upturned face. She was shorter than him by half a foot, but then again, so was the rest of the world. She had sandy blonde hair which was curled into ringlets that were starting to go straight and limp with the passing of the night. She didn't normally wear makeup at work, at least not anything overly noticeable, but she looked... she looked beautiful at the moment. Red lipstick set off a pair of seductive lips. A hint of blush defined high set cheekbones. Her cornflower-blue eyes looked bluer due to dark eye makeup and her lashes were long and thick and dark with mascara.

At the office, Callie always dressed in work attire. He'd never really even taken a minute to notice her before, really notice her. He noticed her at the moment. In a big way.

She had on a tight black dress. It was possibly a little too tight. It pushed her ample breasts upwards so that just the tops swelled above the square neckline. The dress hugged her curves deliciously, like a second skin. It cut off just below the knee where the world's most perfect set of shapely legs began. She had heels on, which he'd also never known her to wear, and they only outlined the definition in her legs.

"I'm sorry," she apologized again in her light, lyrical voice. "I- I didn't mean to bump into you. I-"

"No harm done," he assured her and quickly released her arm. The burn that started making its way up his hand and arm spread through his chest. He realized he might be a little drunker than he thought he was.

"I was just- looking for someone. My friend. I haven't seen her."

"Can I help you get a cab?"

"I really want to find her first." Callie's eyes widened and her lips parted. Her tongue swept out and danced across the most beautiful mouth he'd seen in a damn long time.

His cock jumped to life, already throbbing. The universe certainly had a wicked sense of humor. He'd just promised himself he was done with women. Done with all of it. Of course, whatever forces were out there saw fit to throw the most inappropriate, beautiful, goddess, siren of an admin assistant his way. Why? *Why didn't I ever notice her before?*

He was about to suggest that he take her downstairs and call her cab, when her friend, the girl whose name he couldn't even remember, staggered out of the ballroom and into the hall.

"Oh my god. There you are. I've been looking for you forever," she slurred. It was obvious that she was far drunker than Callie herself was.

Oh god. It's like the blind leading the blind. I'll find them both a cab home. Together. Maybe one of them can get the other one into recovery position if she passes out...

"Chantara? Where did you go!" Callie whirled on her friend. "You knew you were supposed to help me-"

Her desperate statement was cut off when Chantara glanced upward. She giggled. "There is a mistletoe spring right above your head. You guys are standing right underneath it. Go on! Kiss!"

"That would hardly be-"

"I couldn't-" Callie protested at the same time.

"Do it! It's Christmas after all. It will probably be the highlight of this whole boring thing for both of you!"

Matt froze. Callie hesitated. She stepped forward awkwardly, as though spurred by some inner wildness, but she tripped on those heels she had on and tumbled forward. He caught her since she was only a foot away. She hit his chest hard and then her hands were searching, searing, hot. He reacted instantly like she was a match and he was a jerry can full of gasoline.

Her hands hit his shoulders and her fingers dug in. She was probably just trying to figure out what the hell was going on, but her touch did something to him. His head swam and right before he lowered his face to hers, he realized that he was really damn drunk. It was the only explanation. He'd never felt anything close to the crazy physical reaction that was going on at the moment. He felt wild, edgy in his own skin, frantic, animal. He was hot and achy. A shiver tore up his spine. His stomach tightened and his cock throbbed between them. He had a split second to hope that Callie couldn't feel that part of it, or that she was too drunk to notice before his mouth crushed hers.

People talked about sparks and sensation and all that garbage. He'd once picked up one of his girlfriend's romance novels, the real trashy kind about a rancher and his cook, and read a few pages out loud, just to piss her off. It just happened to be about a kiss and some groping. He'd never forget the way the author described it.

Because it was exactly how he felt.

Her mouth was glorious. Her lips were so incredibly soft. She tasted good, a hint of sugar and the underlying bitterness of gin. His eyes were closed, and lights really did flash behind them. It was a damn firework display in his head. Probably because his brain imploded.

It wasn't just his head or his mouth that felt that kiss. It was everything. His entire body. He was completely winded when she pulled away and untangled herself. The kiss lasted only a few seconds, but god, he gasped like it went on for hours.

She put a hand up to her lips, as though they were tingling, shock in her light blue eyes. Eyes that were so blue they were nearly purple. Or grey. He couldn't decide, but he was damn well going to find out.

Behind Callie, her friend laughed softly. What was her name? Chantara. That was it. She hooked her arm through Callie's and urged her away as if nothing had happened. Callie didn't even turn around and look back.

Matt watched them go. *Her eyes. I need to know what color her eyes truly are.* Did they change with what she wore? The lighting? Her mood? *That's ridiculous and completely inappropriate. She's my damn PA.* He was supposed to be done with all of that. He'd promised himself he was going to take a break and get his head on straight. Maybe do what Jason said and figure out how to put out a better vibe so he got better in return.

Not eye up his damn PA. Right after he kissed her. At the Christmas party thrown by his company.

Wrong. Wrong. Wrong. That is seriously all the wrong fucking things to do. He found himself regretting the drinks he had. And the fact that come Monday, the regret wasn't going to be strong enough to keep him from staring at Callie and figuring out just what shade those irises of hers truly were.

CALLIE

*B*y the time Monday morning rolled around, Callie's Saturday morning hangover was long past. What wasn't gone was the slightly foggy memory of kissing someone. She knew she'd done it. Which had been in part because she'd drank down all the gin and tonics Chantara kept handing her. The other part of her... she wasn't sure what that was. She couldn't say what came over her. Maybe it was the fact that she couldn't actually *see* the guy.

No, wait. That made it worse.

Without her contacts or her glasses, Callie had no idea who she kissed. Her hands stayed on their clothes, which felt very much like a dress shirt only. Which gave her absolutely no clue to who it could have been since everyone was dressed formally. He was tall. Taller than her, but so were several guys. He tasted good. *Like that really helps.* His lips were so firm but so soft. *Still doesn't help.* He kissed like a demon. *Seriously that narrows it down not at all.*

The worst part of it was that she knew it had to be someone from work. Really, the odds were completely against it being someone's guest. No one wanted to go to boring office Christmas parties unless they actually worked there.

The guy was probably thirty to forty, but there were a lot of those too.

Callie arrived at work on Monday morning, hoping like hell no one would confront her about what happened Friday night. Maybe whoever she'd kissed had been drunk too and they couldn't remember. Maybe they were embarrassed about it as well. It had kind of just happened.

There were a lot of things that night that just happened. After the DJ screwed up and there was no other alternate entertainment, people pretty much turned to the bar.

Callie made it through Monday without incident. Matt Hilbert, luckily enough, wasn't in. He was away on business. She knew it because she booked his flight for Sunday. Obviously, he didn't get drunk at the party. He had a five am flight to catch.

Tuesday wasn't as easy for her. She got to work early and found a mysterious coffee cup waiting for her on her desk. She removed the lid and sniffed it. It smelled alright. The odds of someone bringing her coffee that had something in it, like something bad, were slim. She took a sip and winced.

Okay, maybe not slim enough.

It might not be drugs or poison, but whoever got her the coffee put a crapload of cream and sugar in it. As in, like, six sugars and half a container of cream.

She appreciated the thought but escaped to the lunchroom. When she was sure no one was there or watching her from the doorway, she dumped the coffee down the drain, rinsed eight inches of sugar out of the bottom of the paper cup, and filled it with the subpar work java. She added a splash of cream and put the lid back on.

There. Whoever brought it will never know I didn't drink it.
She still wasn't sure who could have done it. It really could
have been anyone. There were always things showing up at
work. Doughnuts, fruit, gift baskets. She'd never actually got
something before, but she had only been there for a month.

She'd just sat down at her desk when Matt Hilbert
walked into the office. He was wearing his usual immaculate
black suit and tie combo. He strolled up to her desk and
stopped putting his briefcase down by her desk. She halted,
coffee cup still in hand. She frowned. *Why is he looking at me
like that?* He definitely was- staring at her. There really
wasn't another word for it.

He'd never done that before. Callie cleared her throat.
"Uh... I have your emails sorted out, Mr. Hilbert. All your
urgent messages are on your desk. I ordered them from
most urgent to least, not by date. Uh- I guess- I guess that's it
for now."

He kept staring at her, his face so close that she could
smell his aftershave. Or deodorant. Or shampoo. Hair gel?
She could smell something, and she was ashamed to say,
she liked it.

*What the hell? First, I kiss someone, a guy I couldn't even
freaking see and now I actually like the scent of Matt Hilbert?*

She wasn't about guys. She wasn't about much of
anything since her whole life came to a standstill a year and
a half ago. She was lucky enough Chantara let her move in
to lick her wounds. A year and a half later, she was still
there, still licking away. They might not have been so fresh
or so deep, but those wounds were still there. Common
sense told her that people were untrustworthy. Ben had
taught her not to let anyone in. It hurt a lot less being by
herself, even if it was lonely.

Matt Hilbert cleared his throat and finally must have

realized he was staring. He was probably just jetlagged. "How's the coffee?"

"What?"

"The coffee." He indicated the cup in her hand.

"Oh. Right. It's- uh- it's good now. Or- just good. It's good." Matt blinked. *No, he is not Matt. Don't think of him as Matt. He is Mr. Hilbert or Matt Hilbert or Matthew. Not Matt.*

"Good." He picked up his case, which he had set down on the floor by her desk and walked off into his office.

Callie stayed frozen at her desk for a minute. She didn't know if it was her, or if her boss had definitely just acted really damn weird.

A sudden, horrible thought filled her gut with dread. What if Matt Hilbert had seen her kiss someone? What if he knew how out of line she'd been? Or worse, he could have seen how drunk Chantara was. She could barely stay upright. Thank god there had been no cars for her to dance on. They'd taken a cab home right after her embarrassing kiss and that was that. Of course, just her luck, Chantara didn't remember a thing past eleven the next morning. She was shocked when Callie asked her about the mistletoe incident. Callie hadn't elaborated after Chantara said she didn't remember a thing. Her best friend had been way too hungover to press her for details.

Callie's stomach dropped out completely when she thought about what could happen if Matt did see her kiss someone. Would she get written up? Her job prospects weren't great. She had an English degree, which didn't leave room for a lot of jobs. Ones that paid beyond minimum wage, that was. If it wasn't for Chantara, she wouldn't even really have this job.

Despite the fact that the whole kiss thing was completely out of line, she'd actually enjoyed it. That was the kicker, the icing on the cake, whatever dumb cliché she could think of. She'd spent the entire weekend thinking about that kiss. How she'd felt it in every single limb, right down to her toes and the tips of her fingers. And pretty much everywhere else. She was hot and cold at the same time when she thought about his lips on hers, how his tongue had darted into her mouth just for a second. God, he'd lit a fire in her she didn't realize was even still possible.

And she didn't even know who he was.

If only I hadn't lost my damn contacts.

Callie spent the rest of the week in uncertainty. She felt that around every single corner was a danger waiting in the form of her being fired for what she'd done. Wednesday and Thursday were nearly unbearable. She could hardly concentrate on her work. She was sure her boss was giving her funny looks. She caught him a couple of times, staring at her through the glass of his office. Her desk was right in front of the large glassed-in room.

She tried to pass it off as her imagination. She was being paranoid. That was it. She was seeing things and thinking things that weren't even there. Period. Nothing else was going on.

By Friday, her paranoia got the best of her. She managed to corner Chantara in the hallway when no one was around so that they could talk.

"Hey, what's up?" Chantara's forehead crinkled in concern.

"I... sorry. I just- do you have a minute?"

"Yeah, of course." Chantara shifted the files she was holding under her arm. "I always have a minute for you."

"Thanks." Callie laughed nervously. "So... about that night. The Christmas party- when I asked you if you could remember anything about the mistletoe, there was actually a reason."

"What?"

"Yeah- okay, here it goes." Callie exhaled sharply. "I might have kissed someone. And I have no idea who it is."

Chantara stared blankly at her for a second before she broke into a huge smile. "What?" she gasped. She remembered to keep her voice low, even if it was filled with shock and amazement.

"It was- well- I was a little bit drunk and you were right behind me telling me to do it and before I could say that I couldn't even see anything and that I didn't know who it was, he just kissed me. I was drunk enough that I really don't even remember any details. Like his voice. It's just all kind of foggy."

"Except for the kiss, I'll bet."

Callie knew she was blushing. It was one of the total downfalls of having a pale complexion. "Well, whatever. It wasn't right. It had to have been someone from here."

"Of course it was, who else would it have been?"

'Well, I know people bring friends and stuff, but I doubt that was it. It was getting late. A lot of people already left. We kept drinking after the DJ wasn't playing and I lost you somewhere in the place and I was looking all over, mostly blind because I lost my contacts and you were supposed to stick with me. I ended up in the hall, I think, and I bumped into someone, I think. It's kind of hazy. And then suddenly you were there and saying something about mistletoe and then we kissed, and we left. I think. I don't really know if those are all the details or if they're even right."

"And you were hoping I could help you fill something in?"

"I guess so."

Chantara shook her head. "I honestly don't remember. I don't even know how or why I had so many drinks. I don't remember that either. I guess we started, and they were cheap and they tasted good and it just got out of control from there."

"I think the bartender was free pouring. I seem to remember my first couple of drinks being really strong and then they kind of just went down easier after I got a little buzzed."

"Hmm. Could be. At any rate, that guy and the DJ caused a fair bit of trouble. At least for us."

"What am I going to do? I'm so afraid that whoever it is might write me up. And I'm afraid that someone might have seen it."

Chantara shrugged. "Don't be. Don't be so worried. First of all, I'm sure whoever kissed you had a little something to do with it. You're a pretty girl, Callie. Anyone in their right mind would definitely want to make out with you. If they wrote you up, they'd have to write themselves up too."

"It was one kiss," Callie hissed. "Not a make-out session."

"In your case, I wish it was a full-on make out. You could use a little bit of spice in your life."

"Chantara," Callie said in warning.

"Seriously. I know all about you and what happened with Ben, but it's been so long! You need to get on with your life! You aren't dead, Callie. There are good things waiting for you down the line. You just have to take a chance and put yourself out there again."

"I am definitely not interested in doing that."

"I know. I wish you were though. Then I wouldn't have to worry about you."

"What do you mean worry about me? You don't have to

worry about me." Callie softened her tone. "You're my best friend. I'll be fine. I'm just not interested in doing any of that right now. There are other things in life."

"Like what? Books? You read way too much."

"There isn't anything wrong with books."

"You need more hobbies! You need to get out more. Maybe you'd meet someone then and you'd realize that all guys aren't bad."

"I don't think all guys are bad. I'm just really not interested." Callie wished she could have said that Chantara sounded like a nagging parent or sister or something, but she couldn't. Her family didn't nag her. They didn't know the first thing about her life, because they hadn't been involved in it since her breakup with Ben and barely before that.

"So really, you're just here for confirmation that you're not going to get fired. You don't want me to help you figure out who it is. Because I could ask around-"

"No!" Callie gripped Chantara's arm frantically. The files nearly fell to the floor. Chantara shifted them and grinned.

"Relax. I'm not going to do that. I was just kidding. Don't worry about your job. No one saw. And everyone was doing some really dumb shit that night, I bet. I think that we weren't the only ones who got a little drunk. I've heard a few whispered conversations going around the office. Yours isn't the first mistletoe story that I've heard."

"Oh god. I'm afraid to ask."

"It's probably better if you don't. I think that bartender was to blame for all of it. Let's just go with that. His drinks were waaaay too strong."

"Oh geez. Okay, next year, I definitely am not going to the Christmas party."

"What?" Chantara giggled. "And miss out on all the

excitement! At least you got a kiss. I went home and all I got out of the night was a killer hangover the next day. You at least enjoyed yourself."

"I didn't enjoy myself," Callie protested, face hot again.

"Right." Chantara rolled her eyes. "I'm glad you did. It makes me think there is some hope for the future." She shifted the folders and walked off down the hallway, laughing softly to herself.

Callie gave herself a full minute to try and regulate her heartbeat, return her breathing to a normal pace and try and get her face under control before she went back to her desk. She sat down heavily and brushed her hands nervously over her loose hair. It was a habit and she knew it. She carefully tucked the long strands behind her ears and found something else to occupy her hands.

When she glanced behind her at Matt's office, she swore she saw him look away quickly, back down to whatever he was working on, but she couldn't be sure.

She couldn't be sure at all. Not about the kiss. It drove her nuts. She was going to have to find out who it was, or she was going to drive herself insane.

6

MATT

*H*e wasn't creepy. Normally.

The things he'd been doing for the past week, okay, that was a little weird. Maybe even a little stalker like. No, not that far. He wasn't a stalker.

Matt just wanted to know why his personal assistant, proper secretary by day, wild and sexy seductress by night, was ignoring him after that blazing kiss.

After a quick business trip to San Diego, he wasn't sure what he'd come back to at the office. As it turned out, a whole lot of nothing. Callie ignored him like nothing happened. Maybe for her, it wasn't that good. Maybe that kiss was just a stupid under the mistletoe kiss and that was that. For him though- he'd spent his entire weekend and the rest of the week thinking about it.

He'd never experienced a reaction like that before, physical or otherwise. He tried to summon back the feeling, the exact way his body reacted in the moment, but he couldn't. Of course, he couldn't. That feeling was reserved for kisses like that. Stolen. Illicit. Apparently, ones Callie would rather forget about and pretend didn't happen.

He couldn't pretend. And he sure as hell couldn't forget.

Matt slipped into the office on Friday morning, half an hour before eight. He knew that Callie was always there at quarter to. He placed a cup of coffee on her desk like he had for the past three days. His brain was still buzzing with the information he'd overhead the day before. He hadn't meant to follow Callie. He'd seen her walking to the kitchen and then she changed directions. He was going for a coffee refill and just happened to be on the other side of the hall when she started talking to Chantara.

The whole reason she was ignoring him was because she had no idea it was him at all.

He was stunned when he overheard the conversation. She had no idea it was him she kissed. She hadn't given much away, but from what he could gather, she enjoyed it. She was worried about losing her job. He'd be worried too if he had no idea who had produced a reaction like that inside of him. It was like his entire insides imploded when he kissed her. He wasn't a big believer in romance, especially after his experiences. He'd never liked the whole drama-tized thing about first kisses and sparks and feeling drunk on it.

But that was him in a nutshell. Acting like a fifteen year old boy with his first crush, first kiss, first taste of a woman.

Matt slipped into his office. He set his bag down and waited. He'd been stealing glances at Callie all week, trying to figure out what was going on in her pretty little head. A few times, she caught him studying her.

She's going to find out this morning.

He couldn't let her go on not knowing who it was. That wasn't fair. He'd own up to it and they would have a laugh about it and move on. Plain and simple. It was the only outcome, given that she was his damn admin assistant. He might want a repeat of that kiss. He might want a hell of a lot more, but it wasn't happening anytime soon. As in, never. It wasn't ever going to happen because there are lines and boundaries.

Callie walked in, right on time, at fifteen minutes to eight. She sat down at her desk and eyed the coffee, as she'd done for the past three mornings. She often waited until just after eight before she picked up the cup, went somewhere, and returned with it. She'd sit and drink it after that. It was a strange routine, but then again, nothing about Callie was normal. *Correction. Nothing about that kiss was normal.*

Matt waited. When Callie got up, taking the cup with her, he followed. She went into the break room, went straight to the sink, and dumped the coffee down the drain.

"So that's where all my five-dollar coffees are going."

She whirled when she heard his voice. Twin spots of red appeared on her cheekbones and she stared at him with guilt in her eyes. *Those eyes. Those unbelievable eyes that I was too dense to notice before.* He noticed them now. Big time.

"I..." she turned the cup around. **IT WAS ME** was written in the name spot in black letters. All the other mornings, he'd had the barista leave it blank. "You?" She frowned and something changed in her eyes. The irises darkened, changing from a light blue to something that was nearly purple. It could have just been the lighting, but Matt didn't think so.

"Yeah. Me." He stood back as the dregs of the coffee swirled down the drain.

"I- uh- I'm sorry. I wasn't trying to throw it away. I appreciate the gesture. It's very nice of you to get me coffee. It's just that- there might have been a bit too much cream and sugar. I kind of tend to take it nearly black. Just a little bit of cream for color."

Right. Duh. I should have left it black. "I'm not just talking about the coffee." He stood and waited and when she finally realized what he was talking about, her eyes flew back to the cup, back to those black letters in the name part.

"Oh my god." Her whole face turned a bright shade of red. "Oh. Oh no. No." Her eyes flew around the lunchroom. There was no one else there. "Not here. Your office?"

His stomach lurched and the breath rushed out of his lungs. Imagining her in his office, in a confined space, breathing in the same air, did something to him that it shouldn't have. He knew he was reacting like a- a- well, he was definitely *overreacting.*

She didn't give him a chance to get his shit together and respond. She took off and he trailed in her wake. He tried very hard not to watch the sway of her hips or stare at her round ass, but her skirt was tight, not too tight, just- tight enough that he was able to do both. Her legs- god, her legs were incredible too. He tried *very* hard not to imagine those legs wrapped around his waist. Of course, he failed at that too. By the time he made it into his office, he had to dive behind his desk and pull his chair underneath to hide the fact that he had a damn dent in his pants.

Callie sunk down in one of the chairs. She crossed her legs and clutched her hands nervously. Her eyes darted around frantically before she finally decided to make eye contact. He liked that about her. She always looked at him when she spoke to him.

"Okay- that night- was a- I was a little drunk and I didn't have my glasses or my contacts and I couldn't actually see what was going on. I didn't know it was you. I- the drinks- I would never have done that normally. It didn't mean anything. You're my boss and it's not appropriate. I'm sorry. I-"

He stopped the rambling with a soft chuckle. She stared at him, mouth hanging half-open, as though she couldn't believe he'd actually have the nerve to *laugh* about it.

"I could write you up for this." Her face fell and it sucked the breath right out of him. He rushed on, half in disbelief himself when he heard the words pour out. They weren't at all what he'd planned on saying. "But I won't. If you go on a date with me."

"A- a date?" she said breathlessly. "That's- the- it's the worst..." she took a second to compose herself. "It's the worst idea ever," she finally huffed. "If I don't want you to write something about me, then why would I agree to go on a date with you? That doesn't even make sense."

"Why is it the worst idea?"

"Besides what I just said?"

"Yes, besides that." He liked that she was rapidly losing her composure with every second that passed. She looked cute, damn cute when she was flustered. *Stop. This is so damn wrong.* But he couldn't. He couldn't make himself stop.

"I- well, first of all, you're my boss. Secondly, you're-you're rich. I can tell. Which means that we have nothing in common. I can tell we grew up different. We come from different lives. I'm an admin assistant and you're a DM."

"So? What does that have to do with anything? And how can you be sure that I have money and grew up with it?"

She shrugged. "I don't know," she admitted. She was growing more confident by the minute and he liked that too. Everything she did was sexy. How the hell hadn't he ever noticed before? "There's something about you that tells me you did. Your parents were rich, I'll bet. They probably sent you to the best school. And then you graduated, and they paid for your college. You got a degree in business and you got a good position here because you're both smart and capable and you worked your way up from there. Which means that you have more money. How do I know? Your suits. They're expensive. The fact that I've seen your car. It's worth more than a house. You just walk- I don't know. A certain way. Also, the fact that you didn't thank anyone in your speech at the Christmas party when you won that award. That shows me that you're rich."

"I- I didn't thank anyone?"

"Why are you phrasing that like a question?" Callie glared back at him. She'd picked up steam the whole time and now she was back to being fully confident.

"I- I'm sorry. I didn't mean to not thank people. I just wanted to get away from the front of the room. Some people don't like being the center of attention."

"Oh." That seemed to throw her off, as though she never would have considered it. "But you are rich. And I'm not."

"How is that any kind of reason not to take you out?"

"I don't know. But it's not going to happen. Ever. You're my boss and that's completely out of line. It would be totally cliché. A boss. His admin assistant."

"But that kiss-"

"Was ridiculous. It never should have happened. I'm sorry. I really overstepped."

She really didn't remember what happened. He did. He'd taken the lead. Probably because he also had far too many drinks, but also because he realized, at that moment, that he really wanted to kiss her and if he didn't he'd spend a significant amount of time regretting it. *I might as well take advantage of it.*

"You did overstep. So, I'm going to demand you go out on a date with me or I'm going to file a complaint with HR."

"Are you kidding me?"

"Not at all." He barely managed to keep a straight face.

"In that case, I'll file a counter-complaint. For blackmail. For forcing me on a date. I'll say you've been harassing me and that the kiss was you."

"Oh really?" He raised a brow and shot her what he hoped was an intimidating look. She didn't back down, and damn, it was sexy to see her eyes blazing like they were. Her lips were set in a determined line. One he very much wanted to kiss again. They'd soften under his mouth. He knew they would.

"Really."

They remained like that, locked in a silent impasse, for the next few minutes. He knew he'd lost, but he had other tricks up his sleeve.

"Fine," he said casually. He could tell she was surprised at his easy capitulation. "Fine. You win. You called my bluff. I really wasn't going to write you up. But I'll admit that you have my attention now. I'm not going to harass you or act unprofessionally. That's not who I am. I would never bother you if I thought the attention was unwanted. Just tell me to leave you alone and I will. Tell me honestly that you don't want to go on a date with me and I'll leave it at that. The kiss that happened but was never supposed to happen."

Callie stared at him, lips drawn into an even harder line. Her sweet jawline was clenched so hard he saw a muscle jump below, in the delicate column of her neck.

"So that's how this is going to be."

"No. I just want to know. Have you stopped thinking about it? Do you wish it didn't happen? Now that you know it was me…"

"It doesn't matter if it was you or someone else. The result is the same. It was a mistake."

"It might have been but tell me honestly you don't want to go out with me." He could be charming when he wanted to be, and he flashed her a smile. He waited. And waited. And he knew the exact second she was going to give in.

"I don't want to go out with you," she snapped. "You're my boss. It's wrong."

"Why?"

"I've already given you a list of reasons."

"But the company doesn't have a no dating policy. No one would have to know anyway. And as for the reasons about money- those aren't reasons. At least not valid ones, in my books."

"It wouldn't be an equal distribution of power. You're my boss."

"I don't care about that. I'm not your boss outside of work. And I've never once viewed people who work with me as being below me on any kind of level."

It was true. People always said he was a good manager and a good boss because he was fair and treated people with respect. He was charming and had a magnetic quality that got him far in business. Unfortunately, it hadn't got him quite so far in his personal life. Friends and family yes, romance, not so much.

"Still. It's not right."

"Says who?"

"Says me."

He crossed his arms slowly. "So, you've forgotten all about that kiss. It meant nothing."

"It meant-" She was too honest to lie, and he could tell, from the faint blush that crept back into her face, that he'd won.

He shot her a triumphant smile and she scowled back. "So, you did like it."

"I'm- my god, this is so beyond inappropriate right now."

"It might be but let me take you out. Just once."

"Why? What's the point if it's just once. I know it's not going to be just once."

Because I want to kiss you again. I want to see if I feel the same way, if it- whatever it was, happens again. He could hardly say that, so he shrugged. "Alright. I just thought it would make things less awkward."

"That would make everything worse."

He leveled her with a direct look, and he could have sworn she squirmed a little. "What's so wrong with just going out for one night?" He suddenly had the feeling that Callie never went out. Not with him. Not with anyone. He took a chance. "What's wrong with just living a little?"

She stared at him from narrowed eyes. "Everything," she huffed before she stood and stalked out of his office.

7

CALLIE

allie knew she shouldn't tell Chantara what happened since she'll never hear the end of it, but she also couldn't not tell her.

"Oh my god!" Chantara exclaimed. She pulled a half-burnt pizza out of the oven. The thing was ancient and beat up. It cooked like it looked. "So, of all the people you could have kissed, it was Matt. Your boss." She dissolved into a fit of giggles. It was a long time before she recovered.

Callie didn't laugh. "I don't find that funny at all," she hissed. "The guy had the nerve to ask me to go out with him."

"What?" Chantara swiped away a few tears. She grabbed a knife out of the knife block and hacked away at the pizza. It looked half-frozen on one side, burnt on the other.

"We really should get a toaster oven. I think it would cook far better than that piece of shit oven."

"Nope. No way." Her best friend shook her head. "You are not off the hook. You can't just change the subject like that."

"I wasn't," Callie protested. "But we really should get a

toaster oven. Maybe we can find a second hand one." She liked thrift and vintage shopping. Most of her wardrobe was vintage and the rest was certainly unconventional. When she wasn't at work, she was much more colorful than her black skirt, white blouse, black cardigan combo.

"He asked you out?"

"Yeah. Of course, I said no."

"Why?!" Chantara hacked away at the frozen part of the pizza. "You know, I think you're right. This is going to need to go in the microwave and that part isn't even edible. But-but why would you turn Matt down?" She frowned then seemed to reconsider. "Never mind. I know why. It's not even the fact that he's your boss."

"Or that he wears a watch that cost more than my car like a hundred times over. Who even wears watches anymore?"

"It's not about the watch either."

"Okay, Miss Know It All, what's it about then?"

"It's about the fact that since you and Ben broke up, you've been determined to deny yourself any kind of life. You think that you have to punish yourself or live this barren lifestyle or- or be a saint or something. You're afraid of ever being hurt again so you wall yourself up and you won't let anyone in. You're too scared to take a chance, even on just having a good time. No one said if you went out with him that you would have to date him. It was one night. One time."

"You don't know that! I have no idea what he really wanted! I have no idea why he'd even ask me out. Me! I'm his admin assistant. That's just wrong."

"Maybe that's it. Maybe it's a secret fantasy he's always had, to take down his secretary. Maybe he wants to bring you to work after hours when no one else is there and bend you over his desk and-"

"Chantara! Seriously!"

Her best friend giggled. She stuffed the half of the pizza that was still frozen onto a napkin and threw it in the microwave. The thing didn't work much better than the oven, but it still had enough life left in it to zap their dinner. She divided the food up onto two plates and passed one over. Callie set hers down on the table. She picked up a burned piece and nibbled away at the toppings. She was sure the crust wasn't edible.

"Well, really... Matt is hot. Would it be so bad to give him a chance?"

"Yes! Yes, it would be bad. And I haven't locked myself up in some ivory tower. I just..."

"You have. You haven't been out with anyone or even considered it for a year and a half. You can't let Ben win. You can't let him ruin your happiness. That guy was a pig. I'm glad he left before you married him. God, you dodged a real bullet. It's great that he showed his true colors sooner than later. I never thought you should marry him anyway."

"Yes, I know. I remember how often you used to tell me to break up with him."

"That's because I always knew he was a dick. I never thought he treated you well."

"He was nice enough. At first."

"That's the problem. Everyone says Matt is a good guy. He seems nice. He's smart and capable and has money. What could be so wrong with that? And he's also tall, blonde, handsome, and probably has a big dick."

"That is *waayyyyy* too far!"

Chantara shrugged. She bit off a giant piece of burned pizza and chewed as though she didn't mind the taste of char or the fact that it was hard as a steel band. "There are worse things in the world. Just saying."

"Than fucking my boss?"

"Who said anything about fucking?" Chantara blinked innocently.

"Damn it! You did. When you said he had a big dick and you talked about his desk and after hours."

"Well, I was just guessing at that. I didn't say you had to do it. But really, would it be so bad to go out on a date? Let him treat you nice and spoil you a little? Don't you think you deserve that? You've been through the worst of it, Cal. You're my best friend. You're a great person. I think you do deserve someone good in your life. You definitely deserve to have some fun once in a while. You're not dead. You're still under thirty. Please, live your life before you wind up one morning as an eighty year old woman and you have to look back on it and decide you did nothing with the best years of your life."

"I am doing good with them."

"Uh huh. Books and baths are all well and good, but they shouldn't be all you do. Let him take you out, just once. Tell him once and that's it. I bet he'll do something nice, like the opera or symphony or something. Those are nice rich people places."

"Geez. He'll probably take me for fast food and back to the office right to his desk. Just like you said. Guys like that, they want one thing only. He had me screening his calls, remember?"

"That's probably just because he went out with a few psycho chicks. Money attracts all kinds. Maybe it wasn't even his fault."

"He looks like a god. I'm sure it was his fault."

"A god hey?" Chantara's brow arched up. "So, you have been thinking about him?"

"No, I haven't been thinking about him. But just look at him. He is tall and jacked and he..." *he probably does have a big dick.* She cut that off right there. She couldn't even believe she was considering her boss' dick at the moment. Her entire body clenched. Her heart rate kicked up to a painful level, her pulse slammed at the side of her jawline and there was a distinct throbbing in a distinctly wrong spot.

"See? You want to do it! Do it then! Just go out and let yourself have a good time! It's not like you have any other prospects. I know you don't believe in dating online and you'll never go out and find someone. This is the best case scenario. Besides, don't tell me you didn't enjoy that kiss."

"That's what he said," Callie said grumpily. "He kept getting me to try and deny it and I couldn't because- well, I guess I did. But who wouldn't? It's Matt Hilbert! He's the sexiest man in Denver."

"Is he?" Chantara's lips twitched in amusement.

"Don't laugh at me. I swear if you laugh-"

"What? You'll throw pizza at me?" Chantara giggled. "The whole thing is funny. That kiss. Maybe it was meant to be. Just roll with it for once in your damn life. Stop being so uptight. Stop being a huge martyr. You guys are both adults. One date isn't going to kill you. You can end it at that, and he'll probably leave you alone if you want him to. As it is now, you're only going to have him after you harder."

"That sounds disgusting."

"I didn't mean it like that. What I meant is, you told him no when it was pretty clear you didn't honestly mean it. He's going to keep asking you until you say yes. Most guys like a chase."

"I wasn't trying to be a tease."

"I know that, and he probably knows it, but he also probably likes a challenge. Guys like him don't get where they are by giving up early."

"Guys like him have been handed the entire world," Callie huffed. "We aren't on level playing field. He's my boss and he has money. So does his family. Probably. I don't really know, but it makes me feel weird. Like I'm somehow below him."

"Matt would never make you feel like that. Only you are making you feel like that. You're your own worst enemy, Cal. Just go out there and give it a chance. Going out with him once isn't going to bring the world to an end. No one has to know about it at work and I'm sure he will respect you enough to cut it off after if you don't enjoy it. He doesn't seem like the kind of guy that's pushy or rude or who would take advantage of someone."

"Oh really? This from someone who doesn't even know him?"

"I've worked at the same place for two years with Matt. I get the impression he's a nice guy. Really."

"Oh, do you?"

"Yes, I do."

"Funny you say that now. You were perfectly happy to make fun of him before."

"That was before I knew he wanted to take you out. As far as I'm concerned, anyone half normal who wants to take you on a date is in my good books. Please, please, please say yes."

"Let me guess. If I don't, I'm not only not going to hear the end of it from him, I'm also not going to hear the end of it from you."

Chantara grinned. She picked up another piece of burned pizza and ate it like she hadn't eaten in a week.

"Yeah, that's pretty much right," she said around a full mouth.

Callie let out a frustrated sigh and stomped out of the kitchen. She left her pizza sitting on the table. She had no appetite anyway. She only agreed to have some because Chantara said she was starved and couldn't eat the whole thing.

The worst part about it all, she thought as she slammed her bedroom door and locked it behind her, was that she didn't want to curl up in bed with the book on her nightstand. She didn't want to get lost in a world of someone else's romance and happy endings. She didn't want to take a bath or light a damn candle or go shopping or watch a movie. She didn't want to be by herself.

What she wanted was that date with Matt Hilbert.

She just didn't want to let her guard down. She didn't want to let anyone in. She was scared and she wasn't afraid to admit it to herself. It wasn't just Ben who had done a number on her. Her entire life had taught her that it wasn't okay to trust people. Trust was always misplaced, and she only ended up hurt in the end.

One date though... would it really kill her? A year and a half was a very long time. Would it be alright, like Chantara said, for just one night, to have a little bit of fun? Even if it wasn't appropriate, her best friend really was right. She didn't have a lot of other options.

8

MATT

*M*att couldn't have been more shocked if an actual hurricane blew through his office. It was just after eight on Monday morning. Callie opened the door and as casually as if she was telling him the copier was jammed again or that she'd booked him a flight for his upcoming business trip, she stated that she'd go out with him exactly once.

Those were the words she used. Exactly one time.

Matt struggled to get a hold of himself. It wasn't easy to keep his face composed when she'd just dropped a massive bombshell on him.

"Uh- right. Okay. One time. I get it."

She glared at him like the date was something she was being forced on. "Chantara said that because I said no, you'd only pursue me harder."

"That's not exactly true." His insides tightened.

"Well, I think she's right. She said other stuff too, but the thing is, you can take me out once. Just one time."

"I got that."

"It's not a euphemism for more times."

"I understand."

"And no one can know about it."

"Right." His throat was so dry he doubted he could force anything down, but somehow, he choked back a sip of coffee. He nearly choked on the bitter liquid as he swallowed it the wrong way of course.

"And nothing funny goes on."

Matt nearly spat out his attempt to wash down the first swig of coffee. "Uh- yeah. Right. Of course."

"I'll tell you straight up that I don't get out enough. I can't remember the last time I did something truly fun or enjoyable. I'm using that as an excuse to justify this. So, if you could come up with something that will be a good time, I would appreciate it." Callie rolled her eyes and muttered something under her breath. When she saw he didn't catch it, she composed herself and spoke louder. "Although, at this point, just dinner at a one-star restaurant would probably qualify."

"Right." Matt swallowed hard. Certainly, it was the most unconventional yes he'd ever heard. It was grudging, like she thought that by saying yes, she was weakening herself somehow. "Can I pick you up at least?"

"Uh- no. No, I'd prefer not. I'll meet you here. In the parking lot. Friday night at seven. I checked your calendar. I already know it's free."

He nodded slowly. God, could he make a promise that 'nothing funny' as she termed it, would go down? Normally, yes. Normally he'd have no problem controlling himself. But then again, he didn't normally have a memory of a searing kiss. He wasn't normally burning up from the inside out, day after day, sitting at his desk, staring at his damn sexy secretary through a glass office. Well, yes, he normally was, but after that kiss, everything was different. After he *noticed* her, he couldn't *unnoticed* her. There was something about the way she said that she'd checked his calendar already too- god. It was hot. Real hot. As in, he was glad he was behind the desk again because his cock refused to obey commands and not rise to the occasion hot. *What the fuck is wrong with me?*

So much for not doing this anymore. Although, it was one night. A night out for Callie, because she admitted her life was boring. Whatever reason she'd swept in here and said yes, he wasn't giving her a reason to change her mind. He'd behave, but he'd also make sure that she had a great time. If she changed her mind and wanted to go out with him again, that was fine. *It would be more than fine.* If not, he'd man up and live with it. *Hopefully.*

"Yeah- sure." He realized she was waiting for a response and snapped the hell out of his head. "That's fine. I'll come up with something. Something you'll enjoy."

"Alright." Callie nodded curtly and fled out the door. She didn't go to her desk, but continued on past it, down the hall.

Matt leaned back in his chair. He raised his arms above his head and worked the kinks out of his shoulders and spine. He normally hit the gym at lunch and his upcoming session would do more than just loosen up muscles that were sore and knotted from sitting too long. He'd be able to work out the frustration of having to wait until Friday to take out his secretary.

God, it sounded so bad when he put it like that but was it really? There were surely worse things on earth than taking out a smart, attractive, capable woman who worked with him. He didn't see their positions in the company or the fact that he had more money as an obstacle, though he could understand why she would. He would never use it to hurt her or lord it over her and the fact that someone else might nearly choked him with anger.

Something she'll enjoy. He'd set the bar high because he had to. She'd said once, but his aim was to give her a night she wouldn't soon forget, one that she enjoyed so much there was a second and maybe another time after that. He'd said he was done with dating and all of it, but hell... Callie wasn't like other women. He could tell already she wasn't going to use him for his cash or chew him up and spit him out. She wouldn't string him along or stomp all over his heart. *Would she?* He didn't think so, but there were a million ways to play someone. Just because she seemed innocent and straight up, didn't mean she was.

He gave himself a little shake. He wasn't going to hold it against her that other people hadn't treated him fairly. That wasn't right. He'd take her out and they'd see.

He just hoped that in the next four days he didn't combust at his desk and that he could come up with something that topped her rather low expectations of the stated one-star restaurant. Surely, he could do better than that. He had to. She wouldn't give him another chance otherwise.

9

CALLIE

ear warm clothes. Those were the only instructions she had for the date she already regretted agreeing to. She'd pretty much regretted it from the moment she walked out of Matt's office on Monday morning. Surprisingly, it didn't make things awkward between them, but then again, she hardly ever saw Matt. She booked his trips, went through emails and calls and scheduled meetings, but as for direct contact. It was pretty minimal. It still didn't make her feel better about the date.

Standing in the company's parking lot beside her car, just because she felt she couldn't breathe in there, Callie realized that she was only nervous because she actually cared. It was unthinkable, that one kiss should cause so much trouble.

It was before the kiss. She didn't like the overly honest thought, but it was true. She'd noticed Matt was attractive far before she kissed him. Maybe there was something in her subconscious that night that pushed her into it. To find and kiss him... no, that was just silly.

After a few minutes, Callie checked her phone. She was

way too early, as usual. It was still ten to seven and she'd been there forever. She just couldn't sit around the apartment any longer. Chantara was there and she wasn't going to give her a moment of peace. She was way too nervous and instead of pacing a hole in the carpet of her room, Callie decided to get out and just go for a drive. In the car, there was nowhere she could go where she could escape her nerves, so the drive turned into just driving to work and she'd been far too early.

Her insides felt like they were tied in a hundred painful knots. She hadn't eaten anything all day and she was both starving and so anxious she felt like she could actually throw up. Inside her mitts, her palms were soaked with sweat. Her warm clothes were in the backseat of the car. Her snow pants were the ones she'd had since high school. Her jacket wasn't very pretty either, but it was warm and functional. She'd left them off, since she didn't want to overheat, but also because she wasn't sure how warm *warm clothes* were. She currently had on the knee-length jacket she wore to work every day. It was much nicer, red and black plaid and not ugly at all.

A pair of headlights swept down the street and drew closer. She recognized Matt's shiny black sedan from a distance. It was one of those imports and even though it was a four-door, it managed to look sporty. Somehow, it made its way down the snowy, icy streets, which meant it either had good tires, or it was one of those all-wheel drive cars that she heard people talking about. Probably both. Matt had money after all.

Matt pulled up and unrolled the window. "I hope you brought warmer clothes than that."

"I did," Callie said defensively.

She tried to ignore how good Matt looked in a black

wool jacket. It was pulled up around the angle of his freshly shaved jaw. His ice-blue eyes glistened. His lips, lips which damn well haunted her, turned up in a huge grin. *It's sinful to be that handsome. He probably always gets what he wants because his face looks like it's carved out of stone.* That only made her think about the rest of him and what else was rock hard, like shoulders and chests and abs and- *hell no. Do not go there.*

"Are you going to ride with me or follow?"

"Follow."

"I figured." He didn't elaborate and never lost that charming smile that turned her insides into a hot mess.

"Where are we going?"

He winked at her. "Wait and see. Do you think you can keep up?"

"It's a surprise then," she stated dryly. She left no doubt as to what she thought about that.

"Yup." He rolled up the tinted window so that she could barely see the flash of his teeth. He waited for her to get in her car before he rolled out of the parking lot.

Callie had a feeling that Matt didn't normally drive that slow or that carefully. He probably did it just so she could keep up. Not because he was being nice. She wouldn't give him that. He probably thought her old early nineties sedan couldn't keep up. She'd show him. The tiny little car always started. It might be rough looking, but it was reliable. It had never left her stranded and even after heavy snow, she'd never been stuck.

Matt finally pulled up in an empty parking lot. It felt like they'd been driving forever. There was nothing around them. Callie was slightly worried about driving so far out of the way, but she had to trust Matt. She worked with him after all. He wasn't going to drive her into the middle of nowhere and do something awful to her. That was just her nerves making her extremely and overly paranoid.

When she climbed out of the car and saw the huge hill looming in the distance, her eyes flew around the parking lot. She spotted a sign a few seconds later.

"Sledding?" She turned to Matt, who was just getting out of his car.

He nodded. He seemed far too proud of himself. "I rented the place for the night. It's just you and me and the people who run the place."

Callie nearly snorted. "See! That's something a rich person would say." She did her best impression of his deep, husky, far too self-assured, far too sexy, voice. "I rented the place out for the night."

"You said you wanted it to be memorable. I doubted standing in line and waiting all night was going to be that."

"Sledding?" she asked again. "You mean like, with actual sleds? Toboggans and tubes and stuff?"

"That's what I mean. There's a huge lift so that we don't have to walk up the hill after. More rides that way."

"I haven't done anything like this since I was a kid," Callie admitted grudgingly.

She stared up at the monstrous hill. The idea was a strange one, but it did sound fun. If she was busy sledding down the hill, she wouldn't have to be sitting there staring at Matt like she thought the date was going to be. She thought he'd take her to a five-star restaurant and throw cash around to try and impress her. *Boy, was I wrong.*

"I guess I'll get my stuff on and we can go."

"Great me too."

She went back to her car and dressed awkwardly, hopping on one foot to get her feet into her boots. Of course, her outdoors clothes weren't nearly as nice as Matt's. He had an all black suit on that looked like it was meant for skiing or snowboarding or something. Of course, his toque, mitts, and boots all matched.

"Okay," she said with forced cheerfulness. "I'm ready to relive my childhood."

It turned out, that after a few minutes' ride to the top, sledding down the hill was a lot of fun. She let Matt go first, on a huge black tube, and she followed on one of her own. She went on her stomach and was shocked at how much speed she picked up going down the hill. She laughed and screamed and watched the world rush by. She came to a standstill at the bottom, near Matt, who was waiting for her.

"How was that?" He raised a brow and even though he was smiling at her sarcastically like he could tell she really was having the time of her life, she laughed.

"It was fun," she admitted. "Really fun."

"I guess we can just leave these here and go back up and take something else. The staff brings the equipment back up."

"Okay."

She had to sit beside Matt on the lift, but even that wasn't bad. He remained quiet, content to just watch the lights of the city twinkling below them as they rose higher and higher up the hill.

"Is this place just for sledding?" Callie asked, near the top of the hill.

"Nope. On the other side, there are a few ski runs and courses for snowboarding and stuff."

"Do you come here a lot? I've never been skiing or snow-boarding before."

"Really? We'll have to come again then." Matt's eyes twinkled. His breath fogged out in the air above him and he looked so damn charming and boyish in that moment, Callie was almost tricked into saying yes. Almost.

"No way," she laughed to cover up her discomfort. "This was a onetime thing. No tricking me into any more dates."

"I was hoping you'd agree to come if we had friends join us."

"Nope. No deal. That's still a date. In disguise."

"Darn." Matt grinned, completely unfazed. "I guess I still have a couple of hours to change your mind."

"You go ahead and try. It's not going to happen."

Except that, after two hours of sledding and screaming, rushing down the hill on tubes, toboggans, sleds, plastic disk things and plastic squares which Callie didn't even know the name of, she was tempted to give in. Matt didn't ask her again and she didn't bring it up. She'd had fun. Real fun. For the first time in a very long time. She couldn't remember the last time she'd laughed so much.

"I'm soaked through," she said, as they neared their cars. "Thanks. I had a great time."

"Whoa, there. I didn't say the date was over." Matt's raspy, deep laugh filled up the night. God, he had a nice laugh. It wrapped around her like something soft and warm and did something to her insides yet again.

"What?" She whirled. Her hand fell away from the car door.

"I may or may not have had plans to cook you dinner. If that's alright?"

"I..." it wasn't, but something stopped her from saying it.

Dinner at Matt's house? Cooked by him? It was way too romantic. Although, part of her was tempted to throw caution to the wind and just keep enjoying herself. She was intrigued. She wanted to see what a man like Matt would or could cook. A small part of her wanted to see his house as well, just to get that glimpse into his private life, a life outside of work.

"I promise I have the best intentions only. The rated G kind. It's just dinner. I just thought after sledding we would be a mess, soaked and starving and you might not want to go out somewhere. I would have done it after but sledding on a full stomach would have been uncomfortable."

Callie didn't say so, but she was impressed. Matt really had thought ahead. Truthfully, he'd put far more thought into the date than she ever would have or could have. It touched a part of her, that part of her heart that was hard and cold, wounded and closed off.

"You'll have your car. You can leave at any time." He tried again to coax her into it.

"Uhh... I'm soaked." She looked for a way to back out. "The only clothes I have are underneath these ones."

"I'll lend you a t-shirt and sweats."

His eyes roved over her body, likely just assessing her for size and she shivered. A blast of heat tore at her stomach and that painful pulsing, the throbbing that never really seemed to go away since that kiss, was back.

Just go. For once in your life, do something. Don't be old like Chantara said and look back on everything and regret that it was all wasted. Just live for once. It's just this night. If I don't go, he will probably try and ask for a second date since I bailed on the last part of it.

"Alright," Callie relented. "But it had better be G rated."

Matt smiled and it was the kind of look that melted her insides. Or it would have if they weren't already completely liquid. Her legs felt a little weak like they might go all buttery and collapse. She needed to be in the car before that happened.

"I'll give you my address."

"I don't need it. I already know where you live." He seemed momentarily stunned, but then he recovered.

"Right." His eyes snapped with humor. "Of course, you do. You book all my- well, everything."

"Yeah. Yes, that would be me."

"For tonight, let's just forget about that. You've done a good job so far. Just forget about it for an hour longer. I promise that's all it will take."

He turned around and got in his car with all his gear on, started it and drove off before she had time to protest or change her mind. *Smooth. Real smooth.* It didn't even occur to her until she was halfway to Matt's house, to wonder just what that hour was for. *That's all it will take. What the hell did he mean by that?*

10

MATT

*M*att could tell Callie was thawing out. She'd been pretty frigid at the beginning of the date, but after the first couple of runs down the hill she really opened up. She was laughing and having a good time and he got a glimpse of the woman she probably was outside work. *Or maybe not. Maybe she's reserved at home as well.* There was something about sledding, about just letting go and being a kid again, that brought out the best in everyone. He felt better than he had in ages.

He pulled into his garage and was in the house just long enough to find a spare change of clothes for himself and lay one out on the couch for Callie before she rang the bell.

Matt opened the door, not completely surprised to see that Callie was already back to being guarded. Obviously, she'd thought way too hard on the thirty minute drive over. She hadn't bailed though, so there was still hope for him.

He was in the middle of pulling his T-shirt over his head when he answered the door. He realized, once he finally had the damn thing pulled down, that Callie was eyeing him up suspiciously. He felt her stare, hot and fiery, rake along his body then quickly back up to his face. The blush that always seemed to be there lately, was back. His entire body heated up and since he was wearing sweats, he turned quickly so that she couldn't see that his cock had a mind of its own.

"Here. I found you a change of clothes." He indicated the sweats and t-shirt on the edge of the couch. "The bathroom is down the hall, first door on the right."

"Thanks," Callie mumbled.

Matt figured there was a good chance she wanted to escape out the front door and run back to her car. He almost expected to hear the door slam behind him when he turned his back. It didn't.

"Do you eat pasta?"

"What?"

"Pasta?" He turned half back around, just in time to see Callie kick off her boots. She bent and lined them up on the mat and he tried not to stare at her ass as she did so. Thank god she was wearing snow pants and a jacket still and most of her behind was covered up. "Do you like it? There aren't many things I can cook, but it's one of them. I have red sauce or white sauce. Or... I have a premade bag of salad in the fridge-"

"Pasta is fine, thanks." Callie scooped up the clothes, ducked her head and rushed off in the direction of the hall. She left a wet trail in her wake as her sopping snow pants were too long, dragged down from being wet.

"You can hang your wet clothes over the shower bar," Matt called, but he got no response.

He headed off to the kitchen, trying to damn well control himself. He'd invited Callie over for dinner and that was it. Absolutely it. He didn't want to imagine her in his clothes, wearing his t-shirt and his sweats. He couldn't help it. His thoughts totally went there, and he knew before she even emerged from the bathroom that she was going to be hot.

Of course, he was right.

He raised his head and his hand froze. He had been chopping herbs, but that was quickly forgotten. The knife hovered midair. The clothes were way too big. Callie swam in his t-shirt, even though the thing was one of his smallest ones. She'd tucked it into the grey sweats and tied up the drawstring probably as far as it would go. They rode low on her hips. She looked... god, she was so sexy he forgot to breathe for a minute. He was so used to seeing her in work clothes, nothing but perfection, well put together, composed. It was nice to see her a little- undone.

The ends of her long blonde hair were wet and hung in clumps. The parts that had been under her toque were mussed. He could tell she'd tried to run her fingers through it to smooth it out. He found himself wishing he could have done that for her. Her hair looked like it was soft. Real soft. *It probably feels like silk.*

"I- uh- can I help with anything?" Callie shot him a look that told him she knew he was studying her. Her face burned bright, but he wasn't actually sure if the blush was just her fair skin flushed after being in the cold for so long.

"No- I- I've got it under control. Unless you want to set the table." He nearly winced. He shouldn't ask his guest to set the table.

Callie nodded. "I guess I can do that. As long as it doesn't require candles and we keep the lights on."

It finally dawned on him that she was talking about the whole romantic dinner for two atmosphere. "I planned on leaving the lights on." He pointed towards one of the cupboards on his left. "The plates are in there. And below that, in that drawer, is the cutlery."

"Okay."

Despite the fact it wasn't her house and she was prob- ably nervous as hell, though she did her best to hide it, Callie made quick work of the table. And he managed to put on a pot of water and get the rest of the herbs chopped for the sauce.

"You have a nice place." Callie leaned on the other side of the island. She was attempting a casual pose, but he could see how uncomfortable she was in the rigid set of her jaw and shoulders.

"Thanks."

"I didn't expect anything less."

He rolled his eyes. "Also, thanks?"

"Sorry. I didn't mean that the way it came out. I just- it was what I imagined."

"It was a good deal. I bought it as sort of an investment. It needed quite a bit of fixing up. The previous owners actu- ally foreclosed on it. And before you ask, no, my parents didn't help me out with it. At least not with the money part of it. Some of the renovations, yes." Callie looked a little taken aback. He had to laugh. "What? You can't imagine me lifting a hammer and doing anything myself? I might push paper around for a living all day, but I do have some other hidden talents." He was pretty sure now that the pink hue riding high on Callie's cheeks was a blush.

"I guess I just thought- because you're rich that-"

"I'm not that rich. I make a good living, but that doesn't mean I'm drowning in money. My parents are well off and I had nice things growing up. I also have two brothers. We didn't have the best of everything. My dad worked hard for what they have. And I paid for college by working part-time, and, I went to public school. And I didn't go to an Ivy League before you ask."

"I- well- I wasn't-"

"Yes, you were. I have a regular business degree just like everyone else. I just happen to be good with numbers and better with people and that served me well."

"Everyone says you're a good manager," she admitted, then looked embarrassed at letting that little piece of information slip.

Matt got the sauce going, just premade pasta sauce with a few added fresh herbs, and put the pasta into the boiling water. He made sure everything was at the right temperature and turned back to Callie. She was staring at him but dropped her eyes quickly back to the counter.

"Did you have fun tonight? No, scratch that. I know you did. Was it really so bad? Letting yourself enjoy the evening?"

Her head snapped up and her lips shifted upwards at the corners. He thought he spotted a dimple on her left cheek, but the smile was too small to actually produce it.

"I guess I had a good time. Although, I'm pretty sure that anyone would have. It was a good choice. I didn't even know you could do sledding like that. And not having other people there- I guess that was pretty cool."

"It's definitely better at night. It reminds me of being a kid. My brothers and I would take our sleds to this hill a few blocks from our house. It was in a park, but that's all the park was- a huge hill. We used to spend hours and hours sledding down there. It was always dark, and I thought it was so much better than in the daylight. There was just something- magical or whatever, about the night."

"Really? I was always scared of the dark. My parents always said something would happen to me at night and that I had to be careful. That was when I was a kid. After that- I- I grew up and I guess it didn't matter to them as much."

Callie's eyes flickered downwards, to the granite counter-top. Matt had the feeling that she wasn't just talking about the natural progression of getting older and parental guidance tapering off. It was something else. Something- something worse.

His insides tightened. The urge to protect her was so damn strong he nearly walked over and wrapped his arms around her small, frail shoulders. *Don't. It's the last thing she wants. She's made that real damn clear. No funny stuff, she said. That was her stipulation.* He kept his distance, but barely. He had to grip the edge of the countertop so hard his knuckles turned white.

Callie, clearly not in the mood to say anything else, drifted away to the table. She pulled out a chair and sat. Matt let her have her space. The silence that stretched on between them surprisingly wasn't awkward.

He set the food on the table and pulled out the chair where she'd set his plate. His table was large, in a kitchen that was massive. The huge piece and the eight chairs barely made a dent in the room. It was a good thing the kitchen took up the other half and his mom had helped him pick out a few antique pieces, namely the buffet and china cabinet. He only knew what they were because he'd heard her call them that more than once.

"Look," Callie said quietly as he slid the pot of pasta and the scoop towards her. He wasn't going to be presumptuous and put it on her plate for her. "I- I grew up in a small town. I had a happy childhood, but not after that. It was hard growing up. I really struggled. I was glad to get away. There isn't anything wrong with me now. I- maybe I shouldn't have said anything."

He nodded slowly. She didn't take any pasta, so he filled his plate instead. After that, she slowly added a scoop to her own. She put sauce on, swirled her fork around and tasted a bite tentatively.

"Wow. This is actually pretty good."

"You sound surprised."

"I have to say, I am."

He laughed. "Just another one of those skills that I have that no one knows about. It extends to pasta and toast and other small meals that I use to keep myself alive and that's pretty much it. I could never cook a full-on meal."

"Those are bad for you anyway. At least, everyone says people should eat small meals more often. I think I agree. I hate being over full. The oven at my place doesn't even work. We've decided to get a toaster oven instead. I- uh- I guess you don't care about that though. I don't even know why I said that."

"No, no, it's fine." He jammed a forkful of pasta in his mouth and chewed. It *was* pretty good. Luckily one of his better batches. "So- that small town- was it- was it one of those repressive things where no one minds their business and there aren't any opportunities and if you have an ounce of independent thought, people get upset?"

He grinned and Callie offered a small smile back, but at least it was something. It was enough, at any rate, to get him distracted by her beautiful mouth again. Which got him thinking about that kiss again, which had him rock fucking hard under the table. Again.

"I guess so," she admitted.

"I'm glad I grew up in the city. I wouldn't have done well in one of those places. I was in trouble often enough as it was."

"Really? I can't imagine you getting into trouble."

"Yeah. I never wanted to listen to anything the teachers had to say, but I was pretty charming, so I could usually work my way out of it."

Callie giggled. "I guess not much has changed. Everyone says you're very personable."

"I don't know why. Half the time, I think I'm too hard on people."

"I think you're just right." She blushed furiously and grabbed her fork. "I mean..." she stammered as she twirled it into her pasta. "I mean- uh- okay that came out totally wrong."

Callie's eyes flicked back down, but her fork froze. Her hand, he noticed, trembled. When she looked back up, he was shocked as hell to see tears in her eyes. She blinked hard, letting her fork fall with a clatter, and raised her hand to her face to wipe them away.

"I'm sorry," she whispered. "I don't- I didn't mean to-"

"Don't apologize."

Without thinking, he reached over and took her hand, the other one, the one resting beside her plate. He felt her tremble when he gripped her fingers, but it was something more than that. The shock of the touch sent a wave of something hard and vital racing through his arm. His fingers tingled, the hair on the back of his arm stood on end as goosebumps appeared. Actual. Fucking. Goosebumps.

"I'm just cold," Callie whispered in a shaky voice. "Just-just chilled. I just-" but those tears kept on coming, tracing patterns down her cheeks, falling like rain.

She ripped her hand away and stood, shoving her chair back so hard it screamed in protest even though there were those felt pads along the bottom to protect the hardwood from scratches.

Matt stood up slowly and Callie stared at him, frozen,

lips parted. He took a step closer, hand out, as though she was a frightened animal and he didn't want to scare her off for good. Her cheeks were wet with the constant flow of moisture that tracked down them. She finally reached up to brush them away.

"Callie- I don't know what's going on with you, but- I- I can help you."

She stared at him, as though debating with herself. Her eyes searched his face and he never broke contact. Hers were red-rimmed already, but the irises were even bluer than usual. Something in her changed. Her shoulders fell and her body seemed to cave in on itself. He sensed it and when he stepped forward again, she didn't edge away.

His hand fell to her hip, so gently, her small body covered in his clothing. All he meant to do was offer a comforting touch. Just pull her into a hard hug that wasn't exactly appropriate, but he knew she needed it and he was the only one there.

When he touched her though, felt the warmth of her body burning him through those sweats, he couldn't move. He couldn't do it. He knew if he got closer, he might lose control and that was the last damn thing she needed.

She hesitated, eyes as wide as saucers, but she was the one who made the first move. She swung around, wrapped her arms around his neck and pressed her body into his. She pulled his head down to hers and raised her face. Her lips parted, those sweet, soft lips that he couldn't stop thinking about, dreaming about.

"Callie," he breathed. "Are you sure?"

"Yes." Her breath was hot against his mouth.

What was left of his control, what little he had to begin with, snapped completely.

CALLIE

She wasn't sure when the date went so off track. At what point did Chantara's words from earlier that week really sink in? At what point did she feel so totally alone? Was it during the sledding? Racing down the hill after Matt, laughing and screaming, realizing that it was indeed possible to actually have fun again. To allow herself to live a little.

Was it the clothing he gave her? The soft t-shirt and the warm sweats, the way he set them out before she even got to his house? Was it the glimpse of his rock-hard abs and bronzed skin as he pulled his own shirt on when he answered the door? Or was it that someone was taking the time to make her dinner? To care about her like she was an actual person with thoughts and feelings and dreams? Matt looked so tenderly at her like he actually cared. She'd said something stupid, about her past, and it spiraled out of control from there.

She hadn't meant to cry. It was the last thing she wanted to do. It was just that- the tears had been so long in coming. Callie felt like she'd been holding them back for years.

She knew she had to get out of there, but then Matt rose, and he looked at her and in his eyes, she saw- god, she didn't know what she saw. Pain. For her. Sincerity. Care. Compassion. He cared about her. She wasn't just another notch in his belt or a trophy for his wall. He looked at her like she truly mattered. In a world where she'd grown used to feeling invisible and unwanted, ashamed of who she was and alone for the most part, having one other person there made all the difference.

Matt pulled her into him, and she went, tangling her arms around his neck. He asked her if she was sure, with all the sincerity in the world. She knew that he'd let her go if she wanted him to.

She could have gone. It would have been the right decision for so many reasons. But she didn't. She looked into Matt's eyes and said the word.

Yes.

Yes, she wanted to stay. Yes, she was going to regret what they were about to do, because she made no mistake about the fire in his eyes. Yes, she was going to make sure that after she opened herself up she was protected again. She was just so tired, so very damn tired, of being lonely. She craved that connection with another person. If she was honest, she'd never really had it with Ben. It had been years, *years* since she felt truly alive.

Matt was her boss, but it didn't matter. She wasn't going to see him again after. She'd quit her job and that would be that. She'd give herself this experience, not a night, just the sex, the connection, the... whatever was going to happen. It wasn't about intimacy and it sure as hell wasn't about love. It was because that one kiss would never be enough for either of them. She knew what it meant to give in to something she truly wanted. That it was just a mistake, that it hurt, in the end. But this, this wouldn't be a mistake. She'd be careful. She wouldn't let herself get hurt again.

And then Matt's lips descended to hers, warm and soft and just as incredible as she remembered them. She forgot to think as the kiss went from something that was gentle to something that was searing and wild and hot. She forgot to remember her past. She forgot the reasons she shouldn't be with Matt in the first place. She forgot to think, to remember, to process, to do anything other than surrender.

It felt good. It felt so damn good.

Callie leaned into the kiss, pressing herself against Matt's solid form. He was real. This was really happening. It wasn't a dream that she had to wake herself up from. His tongue pushed between her lips and it was *really* real. She kissed him back with equal ferocity. Her tongue tangled with his and when he withdrew, she nipped at his lips, licking and probing until he opened his mouth to her.

Their teeth clashed together in her haste, but it was nice, that little shock of friction, the urgency. His cheek scraped against hers, his skin soft from a fresh shave, likely done just before he left for their date. She pulled away for a second and smelled pine and woods and the deeply erotic scent that was just Matt. It was raw and unmistakably masculine.

Her senses overwhelmed, all Callie could do was hang on. She sank her nails into Matt's neck and pressed herself against him as his mouth crushed hers once more. His knee came between hers and she felt the hard bulge against her thigh. Her senses reeled at the contact. The throbbing that had been going on between her legs since the damn Christmas party was back. She felt the rush of wetness soak the sweatpants as she ground shamelessly against the rigid muscles of Matt's leg.

She was almost embarrassed at how wet she was. She'd

left her panties in the bathroom, hidden under her wet clothing, since everything was soaked through. She figured he'd never know…

Matt deepened the kiss. His hunger and desperation were evident and she pushed back just as forcefully, their mouths locked in a passionate war that neither of them was going to win. She didn't want to win.

Desire pooled low in her stomach and her insides clenched hard. Her fingers swept through Matt's hair, marveling at how soft it was, despite the product that was there. It was minimal and used on the outside of the golden strands.

He shifted, moving his knee away and she nearly cried out in frustration, but then his hand was there, on the inside of her thigh, and she vibrated with the touch. He explored her through the sweats, the outline of her leg, the curl of her hip, the flat planes of her stomach. She had his t-shirt tucked in to try and keep the too large sweats from slipping down her hips. He pulled it away easily and slid his hand under the waistband. He kept going, exploring her smooth sex.

She nearly jumped when she felt his fingers, as hot as molten lava, lower. He groaned loudly and even she felt the tremble that ripped through him.

"Dear Lord, you aren't wearing any panties."

As if he just realized. But maybe he did. Maybe his brain is moving as slow as mine. Like sludge.

"They were soaked," she panted.

"From sledding," he said huskily, as though he just realized what she was talking about.

"Yes."

"You're so smooth. And wet." His finger moved over her sex and she knew it was true. She was shamefully wet, slick and throbbing. For him. "Are you still cold? Chilled? I have something that would warm you up."

"What's that?" *As if I don't already know.* A bolt of fear raced through her, but she pushed it away. This was her night. This was her one damn night to feel alive again.

"A shower. With me."

"I..." she hedged.

It was embarrassing. She never did this with anyone. She hadn't come prepared, because as far as she was concerned, it wasn't happening. Ever. It was supposed to be a nice, innocent evening. *It was supposed to be, but I don't want that anymore.* She really doubted that she'd ever wanted it if she was totally honest with herself. Which was something she hadn't been in a long time. Honesty was hard. Honesty hurt. Honesty beat the hell out of a person. It was easier to harden off, to block out the past and the painful memory. It was easy to hide behind walls made of stone and not let anyone in.

"What is it?" Matt took his hand away. He brought it up and gently stroked it over her bottom lip. She could smell her own feminine, dusky scent and her body heated up. The throbbing turned into a roar that needed to be sated.

"I- I didn't bring- I'm not on anything. I mean- protection..."

"Right." Matt's eyes darkened with understanding. "I have something upstairs."

"But- I- if we shower?"

"We don't have to do this if you don't want to," he said gently. Even though his eyes burned into her, she knew he would stop if she said the word. She didn't want him to stop. She wasn't going to say the damn word.

"No, I do want to. It's just... I want to be safe. I- I just want to be responsible."

He nodded. "If you still want a shower, I'll do everything in my power to make it the best shower you've ever had. Then we can take it to the bedroom from there. We'll be adults."

Callie paused. She wanted to trust Matt. *I do trust him. He's a good person.* She didn't really know anything about him, but she knew that was true. He wasn't going to hurt her. Nothing would happen. She'd feared it with Ben too, that something unplanned would come between them and ruin them. She'd kept her secrets inside for as long as she could. She knew it wasn't fair to Ben and she'd finally given in and let him in right before their wedding.

As far as honesty went, she knew he wouldn't marry her. She'd told him so anyway. Ben had been safe. He was someone she'd met at the end of college and turned to because he was just... safe. He'd convinced her to go out with him. Him and his black hair and dark eyes and his perfect smile. He had that bland kind of life that she could tell was just... safe. She'd never stepped out of her comfort zone. She wasn't even sure they'd ever actually loved each other. They had no business even getting married...

Callie shook her head and Matt stared back at her. She pushed thoughts of Ben aside. "It's just been... a long time since I've done this." She flushed after, at how bad that sounded said aloud.

Matt didn't wince. He didn't smirk or make a face or drawback. His eyes, if they changed at all, softened a little. "I swear I won't hurt you."

"I know."

He looked like he wanted to say something else, something about there still being time for her to back out, but she stepped in again, braced her hands on his shoulders, and pulled his face to hers. She kissed him like there wasn't going to be a next time. She already knew that with him, there wouldn't be. She drank him in, nipped him and he nipped back. She captured his groans in her mouth and pressed closer.

She let out a gasp as his hands slid around her hips, down to the curve of her ass. He lifted her easily, hiked her onto his solid, rock hard hips. She wrapped her legs around him, and he carried her through the kitchen, through the living room and up a set of stairs. He set her down in the bathroom and set to work on getting the shower going.

It was a stand-up shower, one of those things that were tiled and set off by itself. There was a tub on the other end of the bathroom, a freestanding thing that looked expensive. The countertops were marble or granite or something, in the double vanity. A set of white, fluffy, terrycloth towels hung from the towel bar at the side of the shower. The bath-room was almost so perfect it looked like it belonged in a hotel.

Matt turned back to her and the look in his eyes sent a wave of lust stabbing right through her. "Let's get those clothes off."

Callie froze. *Am I really ready for this? For another man to see me naked?* What did it matter though, if she never saw him again? It wasn't like he would look at her at work and everyone will know that he'd seen her without clothes, that he knew what she looked like underneath those layers. She wanted him. She wanted him enough that she could brave the embarrassment of getting undressed with the lights on.

She gripped the hem of the t-shirt, his t-shirt, and pulled it over her head. Matt froze. The cool air hit her bare skin. Her nipples were hard little buds before the cold air even grazed them. Matt let out something that sounded pretty damn close to a growl.

He stalked toward her and met her hand halfway to her pants. He worked them down her legs with her, let his hand travel over the smooth skin of her thigh and down her calf, as she shed the sweats onto the floor.

"Lord, you are perfect," he growled. Oddly enough, when he said it, she almost believed him. "I haven't been able to get you out of my mind. Not since that kiss."

"Really?" she gasped. She wasn't brave enough to tell him that she'd relived it a hundred times. Or a thousand. More than that?

"Really." Matt tore off his t-shirt and she stepped back, looking on in admiration.

She got a full-on view of that bronzed chest, the hard pecs, the striated muscle of his shoulder, the bunching of the muscle in his arms, the bulges of biceps and streamlined forearms, the hard ridges of defined abs. He was glorious. If men could be called beautiful, he was definitely freaking gorgeous. Her mouth actually watered, and her hands itched just to feel even an inch of all that hard muscle and golden skin. And then he shed his pants. He stepped out of them and let her see what she was really in for. She forgot all about being self-conscious that she was naked. Because he was too.

Her gaze was immediately drawn to his cock, which was so hard it stood nearly straight up along his chiseled abs. Her sex ached at the sight of him naked. He looked good in clothes, but he looked much better without.

When she looked up, she blushed painfully as her eyes met Matt's. He knew she'd been looking at him, studying him, wondering how the hell he'd actually fit inside of her.

"Stop thinking," he said huskily. "I want you to stop thinking and start feeling."

"Feeling?" she asked woodenly.

"Yes. Feeling. I want you to enjoy every single second of what I'm going to do to you in that shower."

A shiver raced up her spine and goosebumps formed all over her arms and legs. There was a promise in his voice, deep and rich and so darkly sexy. It killed the last bit of common sense or reserve she might have had left.

Her legs bucked beneath her, but Matt caught her. He hauled her into him and when he kissed her, it was even hotter yet. He propelled them into the shower, beneath an unrelenting spray that felt like paradise against her oversensitive skin. *I need this. I need him.* She'd promised herself that she wouldn't do this again. That she wouldn't give someone the capability to hurt her, but she couldn't stop.

And then he dropped to his knees and she learned firsthand what paradise truly was.

12

MATT

*S*he tastes so good. So damn good.

Callie melted against him, rocking her hips into his face, grinding against his mouth. He took his time with her, exploring and teasing and tasting and learning. She inflamed every single one of his senses and then some. He felt drunk and dizzy. The whole world felt like it had been tipped on its side and he was doing his best just to hang on.

He swirled his tongue over Callie's sex. She was perfect. Her taste was perfect. The water cascaded down her heaving breasts, over her flat stomach, mingling with the spicy musk of her arousal. It mixed together on his tongue and slid down his throat when he swallowed. Callie's harsh little pants turned to wild moans and matched the groans that were torn from his throat.

For someone who was so proper at work all the time, she was a burning, fiery pillar against him. Her hips bucked wildly, her nails dug into his scalp and shoulders in turns. She writhed and whimpered and moaned as he delved into her with his tongue, lapped at her with his mouth, worshipped her in every way he knew how.

He gently ran a finger over her sex, finding her tight entrance. She gasped when she felt him there. Just as he entered her, slowly, he flicked his tongue over her clit. She vibrated against him and let out another wild moan. Her fingernails dug in so hard, he was sure they made little crescent marks in his shoulders.

"Oh, god," she panted. "Yes. Matt..."

He began to work her with his finger and suckle her clit at the same time. Her body responded eagerly. She came hard a minute later, her cries echoing through the shower. He lapped at her, slowly, gently, and marveled at all she made him feel. He felt alive. More alive than he ever had in his life. He felt... like it was right. Like what they were doing was always meant to happen. He'd never been so fucking turned on from pleasuring another person. He was rock hard and right on the verge himself.

Matt gave Callie a second to recover and then he scooped her up in his arms. He managed to hit the shower dial on the way out. He didn't bother with towels. He carried her naked and dripping wet and entirely glorious, straight to his bed. He didn't flick on the lights since he knew she'd probably protest, and he didn't want to make her uncomfortable. There was a stream of light filtering in from the hallway that gave the room just the right amount of golden glow. Enough to see, but enough that she wouldn't be shy.

She sure as hell wasn't shy in the shower. Matt suspected that even Callie was surprised at herself.

He set her down gently on the bed and she scooted up. He ripped open the drawer of his nightstand. It only took him a few seconds to find the little packet he was looking for, rip it open, and slide it in place.

"Matt- I..." Callie panted. "I haven't done this in a while."

"It's alright," he assured her. "We can take it slow. Unless..." the word was painful. "Unless you want to stop."

"No." She shook her head vehemently, her eyes glassed over with passion. "No, I don't want to stop. I just want you to know. Because I'm probably going to be bad at it."

It was his turn to shake his head in denial. "No way. Not possible." He could have sworn she was blushing, but it was too dark to be sure.

Her hair hung around her shoulders in wet clumps. It was so much darker when it was wet. Her eyelashes were thick and clumped together in little star patterns. Her lips were swollen from his kisses. Little beads of water trailed down her shoulders, her breasts, her stomach, her legs. Every single inch of her was so damn beautiful. *Flawless*. It was flawless. *She* was flawless.

"So- what- uh- do you want to do?" Callie asked. She sounded like she was ready for a negotiation session and Matt paused.

"What do you mean?"

"I mean- uh- what position do you want me?"

He didn't know whether to smile, laugh or groan. She stared up at him, eyes wide and searching. "You don't have to ask me, that," he said gently. "We'll just start and then you can take the lead. How's that?"

"What if- I don't know what you like?"

He nearly laughed. "Trust me. I like everything." *When it comes to you.* He cut that off, not wanting to make her any more uncomfortable than she probably already was.

"Alright," she whispered in a tiny voice.

He knelt on the bed, sure to keep the lower half of him away from her. She seemed shy and nervous, which was a little strange after she'd been so lusty and alive and- and loud- in the shower. He'd bank those fires again. He'd bring her back to the point where she needed him, where she was moaning and whimpering and crying out his name again.

Matt braced himself on either side of her slim shoulders. He bent his head and claimed those beautiful kiss swollen lips before he broke away and moved to her breasts.

"God, you have beautiful breasts," he panted. They were full, but not too full. The little pink buds stood on end and he closed his mouth over each one in turn, licking and suckling.

"Really?" Her little gasp was adorable.

"Really." He bit her left nipple gently just to emphasize his point.

She arched up under him, pushing her breast into his mouth. He licked and suckled her, and she writhed and moaned below him. Her hips bucked beneath him, but she froze when his cock hit her thigh. He froze too, stilled and just enjoyed throbbing against her delicate skin.

"I want to ride you," she said, out of nowhere.

Matt was completely blindsided. He hadn't seen it coming, but damn, he sure as hell wasn't going to refuse. He reached down and gripped Callie's hips, turning her easily so that in one swift motion, she was the one on top. She shifted, untangling their limbs, straddling him. The warmth of her thighs burned right through him. Just when he thought he couldn't get any harder, she gripped his cock.

"Fuck," he ground out as her hand closed over him. She immediately relaxed her hold.

"I'm sorry," she gasped. "Did I hurt you? Oh god, I said I wasn't very good at this-"

"No," he ground out. "No, you did *not* hurt me."

It took a second for that to sink in, but when it did, Callie let out a nervous giggle and her small hand closed around his shaft again. She gripped him tight and he did his best to control another groan. He ground his teeth together so hard that it actually hurt.

She whimpered when his cockhead grazed along her clit on the way to her entrance. She eased down on his cock with absolutely no other foreplay. Which he was damn glad for. If she stroked him any more with that tight little fist of hers, the fun might be over right there. Which would be damn embarrassing.

She took him slowly, inch by inch. She was so tight and warm, it took a herculean amount of willpower just to concentrate on not fucking coming right that second.

"God," he groaned. "Fuck..." It wasn't at all decent language, but he couldn't stop himself. A groan was torn from his throat just as Callie whimpered above him.

She took him right to the base and then she waited. He throbbed inside of her and her inner muscles gripped him in response. Matt couldn't tell if she was doing it on purpose. He didn't think she was, but it felt so damn amazing.

When she moved, he nearly shot out of his skin. Callie, he learned, was the kind of person who knew what she wanted, even if she didn't think she knew. She knew just how to rock with him, how to grind her clit against him, how to use him to find that perfect spot. She rolled her hips, grinding and swaying.

Matt had to open his eyes and enjoy the show. Callie with her hands resting on his shoulders, hips gyrating wildly, breasts swaying, water droplets still sluicing over her alabaster skin from her wet hair- it was all one hell of a display. He had to close his eyes, simply because he couldn't look at her anymore. Not if he wanted to retain any kind of control over himself.

He closed his eyes and it wasn't long before his entire body was vibrating with need. It actually was physically painful for him to hold back. He couldn't stop himself from gripping Callie's hips, from helping her rock and sway with him, finding the rhythm that they both so desperately needed.

Matt felt the pressure building, inside himself, inside Callie. He felt those first little trembles, in her thighs and then deeper. Her muscles clenched around his cock and then she cried out. He thought she probably threw back her head, but her wild gyrations, the way her body trembled around him, treated him to one hell of a fireworks display of his own. Lights burst behind his closed lids and his body went into full spasm mode.

He thrust into her hard, pumping her with every one of her wild gyrations. He was as wild as she was, bucking and grinding into her until with one hard thrust, he came deep inside of her. He throbbed wildly and even with the damn condom on, he could feel all of her, every glorious part of her, every spasm, all the heat and the rush of wetness- all of it. And god, it was amazing.

When she'd finally stopped shaking, Callie rolled to the side. Matt went with her. He grabbed for the sheets and covered them both in an awkward motion. He wrapped her up in his arms and she went, if a little stiff.

"Don't," he whispered pleadingly. "Don't pull away yet. Just stay- just like this... for a few minutes." He could tell she wanted to run. That she was probably already regretting what she'd just done.

And him? He was lying there, marveling that anything could feel so right. It was actually frightening how good it felt, just the two of them. He had never, ever, experienced anything like that in his life. Nothing even came close to what it had been like with Callie.

He knew. He'd known from that first kiss they'd shared at the damn Christmas party, that she would be different. It was why he couldn't stop thinking about her. It was why he'd been tortured by that kiss.

Matt couldn't even explain what the feeling was exactly. There didn't seem to be a word that could encompass the kind of connection they'd just shared. It was fucking earth shattering.

For him, it had been. Did she not feel the same? Or was she scared? After a minute, Callie relaxed against him, and he allowed himself to take a breath. And then he did the worst thing he could have done, but he just couldn't let her leave him like that. He had to know what had been in her past. What made her want to run? What made her afraid? It was more than just the whole boss thing. It was more than what she'd said, about being at different income brackets.

"Please, Callie." He stroked his hand over her wet hair. "I... what is it? I can tell there's something. Something bothering you. Will you tell me what it is?"

She went completely rigid in his arms. Rigid, but she didn't pull away. That had to mean something. He could feel himself losing her, even though she was right there with him and it just about killed him.

The room was silent for a long time. It was just their breaths, which had resumed an almost normal cadence. She let out a sigh, the smallest of sighs. It seemed like she'd debated with herself, silently, and that whatever was holding her back, had crumbled. Either she trusted him, or worse... he didn't want to think about her disappearing and never seeing him again. He didn't want to think about her spilling her heart to him just because she needed it. She needed to tell just one person who would never betray her because she'd never let them.

He was about to tell her she could tell him anything, that he'd be there for her, that it was early, but he already knew that- that she meant something to him. That he felt something he'd never felt before in his entire damn life. He opened his mouth to tell her, but then she spoke, shocking him into silence.

"I- I was engaged once..."

13

CALLIE

"So, you were engaged, but you never got married."

Callie froze. *Is this what people meant when they talked about appropriate after sex talk?* It hardly seemed like bringing another man between them when their sweat was still cooling, his name barely off her lips, their breathing still irregular, her body still trembling, was a good idea.

Matt turned to face her. Callie moved over an inch in the opposite direction. She cursed her tipsy drunk self and the remarks she made. *Why him? Why does it seem like I can tell him anything?*

"Uh- yeah. Something like that."

Matt frowned. Even in the darkness, Callie could see the little lines bracketing his eyes and mouth. "I want to know where you came from. You turned up out of nowhere. I know nothing about you." He reached out and caressed a silken strand that tumbled across her cheek and trailed down her neck. He tucked it safely back behind her ear and the gesture was so tender and kind, she almost believed she could trust him.

Don't. It's a false sense of security. He's my boss. And I'm in bed with him. It's bad enough already.

"Please. I promise, your secrets are safe with me."

"My secrets aren't safe with anyone. I've learned that in the past."

"Yeah, well, whoever they were, I'd like to find them and give them a good pounding. Pound out whatever shit they said to you to make you feel like you had to live alone for over a year."

"I didn't feel that way, I chose to live alone. I was done with it. I was done with all of it. I'm twenty-seven, but I feel like I've lived a thousand years. Do you ever get that feeling?"

Matt stared at her blankly. *How could he? For him, life is endless parties and women and money. Whatever he wants, he gets.*

"I know what you're thinking." Matt ran his thumb across her lips, and she resisted the urge to lick it, or even worse, suck that digit deep inside of her mouth. She knew it would be easy, distract him with sex, tell him nothing. Her lips parted, but he pulled his thumb away. "You think that I'm some spoiled rich kid who had everything in life handed to me. You think that I've never truly worked a day in my life or felt anything at all."

"Something like that."

They stared at each other for a second and then Matt laughed. She couldn't help it, she laughed too. Soon they were both laughing so hard they were shaking, and she had to reach up and brush away a tear.

"Lord, it might be true. Even if it is, one thing I've never done is rat on someone. I've never told a secret that was given to me in trust."

"It's not a secret. Other people know about it, although

they pretend that they don't." She clamped her mouth shut. She'd already said way too much. She couldn't seem to stop though. She sensed, looming in the future, was the release of a burden she'd carried around with her for over a decade. A burden of pain and loss and hurt. "Not Ben though. I told him, the night before our wedding. I thought that I had to. That I owed it to him. That he needed to know since he was going to be my husband."

"And the bastard left you? You trusted him and he just... left you?" Matt's incredulity almost made her feel a little better about it all. "I'd like to find him too. Give him a few thumps upside the head and ask him what the hell he was thinking."

"Not everything is solved by batting someone upside the head or punching someone or fighting. Of course, all guys think so."

"Better to fight it out than keep it in and let it rot you on the inside."

Rot me on the inside. That's exactly what this is doing. Why not? Why not tell him? Callie knew she'd never see him again. She'd given in, given herself one guilty pleasure, the one thing she'd wanted more than anything. She'd given herself a night with Matt. She promised herself too, that if it happened, she'd be gone after. She'd leave before he woke up and she'd disappear. She wouldn't go back to work. She would find another job. *So why not tell him? Just unload it.* She was tired of carrying that grief around with her. More than tired. *Exhausted.*

"Hey..." Matt shifted closer. "Come here. You look like you're contemplating running away forever. I'm sorry. We don't have to talk about this if you don't want to. I just- I- you have me now. If you want to talk, I'm not going to run the other direction."

He would probably leave, just like Ben did. He wrapped an arm around Callie and pulled her close. She went, gave in to the warmth of him, the allure of his body, the hard, broad chest and the crisp smattering of male hair and the delicious scent of skin and sweat and sex. She let him hold her, let herself feel powerless and oddly peaceful up against him. She let him comfort her with his silent strength. *I won't give him the chance.*

"Imagine yourself at fourteen..." Matt's hand paused on her arm. He was clearly confused at the abrupt change of subject. "Go on, imagine it. I'm- I'm going to attempt to talk about it, but... there are other things that need to be explained first." She couldn't really believe how calm she was being. Everything inside of her screamed at her to be quiet, to keep her secrets inside, to not wound herself further with yet another person's condemnation. Her heart ached, and it was that she listened to. Just for one night, for once, she wanted that pain to be a little lighter than it had been for so very long.

"Okay. Myself at fourteen."

Matt stroked her hair away from her forehead. It felt nice, the touch of his firm fingers dancing along her scalp. She turned into him and draped an arm across his chest. Her mouth was right above his nipple and she tried not to look at it, the way it was still slightly hard. Worse, she had to control her tongue from snaking out and tasting it. *What is wrong with me? God... one second we are talking, the next I'm so distracted I can't even think straight. It's because I'm a mess. One hot mess.*

"Myself at fourteen..." Matt went on. "I guess I would have fucked everything in sight. Or at least tried to. Teenagers are horrible. They are these walking- just-walking hormone bags."

"You wouldn't if you grew up in Hundville."

"Where? Hundwhat?"

"Hundville. Population of four hundred. Half an hour north of St. Paul, Minnesota. For the town being as close to a large city as it was, it was so- backwoods."

"I would have expected that down south, but really? Up there?"

"Yeah. I- it was a crazy religious town. Not the kind that does bad things. At least, not overtly. The kind that kills with silent judgment. I swear you couldn't even be in your house and take a breath without someone knowing and talking about it."

"Oh. That kind of thing."

"Yeah. The kind where everyone goes to church on Sunday, there were two churches and no bars, but then the rest of the week they just forget that they are supposed to be nice good people. Unless their neighbor or someone else messes up. Then they are pretty quick to remind them."

"So, you grew up there?"

"My mom and dad worked in St. Paul. They commuted since that was less than the cost of houses in the city. I hated Hundville. I hated that they made my sister and I live there. I hated that there was nothing to do and nowhere to go. It got worse as I got older. I was always a deep thinker. I had too much independent thought, that was the problem."

"I could imagine it, in a small town like that."

"When I was fourteen, this family moved to town. It was actually the church closest to our house. It got a new pastor and that pastor had two sons. One of them was in my grade. Johnathan. He was- he was incredible. My fourteen year old self thought so. I started taking notice of how I looked. I started doing my hair every day. I started caring about what

I wore. I wanted to wear makeup, but that was out of the question."

"It's hard being fourteen," Matt said sympathetically.

"It gets worse." She braced for judgment, for a stream of questions, but none came. *No, of course not. He hasn't heard the worst of it yet.* "So, it turned out, that what they said about pastor's kids was true. At least, it was about Johnathan. He noticed me too. I probably wasn't very subtle. It wasn't long before we were sneaking out. I said I was at volleyball practice or basketball or going to do homework or watch a movie at friend's houses. My curfew was eight and I was always home before that."

"Sounds like something kids do."

"Not in Hundville. It wasn't the kind of town where anyone did that. No one cheated, no one got divorced. People didn't drink. They didn't do drugs."

"Are you sure? Maybe they just did all that shit in secret."

"No, I'm sure. The shaming would have driven them out of town." Matt stiffened, as though he knew what was coming next. He stayed silent though, which was a small mercy. Callie took a deep breath. Her arm tightened on Matt's chest and reflexively, or maybe because he wanted to, there was more pressure in his arm around her. "I- well, I found out I was pregnant. I knew right away. Even though I was young I'd had my- uh- cycle for a year and I missed it. That never happened. I couldn't ask anyone, and this was before we really had the internet out there. I would have been too afraid to google it."

"You were- pregnant?" Matt asked, amazement in his voice.

She expected him to thrust her out of bed, to stare at her and tell her what a wretched person she was, but he didn't move. He didn't move at all, just stayed with her, comforting her and protecting her with his solid presence. *I'm never going to see him again. I can tell him the rest and then maybe, maybe I can stop thinking about it all the time. Maybe I can just let part of it go...*

"I had to tell my mom. She told my dad. They talked with Johnathan's parents and of course, they wouldn't do anything about it. They denied everything. Even Johnathan."

"What? A pastor?"

"Yes."

"Figures."

"Does it?"

"I don't know. I'm sorry. I won't interrupt you again." There was no judgment in Matt's voice and Callie felt safe enough to continue.

"My mom said she knew for a fact that her daughter wasn't a liar. She swore everyone to secrecy, and she did what she thought was best. She tried to spare me the shaming of the entire town. Of having to go to school, at fourteen, pregnant. The town probably would have driven my parents out. Not with pitchforks and fire, but with angry glares and harsh words. It's just as bad you know. The shame of it."

"Yes. Words hurt far worse."

"I got sent to live with my mom's sister in San Diego. It would have been a nice vacation. I liked my aunt. She was nice to me. She never once made me feel like I was an evil person. I guess she figured the damage was already done. She wasn't like my parents. She didn't have that small-town mentality. She wasn't judgmental or harsh. I went there because she really wanted to help me."

"Sounds like she was a good person when you needed her most."

"Yes. She was. And then- at two and a half months, I started bleeding. It was just a few spots. My aunt freaked out and even though the nurses we saw at the hospital said it was normal for a bit of spot bleeding, I had an ultrasound and there was no heartbeat. None. They sent me home. They thought I would miscarry there, but I didn't. I went to the hospital two days later. They did- well they did the surgery to remove the pregnancy. My aunt was there the entire time. It was just a short procedure, a few hours. I was out for it and when I woke back up, I needed a few hours to recover and then she took me home."

"Jesus- Callie…"

"I went back home after. To my parent's house. They all pretended like it never happened. I wasn't gone long enough for anyone to think anything of it. My parents had made something up about an exchange program or something or trying to go live in San Diego with my aunt because I wanted to take some more challenging courses than what was offered in a small town, some bullshit like that. Everyone believed it. No one knew. And those that did, my mom, my dad, my sister- they never talked about it. I- I went through this thing, this horrible thing, and no one would say a word to me. I had to grieve completely alone. I didn't know how to do that at fourteen."

"Does anyone at any age?"

"I had a life inside of me. A baby that I wanted. I was fourteen, but I would have fought for it. My mom didn't go that far as to talk about options, but I knew that I was keeping it. I would have done anything, anything for us. For me and that child. Anything it took to survive and keep us together."

"Of course. That's what being a mother is."

"And I've been alone in it. So alone. For the past ten years. I told Ben the night before our wedding, like I said, because I thought he should know. He left."

"How could he just- how could he just leave you?"

"I don't know. Maybe he never wanted to be married to me in the first place. Things were- stale anyway. It wasn't right. It was probably a blessing."

"Still. He should have had the balls to break up with you properly over it not being the right thing for the both of you. Not just take the easy way out like a damn coward."

"So now you know," she said softly, eyes closed.

The weight hadn't left her heart like she thought it would. It was worse, that pain, the burden of grief. She doubted it would ever go away. People were wrong. Talking didn't help. It didn't fix anything at all.

14

CALLIE

"*Y*ou did what?" There weren't many times Chantara was shocked. She was one of those live life to the fullest type of people and little surprised her. She wasn't exactly wild. Well, maybe most people would call her that.

"Yeah. I told him."

"Everything? About- about the miscarriage?"

"And about Ben."

Chantara wiped sleep from her eyes. "Jesus. I thought when you rolled in at four in the morning you were going to have something to tell me about getting laid for a change."

"Oh, we did have sex."

"And after you told him? You told Matt Hilbert things you wouldn't even tell your own family?"

"I guess that I did."

"After you had sex."

"Yes, that's pretty much right."

"Hold on. I need to make us some coffee." Chantara flew around the kitchen, gathering the things she needed to put on the dark roast she loved. "So, you told him everything, everything?"

Callie could really use a stiff cup of something black and bitter. Maybe she could scald herself back to reality. "Yes. Pretty much."

"Why would you do that? Tell him, I mean? You haven't even really told your family what went on with Ben."

A heaping spoonful of grounds was dumped into a filter, followed by another. The filter was placed in the machine and the on switch was pushed. Chantara did this weird thing where she always had the thing filled up with water and ready to go for the next time she used it.

"Honestly, I don't know. I- maybe it was the sex. I felt- screwed up after. He was the one who started it and I had my guard down. I felt- all soft inside or something."

"Definitely the hormones. Or the orgasms. How many were there?"

Despite everything, Callie had to bite back a smile. *Typical Chantara.* There was no one else on earth she could talk to like she was; with her guard down and her heart wide open. "Four," she admitted.

"Four? Holy shit. Mr. Hilbert is a demon in the sack. Good god, you kissed the right guy that night, that's for sure."

"Please, don't call him that. And I might have kissed the right guy. The orgasms might have been good. Really good. But that's it. He started asking me questions about where I came from and I just- I told him. It just kind of came out. I thought it would make me feel better about the whole thing. About Ben and everything too. It didn't. I still feel exactly the same way. Talking doesn't fix things. It only ruins it."

"What?" Chantara's eyes softened. "I'm sorry. I- that

sucks. It's really shitty. Maybe you should see a therapist or someone professional who can actually help."

"No. I didn't before and it's probably too late now. I'm just going to carry this around with me forever."

"That's terrible. I didn't honestly realize it was still that bad. I- I thought it just kind of went away with time and got easier to bear. And Ben- well that guy was a prick. Good riddance."

"I'm over Ben."

"Are you?"

Am I? Callie stared at the slow drip of the coffee, making its way down into the pot below. It seemed infinitesimally slow. "I'm over Ben," she said carefully. "But not over what he did. I think we both know that. It's why I haven't been with anyone else. I don't trust them."

"But it's different with Matt?"

"No. No, it's not. I should never have slept with him. I should never have kissed him. Good god, he's my boss. How much more inappropriate can I be? Which is why I'm quitting. As of this morning."

"What? No!" Chantara's blinked eyes that were red-rimmed from lack of sleep. "You can't! I'll be all alone there again. I love working with you. So what if you slept with him? It's not like he's going to tell anyone. He won't want a sexual harassment suit on his hands."

"It's not that. It's that I told him everything about- well. You know. I shouldn't have. I just- I knew that I was going to do it right after I slept with him. Quit. I can't face going back there and seeing him after I- well it's going to be so awkward. You can't sleep with someone and just pretend it never happened."

Finally, the coffee was ready. Chantara poured two mugs and handed one over. Callie took it gratefully. She held it between her palms, even though the heat was scorching. That little burst of pain felt good. It was something else to think about other than the shit that was going on in her head at the moment. Her head and her heart. She wasn't sure which one was worse.

"You could if you wanted to. It might be awkward, but you could get on with it. Maybe he'd want to see you again. If you like him and the sex is good, what's wrong with that?"

"Everything. He's still my boss and now, he knows what happened too."

"Well, did he say anything? Did he say it was your fault or that you were a terrible person or that he wanted you to leave?"

"No," Callie confessed. "I waited until he was asleep and then I snuck out. He just- kept holding me like he was doing the entire time. I think he did say something that it wasn't my fault or- I don't know. I don't even remember. It's like a blur. I was saying those things because I thought if I did, it would help me. It- it didn't. I feel exactly the same."

Chantara set her cup aside and wrapped her arms around Callie. "Oh, honey. It will be okay. Everything will be okay. If you don't want to work there anymore, I get it. But sneaking out at four in the morning after some great sex? Four orgasms! What's Matt going to think when he wakes up?"

"I don't know. It's not my problem anymore. He'll think that we had a great night and then I left and that was that. He will probably be relieved that I quit. Or maybe he won't even care. We all know he likes the ladies. He'll probably just hire another assistant and be in bed with her in no time. Maybe that's why I felt I could tell him those things. Because he'd listen and then just- forget. Like he'll forget all about me."

Chantara's arms tightened around her waist. "That's a terrible thing to say."

"But it's probably true."

"Don't you think this is odd? That I'm the one comforting you after a one-night stand? Usually, you're the one wiping my tears and offering me popcorn and a movie or wine and tissues. You're always the one telling me everything is going to be okay."

"Yes, well, your sex life is a little more vibrant than mine is. Has been. Will ever be."

Chantara laughed softly. "I know it's five-thirty in the morning, but with another cup of coffee, we should be good to go. How about a bowl of popcorn and our usual break up chick flick?"

"Popcorn? Isn't it too early for that?"

"It's never too early for grease and salt. I'll make us up a batch."

"The neighbors might complain about the noise. We should at least wait until eight."

Chantara pulled away and shot Callie a look that was absolutely hilarious. "No way. This place might have paper thin walls, but if anyone complains, I'll just talk about how Mr. Jones gets up to pee eighteen times a night above us or how Mrs. Fredrick stomps around swearing at her husband until the early hours of the morning."

"I swear, there might be a frying pan related death there someday."

"Right. And that girl down the hall, the one who we don't even know her name and we never seem to see her, but we always hear ..."

Callie winced. "She had someone over again?"

"Oh god. All night. I think she might have rivaled your

four orgasms if all that screaming, and moaning was to be believed."

Callie allowed herself a small laugh. If there was one safe place left in the world for her, it was home. Not the home she'd grown up in, but her dumpy little apartment she shared with the best friend anyone could ever ask for.

"Alright, alright." She capitulated. "Make the popcorn. I'll get the movie."

She relaxed against the counter and let some of the stress melt away. She noticed, with the movement, how sore she was, in spots she didn't even know she could be sore in. Her nipples chafed against the lace of her bra and between her legs... well, she wasn't even going to start thinking about that. Of course, *that* hurt.

She knew it wasn't allowed, really. There were rules, unspoken, invisible, in her own life and governing her professional conduct. She'd crossed every single line. Other than the aftermath, the part where she'd spilled the most private details of her life like it was safe for her to do it, she couldn't regret the sex. Who knew? It might be another fourteen months before she enjoyed anything that much again.

15

MATT

The first thing Matt noticed on Monday morning was the empty receptionist desk. *Of course, she called in sick. I should have expected it after she ghosted in the middle of the night.* He had to admit that as good as the sex was- and it had been fucking mind blowing phenomenal, he felt like he'd fucked things up a little.

He kind of got the feeling that Callie was telling him that stuff about her past life kind of as a goodbye. Like she was getting ready to disappear out of his life completely and she felt safe telling him before she left.

Matt didn't really want to believe that, but then Jenny from HR knocked on his office door at ten minutes after ten.

He let out a groan and motioned her in. *Fuck, did Callie go to HR? Is she filing harassment charges against me? Is consensual sex harassment?* The fact that he didn't know, only proved to him how inadequate his knowledge about that kind of thing really was. He knew better, keep it out of the workplace. Callie had said so as well. *And then we didn't. We freaking didn't.*

"Hey, Matt, do you have a minute?" Jenny smiled at him

and Matt's cramped stomach eased a little. She probably wouldn't be smiling if Callie had accused him of doing something vile to her.

Which I did not fucking do. And would never, ever do. She was into it. She was. You can't fake four orgasms, thank you very much. Still. They wouldn't be nearly as good if he got fired over them.

"Sure." He shut his laptop and closed down the screen desktop beside it. He pasted on a face that was what he hoped could pass for bland and stared back at Jenny, who took a seat in front of the desk.

Jenny was one of those proper women, even though she was young, probably not more than thirty. She had nice blonde hair but always wore it in a severe bun. She could have been pretty, but her features were always so intense it was hard to find her that. *Not that I want to.* It was just a casual observation, like looking at a paint job and noticing it could have fit better with the décor if it was a different color or something.

Jenny always wore matronly clothes as well. A white blouse and a black skirt, which on her, were somehow not the whole typical secretary garb. She never wore anything else. She was always all business, and she was damn good at her job. Guys who might have thought she was attractive, he'd never been among them, learned fast to steer clear. She wasn't interested.

Because she is a professional. Unlike me. The perv who fucks his secretary. Total cliché. Fucking totally fucking cliché.

"I just wanted to inform you that your secretary, Callie Canahan," she said the name like he didn't know who his own damn admin assistant was, "phoned in her notice this morning. She said that she had some personal issues come up. She's very sorry, but she's resigning as of this morning. As in, she's not coming back."

"Oh." His stomach hollowed out. It absolutely winded him to find out that his worst fears had come true. "I- I see."

"I'm sorry. We are working hard on finding you another assistant, but it might take a few weeks. And then there is a matter of training her. So, you may find yourself with a heavier workload. I'm just wondering if there is anything I can do to help out."

Matt thought fast. He was usually intelligent. Witty. On top of things. He hadn't felt that way since he met Callie. No, since that kiss at the damn Christmas party. He'd barely noticed her before then and she'd been working for him for three months. She'd been so damn mousy and polite, just like Jenny, that he'd paid her almost no attention. He knew she did good work, but that was about it. He'd taken no other interest in her. Then she'd shown up at the party wearing that little tight black dress and she kissed him, and he was just... gone. He was lost from that point on. His equilibrium was definitely off and he wanted, desperately, to get it back and get a hold of himself and the situation.

"I- yes, there is something you can do. Can you ask Jeff if he'd be willing to lend me his admin assistant just to catch up on emails and the more pressing things? Two afternoons a week would be great if he wouldn't mind."

"Right. Chantara?"

"Yes."

"I'll go ask him. That's a good solution. She's been with the company for a long time. She can probably help with some training as well, so that frees you up."

"Right. Thank you. That would be great."

"Thanks, Matt, for taking this so well. I'm sorry again.

We'll get you a replacement and have everything flowing smoothly again in no time."

He nodded and watched Jenny as she stalked swiftly out the door, ready to solve all their corporate problems. He liked that about her, her efficiency, but at the moment, he didn't want everything flowing smoothly. Not if it meant not having Callie there.

She ran. She got too close and she ran. She's like the damn moth that got singed in the flames. Bad analogy. That would be assuming that I'm good enough to be a flame and she's helpless like the moth. She could have left for other reasons. Maybe something personal really did come up. Matt doubted it. She'd told him about her past and he got the feeling she didn't tell anyone about her past.

It made sense that she'd do something she regretted, namely sleeping with him, likely because he was her boss, and feel obligated to resign. Which meant when she told him about the things that had happened to her, she already knew she wasn't going to see him again.

She'd used him like a confessional. She'd poured her heart out to him, or something like that, because she knew that he'd never tell anyone because he wouldn't ever get the chance. It would make no difference. She'd unloaded her burden on him and walked away, just like that, without a backward glance. She hadn't even stayed to tell him. She'd waited until he was sleeping and left.

No. No way. I'm not going to let her go like that. For one, he wanted to tell her he wasn't her emotional punching bag. Two, he needed to let her know leaving him up shit's creek workwise wasn't appreciated. And three, he had to find her because he needed to see her again. He needed to assure himself she was going to be okay. He did care and that hurt. She obviously wasn't used to opening up and he wasn't used to having that matter. *Caring. I'm not used to caring and worrying.*

Really, that was the only reason. He'd just use the other two points as a way to try and pretend that the third reason didn't exist. He could admit to himself that deep down and not so deep down, he was a lot like Callie. Afraid. The whole once burned, twice shy deal.

He nearly grinned when Chantara pushed open his office door without knocking. She put her hands on her hips and glared at him with the evil eye. That girl was a force to be reckoned with. He was glad that Callie had someone like Chantara in her corner.

"I know what you're doing, Matt Hilbert. It's not going to work. I am not going to tell you anything. Anything at all. I'm here to help you catch up on your emails and all that, but you are not going to get anything else out of me."

He stared at her flatly, so composed that he could see the very second she began to doubt herself and her outburst. "I have no idea what you're talking about."

He could see he wasn't going to get answers out of Chantara right away. Neither of the women knew that he knew that they were more than work acquaintances. He'd have to work her up to it, cajole and maybe even plead and then, after all of that, he'd convince her that he genuinely cared about Callie. Because he did.

And then, hopefully, because it truly was his only hope unless he wanted to break into HR and steal Callie's file and find her address, Chantara would tell him where her best friend lived.

16

CALLIE

*L*ife without a job turned out to be not so great. There wasn't ever really a time in her life when Callie didn't have somewhere to go. She'd always given proper notice, her two weeks, and then gone straight to a new job.

She felt horrible, listless, lacking energy. She couldn't get out of bed and then when she did, there was nothing to get up for. She dreaded the fact that it could take weeks to find another job. She'd already spent two days with her laptop open on the kitchen table, checking the job sites every few hours. Not that there was much else to do.

Finally, mid-afternoon, Callie forced herself into the shower. She emerged feeling slightly better, but no more hopeful. The apartment was quiet. Way too quiet. Whoever thought sitting around home all day was a good idea- well- it wasn't her. She couldn't imagine this being her life.

Everyone else was at work. Her family. Chantara. All her other friends. Short of going out and doing a few errands, meaning aimless shopping, which she couldn't really afford to do without a job, there wasn't much to do but turn on the TV and stare at the screen blankly or pick up a book and read it without really reading anything at all.

Since the whole getting out of the house seemed like a better idea, and she had a full tank of gas, Callie was just picking up her car keys when the buzzer sounded through the apartment.

She jumped, nearly sending her laptop flying off the kitchen table. *It's the middle of the day. It's probably just someone with the wrong apartment number.* That happened occasionally. It wouldn't be Chantara. There was no way she could lose her key. It was attached to the same ring as her car keys. It wouldn't be anyone else she knew or even the mailman since he always just put a slip in the box and never bothered with ringing anyone to deliver packages. People in the building complained about that all the time.

Callie waited, her keys in her hand, her purse on her shoulder. She was sure that whoever was down there would figure out they had the wrong number and the buzzer wouldn't sound again. She was wrong. The buzzing ripped through the apartment, shrill and annoying, three more times.

"What the hell?" Callie muttered under her breath. "Seriously? Take the hint already." Whoever was down there clearly wasn't in tune with her mutterings, because the buzzer rang another four times. "Unbelievable!"

Callie stalked over to the intercom panel and pressed the TALK button down hard, so hard, that her index finger stung. "Hello there," she said in a tightly controlled voice. It would do no good to scream into the thing. "I think you have the wrong apartment."

There was a second's pause, then a deep voice drifted

over the speaker, crackly because the thing was a piece of shit, but unmistakable. "Actually, I'm pretty sure I have the right one."

Callie nearly fell over. "Matt," she breathed before she thought better of it. She realized she was still pressing the button down and he could hear her.

"Yeah," the answer drifted back. There was a hell of a lot of snapping and crackling mixed along with his heavy breath.

"What- what are you doing here? How do you even know where I live?"

"Are you going to let me come up? I just want to talk."

"No. Not a chance. How did you get my address? If HR gave it to you, I swear that I'm going to file a-"

"They didn't. It was Chantara who gave it to me."

"What?" She nearly died of shock. There was no way in hell her best friend would have given Matt Hilbert their address, not knowing fully well that Callie never wanted to see him again. *He's lying.* "Look, I don't know how you really got my address, but I don't want to see you. I thought that was pretty clear."

"Quitting your job isn't the answer." There was more static and crackle. "Will you please just let me in? If you don't, I'll stand out here for the rest of the afternoon ringing your buzzer."

Callie considered how angry the neighbors would be if that happened. The walls were paper thin and there was no doubt they could hear the buzzing. She knew it wouldn't be long before someone was banging at her door asking why it was so hard to obtain a few minutes of peace and quiet.

"I'll call the cops if you do that."

"No, you won't." Even past the static, she heard the smile

in his voice. It annoyed her that he sounded like he was laughing at her.

"I will! I'm going to call them right now."

"No, you won't. Now, will you please just let me in so we can talk? Five minutes. That's all I'm asking for and then I'll leave."

Callie hesitated. She didn't want Matt there. She didn't want to see him again or talk to him again. *Liar. Yes, I do. I want to see him more than anything.* She hated that. She hated that it did something to her stomach to recall his face, that her skin burned with the feel of a touch she'd never forget, that her lips tingled and her legs suddenly felt like water and her stomach hollowed out and that throbbing was back in all the wrong places. *He's dangerous. This isn't right. It was never right.* She knew that, but she'd done it anyway. *Now, I have to clean up the mess.* She thought she'd done her damage control by resigning from her job, but clearly not.

"Fine," she ground out. "Five minutes and that's it. If you aren't gone by then, I'm locking myself in the bathroom and I really will call the police."

"Alright. Deal. I'll start timing myself the minute I walk through the door. No, wait. That's hardly going to work. I'll set the timer on my phone from the minute we start talking because you need to hear what I have to say."

Callie really doubted that she really did need or want to hear what Matt was going to tell her, but her finger moved, pressing the button that released the front door lock. *He's probably just going to come up here and try and convince me that what I did with him wasn't a mistake. Or that I don't need to feel ashamed about it. Maybe no one has ever left him before. Maybe he just wants to have the last word.* If that was true, she could deal with that. Even if he tried to come up and change her mind, she could deal with it, because she knew that there was no changing her mind. She might want to have a repeat of that night with Matt, minus the end when she told him things she shouldn't have, but it was never going to happen. The sex might be good, but that didn't mean anything. *Well, it shouldn't at any rate.*

She flew around the apartment, straightening things up for the few minutes it took Matt to walk up four flights of stairs and knock on the door. There were still dirty dishes in the sink and the kitchen was a mess, but she couldn't do anything about that. At least the living room was kind of clean. She'd steer him there.

Callie pulled open the door, annoyed that Matt wasn't even breathing hard after that long walk up. He wouldn't have taken the elevator. She knew that because the damn thing was out of service at the moment with no signs of being fixed despite the hazard it caused for those living on the upper floors.

"I was just about to go out," she admitted. "So, you had better really only take five minutes."

"Going to another job interview?" He looked her up and down and she burned under the intensity of his gaze.

"No," she mumbled. "Not in jeans and a sweater I'm not."

"You never know. Some people don't require a formal setting or attire."

"Still. I would at least wear black pants. Even if they were yoga pants."

Matt got this funny look on his face and she realized he was probably imagining her in yoga pants, which would undoubtedly be tight and outline the curves of her ass and the shape of her legs. *I'm an idiot.*

"Anyway..." Matt stepped in. He glanced around and

slipped out of black leather shoes that were so expensive they probably cost more than her share of the monthly rent.

"Yeah, I know it's not a nice place. You don't need to tell me that or comment on the overall shittiness of it or how much worse it is than your place or how shocking to find out it is that you had relations with someone who is clearly so out of your income bracket."

A wry smile slowly spread across Matt's face. *Lord, he's handsome. Far too handsome. Why does he have to look so good?* She didn't dare breathe in. She knew exactly what he'd smell like. God, she knew what he *tasted* like. Everything had changed between them. *I've had him inside me.* It just proved she was right in quitting her job. There was no way she could work with him after what they'd done.

"I wasn't going to," he assured her. "If you're done trying to push me away, there is something I really want to tell you."

"If you came here to try and convince me to take my job back, that's not going to work."

"Nope. Not here for that either. HR is already trying to find a replacement. I don't think they'd give you your job back even if you asked nicely."

"Oh." Callie felt strangely deflated. She hadn't been hoping for her job back, but it hurt, when it really shouldn't, to hear just how loud and clear that door slammed in her face.

"Can I sit down? Will you offer me a glass of water?"

"No. I- you can sit, but I'm not giving you a drink. I don't work for you anymore. I don't have to wait on your every need."

He nodded. "Alright. That's settled." It was unnerving to see that though he kept a straight face, his eyes sparkled like he was laughing at her on the inside.

Callie turned and led him past the kitchen with the overflowing sink of dirty dishes, hoping he didn't look in, to the living room. She pointed at the couch, which was a sectional she and Chantara got for free. The bonded leather had peeled away in spots, so they'd devised a system of old quilts to cover it. Through careful tucking and continuous adjustment, the blankets stayed in place. It actually looked kind of cool, in a really shabby sort of way. At least the thing was comfortable.

Matt sunk down without a second glance at it. He didn't look around the living room, at the vintage oil paintings or the area rug or the small TV and beat up stand. He didn't stare at the coffee table, which had been repainted but was badly in need of another coat. He waited until Callie sat, a safe distance away. His gaze remained fixed on her.

She wanted to squirm under the heat of his stormy eyes, but she didn't. She remained seated, back straight, hands tucked between her legs.

"So, set that timer." She didn't know why she was being rude. *It's a defense mechanism.*

"I don't need to set it."

"Yes, you do. You said you would."

"I know, I said I would, but I don't need to. What I have to say won't take me five minutes."

"Alright, spit it out then." She held his gaze, even though she wanted to look away, at anything else, anywhere else. Her stomach hollowed to the point where it felt like she might have eaten bricks for breakfast. Or glass. Or a damn lead pipe.

"I came to tell you, that what you told me a few nights ago... you need to forgive yourself. You won't be able to let it go until you do. Even if you move on, it doesn't mean you have to forget. It doesn't mean you have to stop loving- what

you lost. You can be happy if you give yourself permission
to. It wasn't your fault. You need to believe that and embrace
it. I know why you told me. It was because you never
thought you'd see me again. You felt safe in that. I know you
haven't told many other people. So that's the only thing I
can figure. It wasn't that you trusted me. It's that you wanted
to get it out because you thought it would make you feel
better. My guess is it didn't. Because you need to forgive
yourself and you need to give yourself permission to be
happy and embrace life."

Callie had no idea what she looked like on the outside,
but she knew she was a damn mess on the inside. Inside her
head, she was screaming. She was screaming and wailing.
She was drowning. Drowning in grief. Drowning in guilt.
The fact that Matt got it so bang on, what she'd done,
astounded her. She was ashamed to admit that she thought
he was just some spoiled rich kid who liked to fuck pretty
women, who of course fell all over him because he was
attractive and had money. And occasionally, he liked to take
down his secretaries, because that also somehow fit with the
MO. *I was wrong. I was so wrong.*

Instead of admitting it though, it was easier to lash out.
It was easier to drive him away. Callie blinked back the tears
burning up the underside of her eyelids. She swallowed past
the massive lump in her throat.

"What do you know about embracing life? You've had
everything handed to you. Everything was easy for you.
Women, people, they were just conquests. Yeah. I know
about you. I know about your reputation. I was warned off.
Don't think I ever took it seriously. I knew you wouldn't stick
around. I wanted to keep it professional, but you wouldn't
let me, and you got what you wanted. I think that's probably
enough, isn't it? You don't have to feel bad for me. You don't

have to show up here like some fucking knight on a white horse and tell me everything is going to be okay. I'm a big girl. I can take care of myself. I'm sorry if I didn't make that obvious, so I'll make it clear now. I'm fine. I'm going to be fine. Telling you did help me that night and I am moving on."

Matt never broke eye contact. He stared at her and the seconds ticked by in painful, horribly awkward silence. "Okay." He stood slowly.

Callie didn't dare move. She barely dared to even breathe. She wanted to take back her angry outburst. What she wanted to do was cry. She wanted to release that flood of tears that she'd never truly let herself cry. Not over the loss of her child. Not over Ben leaving her the night before their wedding. Not over her family. She wanted to let go and just weep like everyone else. She wanted to tell him she wasn't okay. That she doubted she'd ever be okay. She wanted to tell him she was sorry and that she knew he was just trying to help. *He's the first person I've wanted to tell.* The realization shook her. She hadn't just told Matt that night because she was never going to see him again. *I wanted to tell him.* She couldn't even begin to process what that meant. Especially since Matt was already halfway across the living room.

She thought about him leaving like that, silent, just slip into those expensive shoes and let himself out and that she'd never see him again. The pain that blossomed in her chest was violent and not completely expected. When she actually allowed herself to *feel,* it really did hurt.

Matt turned and their eyes locked. *Can he tell? Can he tell how much I really don't want him to leave?* She'd never tell him. She'd never let him know. In her experience, opening yourself up always meant getting hurt. Trusting someone always meant being betrayed.

"You know, Callie, not everyone is like Ben."

He left her with those words, softly spoken, but they echoed through the apartment like a yell. Just like the sound of the door quietly closing at the entrance was as loud as a clap of thunder.

17

MATT

*A*s soon as Matt walked into work the next morning, he knew he was in for it. Chantara sat ready and waiting behind the desk that used to be Callie's. She eyed him up under half-closed lids as he walked by, scowling fiercely. The minute he made it into his office, she darted in behind him.

"Literally what the hell? I gave you Callie's address because you said you wanted to make things better. You told me that you cared about her."

Matt sighed. He hefted his bag onto the desk. He didn't sit. He thought it was better if he remained standing so Chantara couldn't look down and rain insults on him. Not that he didn't deserve it. Because he fucking did.

"Look," he tried to explain. "I've been playing it over and over in my head. I... I thought if I spoke to her that things would be okay."

Even to him, his words sounded pathetic. What he thought was that they'd reach a resolution, tearful on her part, where she said he was right, thanked him for his insight and agreed to see him again. *I'm an idiot.* He cursed himself for actually expecting it to happen, as though thinking it would make it true. What transpired was obviously not the scenario he'd played out in his head. He'd only made things worse.

"And obviously it wasn't. I came home last night, and she had locked herself in her room. She said she didn't want to talk, but I could hear her crying. I know you went there yesterday, as soon as I finally gave in and gave you the address. She never came out once. I've never seen her do anything like that, not even when Ben left."

That choice bit of information hit Matt right in the chest. He felt more than winded, he was floored. "I- I'm sorry. I really did try to talk to her. I wasn't mean or anything."

"You and your kind have a different way of being mean." Chantara glared at him fiercely.

"My- my- kind?" he stammered.

"You know what I'm talking about."

"I'm afraid I don't." He eyed up his chair, really wishing he could sit, since at the moment, his legs felt like they were going to give out, but he didn't.

Chantara crossed her arms. "Of course you don't. You've had everything given to you forever. You haven't ever had to worry about anything. Ever."

"How would you know that exactly?" His words were flat and betrayed nothing. He found it completely ironic, almost funny in a horrible kind of way, that Callie had pretty much accused him of the same thing the day before.

"Just look at you!" Chantara spat. "You probably got this job because your mom or dad or someone you knew pulled some strings for you. Unlike the rest of us who have to work hard for every single thing handed to them."

"Actually, neither my mom or dad got me this job."

"They paid for your college then, so it's the same damn thing."

"They didn't do that either. I paid my own way." He could tell that Chantara was getting more worked up as the seconds went on. It wasn't a good idea to piss off the only person he might have on his side when it came to Callie, so he changed tactics. "I might understand what you're talking about. I grew up in a good neighborhood. I definitely had advantages that other people didn't."

"Privilege."

"I don't know-"

Chantara's jaw ground together so hard it was nearly audible. "Did you ever think that having money is a privilege? You have a reputation for-well- for the women liking you. Why do you think that is? Don't tell me it's just because of the way you look, because I'll tell you right now, it isn't. That whole thing- don't think it's not on Callie's mind. I don't know what you did or said to get her to- to sleep with you," she lowered her voice for that part, "but it's probably never going to happen again. She's been hurt enough. She doesn't want to be rejected by another guy. Ben threw her to the curb. She had to explain to people why he left her. Do you have any idea how hard that was for her? I mean, her family knew, but other people? His family? It was a fucking nightmare."

He winced. "I can imagine."

"Can you? Mr. Easy Ticket, Golden Boy, Whatever..."

"Okay-" he put up a hand to stem any further choice words, but also to cut Chantara off before she really got going and the whole office heard their conversation. The walls of his office were only so thick. "Okay. I can see this isn't a conversation I would ever win. Not that I'm trying to. I'm trying to tell you that I never meant to hurt Callie. I know what you think. That I wanted to sleep with her as some kind of conquest and be done with it, but I told you before, that's not what I want. I'm not going to lie. I haven't set the best- example when it comes to that in the past. I can see how you both would think that and she's right to have doubts, but I do care about her. She's- she's different. There is something about her, Chantara, that I can't even explain to myself. You might not believe anything else, but believe me, what I told you was true. You gave me her address-"

"It's my address too and you promised not to abuse it."

"Yes, I know," he sighed. He hadn't known they lived together until that morning when Chantara talked about Callie not coming out of her room. He quickly put the pieces together. "I wasn't trying to abuse it. If you don't hear anything else, I need you to believe that I really wanted to help her. I still do. I- I am just at a loss here. I was not unkind yesterday, whatever you think. I read all these articles about grief and moving on in the past few days and I was just- just trying to- to help." He knew it was lame. How many times he said help, but he didn't know how else to put it.

"So even if she didn't want to see you again and she doesn't want anything more to do with you, you were just trying to be there for her?"

"I told you that before too."

"I didn't exactly believe you, but I've seen the way she looks at you and I've heard what she isn't saying when she talks about you. Callie likes you. And she doesn't just like anyone. She hasn't been interested in a single person since Ben. She's been closed off and shut down when it comes to guys or dating or any of that. I was really surprised when she started talking about you, even after the Christmas party. I was shocked when she said that she-"

"Yes..." Matt cut her off, afraid that the walls of his office really weren't thick enough for her to mention *that*. "I know. I- I really don't know what to do. I wasn't trying to hurt her. Then or now. I know you don't believe that. She probably doesn't believe it. I was- I wasn't trying to use her. I wasn't trying to make her into a conquest. I knew it was wrong because we worked together. I should have figured out a different way, but she was... I don't even know." He gave his head a shake. "She's- well, she's just- she's not like anyone I ever met."

Chantara's eyes narrowed further. Her lips parted in surprise. "Oh my god," she breathed. "You're really into her, aren't you? And you have no idea what to do with that?"

"I-"

"No, don't answer that. Callie is- well, she can be difficult. She's my best friend, but she hasn't had an easy past couple of years and that whole thing with the miscarriage and her family, she was young. Really young to have to go through that. I think it's harder for her to let go of it and truly just be happy because she learned at such a young age how not to be. She's carried all that guilt with her for her entire teenage and adult years."

"I told her yesterday, that it was okay for her to give herself permission to be happy. I said that moving on doesn't mean that she had to forget, but she deserves something more. And I told her that not everyone was like Ben. Because there are good people out there. Even if it's not me, she deserves to be happy." It would kill him if she was happy with someone else, but he wanted to see her smile. Those smiles of hers were too rare, too few and far between, but when they happened, they were dazzling.

"That's what you said yesterday?"

"Yes. I only spoke with her for a few minutes. Seriously. I just wanted to-"

"I know. To help."

To his surprise, he felt his face heat up. "Yes," he said lamely. "I didn't realize I was going to upset her so much. She was very defensive. She clearly didn't think I was there to help at all."

"Or maybe she thought you were a fine one to preach at her."

"I wasn't preaching- but- but maybe you're right. I could see now how she would think that. I didn't even think once that I was going there to try and be better than her or tell her that I had all the answers. I don't think I gave off that vibe."

"Yeah, well, you might not have, but Callie, when she gets in a mood- I shouldn't say that. It's not fair for me. I had a good family. I grew up and I was fairly happy for a teenager. I met Callie in college. It was hard to get to know her, but then she decided to let me in, and we've been friends for years. I know her well enough to say that she does have some dark times and when she gets into that, no matter what you say or do, she might take it the wrong way. It's not because of you. It's because of where she goes, in her head, or worse, into her heart."

"I can tell she feels a lot of guilt. I said that she told me that stuff because she wanted to feel better and she thought she'd never see me again, so why not?"

"That's weird. Because that's exactly why she told me. She said she didn't really know why she did it, she just wanted to feel better."

"She's obviously searching. Maybe she's ready to try and get better, or at least, get some kind of help. I thought she wanted to move on, really, and I tried to tell her she could. She just needs to let herself."

"She doesn't know how though. She probably does want to, somewhere deep down, but she buries that with guilt and with pain."

"So, what are we going to do?" Matt finally sunk down, slowly, into his office chair. He felt defeated, winded, far worse than he had all the evening and the night before.

"We?" Chantara raised a brow.

"Yeah. *We*?"

Chantara stared at him, pinning him with her dark, not so angry gaze, for a long time before she finally exhaled. "I wish I knew. Seriously. I would have done it a long time ago."

CALLIE

*A*fter three days of moping around the apartment, apparently, Chantara had enough. She swept in after work, took one look at the dirty dishes in the sink, the empty pizza box and sandwich wrappers in the living room and two bags of shopping that had yet to be unpacked.

"Get yourself in the shower, I'm taking you out."

"What?" Callie stared at her best friend incredulously.

"Look at the place," Chantara commanded. "God, it's a mess. You've been wallowing around in it long enough. Go have a shower. We're going out. I'm going to see if I can instill a little life into you yet."

"No, really, I don't want to go out." Callie turned her attention back to the program on TV, something about fashion design and runways. She thought Chantara would leave it at that, but it must have been bad because she snatched the remote off the coffee table and turned the TV off.

"Seriously, honey, I love you, but you haven't washed your hair in like, four or five days." She sniffed. "Probably not anything else either."

"Hey!"

"I'm kidding about that. Kind of. But really. You need to get out of the house. Now. You can't keep sitting here day after day hoping that things are going to get better."

"It's not like I haven't been trying. I've applied for a ton of jobs, but no one has called me back yet."

"Well, we're going out so you won't have to think about that and everything else. It's you and me like it used to be."

"No, I really don't want to go out *out*."

"Relax. I'm not taking you to the bar. I'm too old for that shit."

"Yeah right. You're twenty-eight."

"So are you. Which is too young to look like you've gone and given up on life."

"I haven't given up on life," Callie protested indignantly.

Chantara moved her hands to her hips in that no nonsense kind of way she had that let Callie know her best friend wasn't going to argue anymore.

"Then prove it. Go have a shower and put on something nice. We'll go out to a pub or something for a drink and some onion rings."

"A drink and onion rings? Why don't we just go to the beer store and order something in after?"

"You're missing the point here."

"Which is?"

"That I want to get you out of the house."

"Going to the beer store is getting out of the house."

"Not like that. I want you to have a good time. We haven't done anything together in a while. Let's go to the pub and we can watch whatever shitty sports they have playing and have a few drinks and we'll cab it back." Chantara seemed to reconsider and for a moment Callie was hopeful she'd get out of it, but that hope faded as quickly as it had come.

"Scratch the onion rings. I want fish and chips. You know that little Irish place a few blocks over? We can go there instead. Then we can walk back."

"You do know that place isn't even really Irish right?"

"But it plays Irish music and the servers wear those plaid skirt things."

"Yes, well, my point exactly. Don't you think it's more of a sexy looking uniform than it is culturally accurate?"

"I don't know. Anyway, stop arguing. Go get in the shower. Wash your damn hair and blow-dry it. Put on some makeup, even just some mascara or something. Get a nice dress on. You'll feel better after, trust me."

"Why a nice dress? Why not just something normal like jeans and a sweater?"

"Because that's what you've been moping in for the past few days. I want to see you in something else. Trust me, *you* want to see you in something else."

Callie pretty much knew it was hopeless to argue any further, so she did as Chantara asked. She had a long hot shower, shampooed her hair, twice, let the conditioner sit in, then rinsed. She stood under the hot spray, mostly just because it felt good. She hadn't been clean and wrinkly for ages.

After she was sure she had just about exhausted their hot water tank, Callie switched off the shower and climbed out. She didn't really want to blow dry her hair since it took forever, but she didn't want to go out with it wet either.

Surprisingly, when it was blown out, her teeth brushed and her mascara and lip balm on, she did feel a bit better.

Chantara was waiting for her in the hall. "Here." She held up a dress. It was one of hers, one of her favorites. It was a little too tight in the bust, but it was cute. It had little beaded fringes on the bottom. Callie remembered the day her best friend bought it. It was definitely a splurge after Chantara got her first real job after college. The same job she was working now. The same job Callie *wasn't*. "Put this on."

"But that's your dress," Callie protested. She didn't want to think about work and she certainly didn't want to think about Matt and the dress reminded her of both in a shitty indirect way. *What doesn't, lately? Just put the damn thing on.*

"I want you to wear it tonight. Come on. Drop that towel and get into it."

Callie snatched the dress and disappeared into the still steamy, too hot bathroom. She emerged a few minutes later and Chantara clapped triumphantly. Her face broke into a huge smile.

"There. You look amazing. How do you feel? Better? Was I right?"

Callie had to grudgingly mutter something about Chantara being right after all, which caused a volley of cheers to erupt in the hall.

"Okay! Let's go." Chantara grabbed up her purse and took Callie by the hand. She managed to shrug out of her friend's vice-like grip at the door so she could put on her shoes.

They walked down to the pub together and Callie had to admit, by the time they got there, she was feeling better. She wasn't trapped in the stuffy apartment, hoping that she could find another job before what money she had in her account was eaten up by rent and bills.

Chantara led the way over to a small table in the corner. Callie had only been to the place a few times before. The place had good draft beer, even though the music was corny and a little annoying. The servers walked around as always, in their little skirts and too tight black tops that showed off their midriffs. She'd remembered correctly. Definitely not culturally correct attire, whatever period of history they were going for.

There were huge TVs around the place, turned to this or that soccer game or rugby. She wasn't actually sure which. Must be rugby, because the guys were carrying the ball. That wasn't allowed in soccer, was it? The bar itself was off to the side, a huge wood monstrosity with bar stools lined up in front, like every other bar. The tables were old and scarred, but they were well built and were actual, dark stained wood.

Callie pulled herself onto one of the high bar stools and braced her feet on the rung at the bottom. She was glad she'd worn flats. The kind of chairs where your feet didn't touch the floor were horrible with heels. She faced Chantara, who gave her a strangely triumphant smile.

One of the serving girls, a cheerful, tall, pretty blonde who looked to be just old enough to be of legal age to even work in a pub, came round. She smiled at them and the smile was genuine. Which also meant that she probably hadn't been working in the pub long enough to be jaded by the clientele. Maybe it wasn't so bad, working in a pub instead of a bar.

"Hello ladies. My name's Anna and I'll be your server tonight. I'm happy to inform you that your first round of drinks is paid for. That said, what can I get you? The blonde beer we have on tap, the one on the little card there in the middle of the table, is excellent."

"Uh, what? I'm sorry, could you tell me- uh- why are our drinks paid for?" Callie stammered. She was so confused and was trying not to make it obvious but failing miserably.

"Oh. That guy in the corner there paid for them."

Callie turned to see where Anna was pointing. And nearly fell off the barstool.

19

MATT

"No! No, Chantara, let's go." Callie tried frantically to convince her best friend to make a quick getaway as soon as she spotted Matt.

He was too quick for that. He rose swiftly and cleared the distance just as quickly. He pulled out one of the two empty chairs remaining at the table where Callie sat. She looked nice, dressed in a tight-fitting black dress again. Lord, she was the queen of those things. If there was a woman who looked better in one, Matt had yet to meet her.

"Hey, there." He sunk down in the chair. He flashed a grin at Chantara and saved a soft smile for Callie. She glared back at him.

"No. No *hey there*. You don't get to just pretend that you just happened to be in this very same pub at the very same time as us." She stabbed an angry finger in Chantara's face. "And you! You had to have been in on this. Wear that dress, you said. Go out, you said. Yeah right! You had this whole thing planned!"

Chantara just shrugged innocently. "I don't know what you're talking about."

"Yes, you do!"

"Nope. Maybe Matt just happened to overhear me say something about how great this pub is and decided to check it out for himself. I was just talking about it over lunch break."

"You were not," Callie ground out. She stared Chantara down, who slipped easily from her seat. She didn't manage to keep the guilt off the twist of her lips that passed as a smile.

"I'm going to the washroom- for like- you know- thirty minutes. So- uh- enjoy."

"What! No, you're not!" Callie made a frantic grab for Chantara's arm, but her friend danced away. Callie watched her retreating back helplessly. She finally turned her eyes his way.

Matt had to say he was impressed at Chantara. She said she'd get Callie to the pub at seven and she had. Callie looked- god, she looked *good*. Her hair gleamed gold, shiny and lustrous. She had on a dash of makeup and if she looked slightly pale, as she had the other afternoon when he'd seen her last, he couldn't tell. She was wearing red lipstick. Like she had on the night of the Christmas party. He breathed in and it wasn't just his imagination. She smelled good too.

He felt himself go hard under the table and he was glad the thing was there to block Callie's view. The last thing she needed to see was how tight his jeans were strained over his damn groin. He didn't like the instant reaction, but he could do nothing about it. It felt wrong, given that he was there to apologize.

"Chantara and I might have set this up," he confessed.

"No, really?" Callie rolled her pretty blue cornflower eyes.

"Yeah, I know. Hard to believe." He had a laugh at himself before he studied her. She shrank back an inch from the sudden intensity. "All joking aside, I needed her to help me. I knew there was probably no way that you'd agree to see me again. I needed her to get you here so that hopefully I could do the rest."

"The rest?"

"Yeah. The rest. I- I want to apologize to you, Callie. For the other day, and really, for everything. I pursued you when you said that it wasn't right for us to have a relationship since we worked together. I couldn't let it go. I couldn't let you go."

Callie blinked. "Why not?"

"Why not?" It wasn't the response he expected.

"Yeah. Why couldn't you let it go?"

And there it was. The shocking truth that he was hardly even able to admit to himself. "I- I- don't know why." It was lame and he knew it. A cop out. Callie pursed her lips and he could tell that he'd made her angry. She wasn't going to be honest with him if he couldn't be honest with her. "I honestly don't know," he rushed on. *What the hell am I doing?* "You're just- different. I can't put my finger on what it is, but ever since that night at the Christmas party, I haven't been able to stop thinking about you."

"What about before that? You never realized I was even alive."

"Because you worked for the company! And directly under me. Contrary to what the entire world thinks, I'm not someone who likes to make conquests or take people down just for the sake of it. I do want it to mean something. I- I really- it wasn't that I didn't see you. I was trying to be professional, but you woke me up at the Christmas party. Big time."

"I was drunk. I didn't even know who I was kissing!"

"I know. Believe me, I know all about how alcohol can lower the inhibitions."

"Then you know that I wasn't- well- that I never tried to-"

"Yeah. I'm not coming here to split hairs or discuss what happened that night or who wanted to kiss who or who drank too much or how it happened. I'm coming here tonight because what happened that night started this whole thing. I did notice you. In a big way. That might not have been your intention, but it happened. I'm *glad* it did."

"So- why are you really here?"

"I'm here to apologize. I didn't mean to come to your place the other day and try to tell you how to live your life. I don't want you to think that I know better than you. Because I don't. I know I'm the last person that should give advice. I really was just trying to help you. I- I wanted to try and make things better for you because I didn't want- it hurts me to- to see you hurting."

Callie blinked, as though she had never really considered that he might actually have any real kind of feelings attached to the whole thing. Or to her. The look of disbelief, the glow of tears in her eyes, it all hit him right in the gut and he found he had to struggle to take his next breath. *Not every guy is Ben.* That's what he'd said to her. He hadn't meant it as a parting shot. He wanted her to know, truly, that people did care. *But have I ever cared about anyone before? Truly?*

"I don't know what to say." Callie looked down at her hands, which were folded in her lap. "I feel like both times, this and the other day, it was just kind of sprung on me. I didn't really think I'd see you again."

"Is it really so terrible? No, wait. Don't answer that." He

tried to smile, attempting humor, but the sad look in Callie's eyes never went away. She did look up though, which was an improvement.

"I guess I just don't know what you want from me."

"I really just want to make sure you're okay. Even if you don't want to see me again, I need you to know that you're a great person, Callie. You really do deserve to be happy. I need you to know that and I really hope that you'll believe it."

"It doesn't just happen, just like that. I can't erase all those years and all the things that happened. I can't just learn to trust overnight."

"No, of course not," he said softly. Even though Matt was tempted, he didn't reach across the table. That would be too much, expecting her to take his hand. He wanted to touch her though. He craved that contact, even just an innocent brush of their fingers, or his knuckle against her cheek, more than anything in the world. "I just- I care that you're okay. Really."

Callie shrugged. She stared off to the bar for a second before she tore her gaze away and pinned him with eyes that were entirely devoid of emotion. "Why? You don't even know me. We had- we had a few days of flirting and then we had sex. It wasn't more than that. It was never going to be more than that."

Matt searched her face for some sign that she was lying. For a sign that she maybe didn't mean what she said. For something... anything. He found nothing. Just a blank wall that he butted up against every single time. There was nothing more he could do or say. It hurt. It really fucking hurt. He'd never felt so useless or helpless in his life and he didn't like it.

"Okay." He nodded. He realized he was bobbing his

head way too hard and forced himself to stop. "Okay. I get it. I- I really do wish you all the best, Callie. I won't try and contact you again. I won't bother Chantara again either. If you end up needing a reference to find another job, let Chantara know and I'll write one and give it to her. I hope that you can find what you need."

She blinked hard, just once. "I hope you can too," she whispered. The sincerity in her voice nearly knocked him over as he got up to leave.

20

CALLIE

*L*uckily enough, after several more days stuck in the apartment, one of the zillion resumes Callie sent off finally landed her an interview at a secondhand store that dealt primarily with vintage clothing and other small antiques. It was right up her alley, even though it didn't pay more than minimum wage. When she was offered the job the day after her interview, she took it without hesitation.

After a week of training, she felt confident enough to be left alone in the store for her first shift by herself. She was just finishing getting the mannequins dressed in new outfits when Chantara walked in through the front door.

Callie turned around at the sound of the bell at the door. She was so surprised to see her bestie that she nearly dropped the mannequin. She caught it at the last second, heart racing.

"Oh god, that was a close call. If I damage one of these things, I'm not sure how much I'd get charged. Probably my first whole paycheck."

Chantara looked around, surveying the pink floral wallpaper, the black and white checker pattern on the floors, the red countertops and all the racks of clothes and oddities tucked in corners and on stands throughout the store.

"Wow. This is really cool."

"See, I told you. You didn't believe me that it would be better than another boring admin job."

"You're right. It wasn't really that, I just know how much money you were making before and-"

"It's okay," Callie hurried to assure her. "I didn't want another admin job. I've always hated sitting behind a desk all day and I just finally realized that I was never going to like it, no matter how good the pay was. All the extra money just goes to taxes anyway. I'll be okay."

"Really? Because I can pay more than half the bills and-"

"No. Really. It's okay. I like it. It's funky. And I get the clothes for half off. I'm not allowed to give anyone a discount, friend or not, but if you see anything that you think looks good on me. You know- really, really good and you think it would just be stunning on and would be something you'd ever like to- uh- borrow- you can let me know."

Chantara grinned. "Yes. Right." She took her time browsing around.

Callie finished up the mannequin and came over to help sort through clothing racks. "Are you on lunch time? It's early. It's only eleven."

"Yeah. I took it early and saved up my breaks for the past few days so that I could have a little bit of extra time to get down here. I really wanted to come see where you work."

"Awww. Next time, can you bring me a latte? Those green tea ones I like?"

"Sure. My treat."

"No way. You don't have to-"

"Seriously, it's a latte. You're my best friend. You should

let me treat you once in a while." The look Chantara gave her spoke volumes. It said that it wasn't all about overpriced green teas. It was also about life. Like- all of it.

"Right." Callie was sure she was a little bit red. She felt her face heat up and carefully looked away, searching for some kind of project that needed her attention. She tried and failed to come up with something. The store was clean. Everything was organized. There were no other customers.

"I totally forgot I wanted to show you this dress," she finally mumbled.

It turned out, she had, and she remembered just in time. She pulled out a purple dress with white polka dots. It wasn't her style, but she knew Chantara would love it.

"Oh!" Callie could see Chantara tried not to be swayed by her distraction. Tried and failed. She came over and touched the dress. "It's soft. I thought all vintage clothing was itchy and scratchy."

"Nope. Not always. Though some of it really is. I have to wear it to work here. I can borrow it and bring it back after I wash it. I don't have to buy it since it is a minimum wage job and the owner knows I wouldn't be able to afford it right off the bat. I've pulled some things out that I liked, but god, they were horrible. Just like, flake your skin right off itchy."

Chantara winced. "I can see that. I like that plaid skirt over there, but I'm not even going to give it a try."

"Yeah. Not that one." Callie nearly laughed. She knew Chantara would see that skirt if she came in when it was still in the store. It nipped in at the waist and flared out at the knees. It was adorable, red with little green and yellow plaid stripes. "But it's straight wool. It made my fingers fuzz just to hang it on the hanger."

"Alright, I'll take the dress. You don't have to worry about getting it for me. I can support your shop. It's a good deal. Thirty bucks is a steal."

"Are you sure?"

"Absolutely."

As Callie walked to the till, rang the dress in and bagged it up, she felt a little bit like crying. She couldn't say what it was. Maybe it was everything. Chantara's absolutely kindness. Her willingness to always be there no matter what it took, including all the little gestures that no one else would even think of. It was everything else too, but she didn't want to think about that.

She didn't want to think about how she lays awake well into the night, thinking about Matt, wondering what he was doing. She didn't want to admit that she wanted to tell him she was sorry too, for the fact that she'd been fairly rude and lost in her own pain. She wanted to tell him thanks, at the very least. She wanted to tell him she'd be okay, even if she wasn't sure she would be. She wanted to tell him so many more things, how she wanted to believe that what he said was true. That not all guys were Ben. How she wanted so desperately to trust. How she was lonely, but not just any kind of lonely. She missed *him*. The things he'd said had really sunk in once she'd given them a chance. She just didn't know what to do with that exactly.

"Just so you know," Chantara said softly as she took her debit card back and tucked it in her wallet. She slipped the handle of the bag through long slim fingers. "When I bring you that latte, I'm going to get the barista to write, Master of Deception, in that little name section."

Callie was so startled she almost slammed the till drawer on her fingers. She recovered enough to giggle. Chantara always knew just what she needed. She never gave up on her. Ever. "You could try, but I don't think it would fit. Those little spaces are pretty tiny."

"You'd be surprised." Her best friend winked and walked to the door. "Oh, by the way... I promised myself I wasn't going to tell you, but I know you'll want to know. Matt looks horrible. He always has these black smudges under his eyes like he isn't sleeping. I know you didn't mean to. I know it might be amazing for you to hear it, but I think you really did a number on him. That's all I'm going to say." She held the bag in the air like a trophy and grinned. "Thanks for the dress."

The jangle of the bell on the door handle lasted for only a few seconds, but it resonated with Callie for the rest of the afternoon.

21

MATT

*T*he bell on the door that opened up into the little vintage store made a little jingling noise when Matt stepped inside. He paused, his eyes doing a quick sweep of the store. He didn't want to be there if the place was full. He'd come back in a few minutes when there weren't customers, but he was lucky. The place was empty.

He wasn't even sure that Callie would be working, but then she appeared from the back. She never failed to take his breath away. Her hair was swept up on top of her head, piled up and tied with a sweet little scarf. She had on a vintage green dress that fell to her knees and a pair of white high heeled, platform boots that nearly reached to the hem of the dress. She looked like she'd stepped right out of the past, obviously a look for the boutique, and she was absolutely adorable.

Matt couldn't help the way his heart raced in his chest. He didn't want to hope, but he couldn't help how he felt.

Callie froze when she saw him. Those cornflower blue eyes that he adored, widened prettily. Her lips parted, but no sound came out.

"Hey," he said softly. "I know I said I'd leave you alone, but Chantara told me to come. She told me where you are working and when you'll be on shift."

"Oh... I- she- she shouldn't have..." her stammering trailed off right around the same time her hand snaked out and gripped the edge of the counter for support.

"Maybe she shouldn't have," Matt admitted. "But I'm glad she did. I need to say something to you, and it's been bothering me for quite a while. Will you please hear me out?"

He half expected Callie to tell him to get lost and was almost surprised when she nodded. "Alright." Her voice shook.

Matt took a deep breath. He knew he ran the risk of really offending Callie and of losing her for good, but he had to try. Nothing else had worked. "I just wanted to say that I know the past might have been shitty for you. Okay, it was shitty. But it wasn't all roses and what not for me too. Having money doesn't fix all your problems. Actually, I'm pretty sure it's the rich people in the world who are the loneliest. Every single person I've ever been with used me for my money. They were only ever with me because they could get something from me. I might be successful and have a good job and a house and a car and all those things that you already know about, but it doesn't mean that I'm happy or that I can't be hurt. So, I want you to stop using that as an excuse to stay away from me. I don't care that we come from different income levels. I- I might have been spoiled, according to you, but that doesn't mean that I don't have feelings."

"Matt, I-"

"No, just let me finish." He felt like gripping something of his own for support, but he didn't think that the mannequin to his right was going to do the trick, so he stayed right where he was, braced in the front entrance, his hands tucked against the suit he had on, since he'd just come from a meeting. "That night that we were- uh- together, you used me for something different than anyone else has. You used me for- for therapy. As a way to make yourself feel better. A way to try and move on from your past. Which I wouldn't have minded, if you hadn't run, but you did it, knowing that you'd never see me again. What we shared that night- maybe it was only me who felt it- but it was incredible. It was amazing. I've never felt anything like that in my life. And then you left. In the middle of the night. You couldn't even face me to tell me the truth in the morning. Honestly, it hurt, Callie. It really did."

Callie's features tightened. Her lips thinned into a hard line and her eyes darted away, but not before he saw the guilt there. He didn't like it. He didn't want to hurt her. He just wanted to try and make her understand.

"Matt..." she lifted her head and took a step forward. "I- I'm sorry. I didn't mean- I- the whole thing shouldn't have happened. I- it took me by surprise as much as it probably did for you and I agreed to your request thinking that I could just give you one date to stop you from asking and then that changed into something else. I wanted- I wanted to just live. For one night. I wanted to just let go of everything and just be alive. I wanted to let myself feel something for the first time in a long time. It wasn't supposed to happen. I panicked. I didn't know what to do. It just kept changing for me, and I kept trying to justify it to myself. And you're right. I did use you. I wanted to feel better. I've realized that I'm really good at self-sabotage. A lot of people have told me that I have no right to be happy in my life and I believed them for a long time. People hurt me and I walled myself up so it wouldn't happen again. I never saw you coming. But you were right. About everything you've said."

He blinked. He hadn't expected that. He hadn't expected any kind of confession or apology. He wasn't even sure why he'd come. He just knew that neither of them had what they needed. Not yet. Chantara knew it too. She knew her best friend better than anyone in the entire world. She'd told him to try one more time and he had.

He wasn't sure what had changed, but something had. He could see it in Callie's eyes when they swept back to his face. He heard it in her voice and read it in the way her shoulders drooped.

"I'm sorry, Matt. I'm sorry that I hurt you. I'm sorry that I'm screwed up. I'm sorry that I'm scared and that I- that I've been walking through life like a zombie for a long time. I'm sorry that I ran. I never meant to use you. I never meant for any of this to happen. I don't even know, right now, how to admit to myself that I do feel something for you-"

He didn't let her finish. He marched across the store, closing the distance between them. He swept her up in his arms and as she gasped, he brought his face to hers. She was breathing rapidly, so rapidly that he could feel the rise and fall of her shoulders, the rapid thump of her heartbeat against his arm where he held her.

"Do you, Callie? Do you feel something? Do you want this, even if you have no idea how to get it? Even if you're scared? That's all I want to know."

She blinked up at him. She knew she had the power, with a single word, to send him away for good. Yes or no. That's all it was going to take. That's all it had come down to. One single word.

The shop was silent for what felt like an eternity. He watched an array of emotions flicker across Callie's face.

Fear, sorrow, shame, maybe even anger. But then she smiled and something else passed across her face that chased all the shadows of darker emotion away.

"Yes," she whispered. "I'm a mess, Matt. I have no idea how to trust again or let someone in again or- or love again." She swallowed hard.

"It's okay." He brushed a finger over her trembling bottom lip. "It's all going to be okay. We'll figure it out. Just-just stop running from me. I'm not good at this either. Honestly, when I met you, I said that I was done with it. All of it. And then that kiss happened. Maybe it shouldn't have, or maybe it was meant to happen all along. I'm glad it did. I'm glad it started all of this."

"I- Matt- I don't even know what any of this is. It's all so-"

"I know. You don't have to stop feeling what you're feeling. I get that you're scared and hesitant, but work with me, Callie, not against me. I do care about you. I want that to grow. I want to- to get to know you. All of you. Whatever you want to share with me, the good, the bad..."

"I'm going to go talk to someone." She shocked him. "I'm going to go to therapy. I need someone to help me. I'm tired of doing this alone. All of this." She looked up at him, her eyes huge and tear-filled. "I'm tired of doing all of it alone. I do want you, Matt. I've tried hard to tell myself that I don't, but I do. I'm- I've lost. You wore me down. You wouldn't just go away and stay away." She laughed and it was a musical sound that he wanted to hear over and over and over.

"Callie, are you sure-"

She shook her head, smiling. It was a beautiful smile, one that finally reached her eyes. "I'm not sure, but what the hell. I might as well give it a try. It can't be any worse than what I'm doing already. The life I was living already."

"I would hope not." He rolled his eyes.

Her hands came up and rested on his shoulders. She blinked hard before her eyes rested on his lips. "Then kiss me already, and let's see if we can make this thing work."

Matt grinned. "I never thought I'd hear you say that. Really. But now that you have..."

Callie stood on her tiptoes and didn't let him finish before she dragged his face down and covered her mouth with his. He might not have been sure, from just words alone, but he could tell in her kiss, a kiss that thawed the parts of him that he didn't even know were iced over, a kiss that held healing and promise, that she wanted him. He wanted her and that feeling he had from their first kiss, that it was right or that it was meant to be, or whatever that feeling was, it sure as hell felt like it was going to stick around.

EPILOGUE
MATT

"Well, my love, did you ever think we'd get there?" Matt indicated the rustic log cabin right in front of them. The trees gave way and it seemed to come out of nowhere. It was homey and inviting, with smoke rising from the stone chimney on the side. The lights were on, shining like beacons in the darkness.

"I had my doubts at some points," Callie admitted. She giggled. "This is just about the nicest honeymoon I could ever have imagined. The pictures don't do it justice."

"No, they don't. It's all ready for us, by the looks of it."

"Then we should go in." Callie slipped her hand through his and squeezed gently.

He almost turned back to the truck to say they should get their bags, but he figured they could wait. He didn't need luggage or anything else, for what he had planned. He certainly didn't need extra damn clothes, and Callie had packed a lot of those.

"Shouldn't we get the bags?" Callie read his mind.

"Never." He breathed in a huge breath of fresh air. Despite the fact that they were only an hour out of Denver, they might as well have been in the middle of nowhere. The cabin had a remote feeling. It was peaceful and quiet, as if they were the only people left on earth.

"You mean after." Callie's smile grew as she looked up at him. She read his mind again. There was no way she couldn't. He'd pawed at her, on and off, the entire drive.

"I mean after. Although, that could take all night. And hopefully all of the next day. And the next."

"Oh really? You think so?" Callie giggled. "I think that I want to be able to walk. Part of the reason we picked this place was so that we could do some exploring and hiking. I wanted to see some real nature."

"I had no idea." Matt grinned when Callie took a swing at him. She hit him lightly in the bicep.

"You are the most impossible husband in the world."

"I like the sound of that. Say it again."

"Impossible?"

"No. *Husband*."

"Husband." Callie's eyes sparkled. Her cheeks were flushed, and it was more than just the effects of the fresh air.

"Wife. I like that. It might have been a long, exhausting day, but I guess it was worth it."

Callie moved her hands to her hips. She skewered him with a sharp glare. "You guess? You guess? It *better* have been worth it!"

"Of course it was." Matt grabbed Callie by the waist and swung her in against him. "You were the most beautiful bride in the entire world."

"Honestly, I'm glad it's over. It was a lot of planning and this and that and I'm exhausted. I was more than ready to make our escape."

"Good thing I had the bags packed and the truck waiting. I'll be your getaway car any day."

"Next time, I'm just going to do a simple backyard ceremony..."

"Next time!" Matt scoffed.

It was Callie's turn to grin. "I'm just kidding. There isn't going to be a next time unless we do a vow renewal. You're it for me, Matthew Hilbert. I love you. I am always going to love you. You are patient and kind and amazing. The best man in the entire world."

"I thought we were done with the vows and speeches."

"Dick."

"What about it? Are you finally ready to go in that cabin and let me make you my wife? Truly? For the entire night?"

The darkness couldn't hide the blush that rose on Callie's cheeks. She looked so pretty, her hair and makeup still immaculate from their wedding. She wore her getaway outfit, a loose-fitting black dress. She'd thrown his suit jacket overtop to keep her warm.

"I don't know about the *entire* night..."

"I do. I can't wait to mess up your hair and smear your makeup and make sure that expensive black dress and this far too expensive suit end up in a heap on the floor."

She laughed. "You're impossible."

"I like being impossible, but I love that you're my wife. I love that we're here, Callie. Finally."

"It only took two years. That's not overly long in some people's books. And we did move in together after six months. Some people would also find that way too short."

"Not me."

"We're here now." Her eyes darkened as she stepped into him again. "And I'm glad. Now, husband, you should pick me up and carry me into that cabin and we'll talk more about all night."

"I'm done talking." Matt swept Callie up in his arms and

kissed her until she was breathless. "But I will take you into the cabin now."

Callie squealed and wrapped her arms around his neck. Despite all her protesting, he knew he wouldn't have to try very hard to make sure that she lost sleep. It would probably be her keeping him awake. He kept waiting for them to become like any other couple who had been together for a longer time. He kept waiting for that spark to wane. But it hadn't. He didn't think it ever would. He would do anything and everything to keep it alive. The fire in Callie's kiss told him she would too.

He was very much looking forward to their night together and every single night after that. He finally realized what that feeling he'd always had with Callie was. She was the one for him. He would have laughed about that before, but not since she came into his life. She was the one. She was his forever, his heart, his best friend, his love, his life. She always was and always would be, just *right*.

The End

ALPHALICIOUS BILLIONAIRES BOX SET 1

We are sworn enemies but she's having my baby.

How you ask? Well, I'm also wondering the same thing.

How the hell do people in that stupid fertility clinic mistake MY sperm and inject it into the wrong woman...

The same woman I fired just the day before for running her mouth off at me.

Free in Kindle Unlimited

ABOUT THE AUTHOR

Lindsey Hart specializes in sweet to extra hot and dirty romances and strongly believes in happily ever after. If you are looking for a page turner, then you are in for a wild and naughty ride with feisty heroines and alpha male heroes.